Foreign Language
Culture
Teaching

外语·文化·教学论丛

A New Probe into English Figures of Speech
from the Perspective of Pragmatics

语用学视角下的
英语修辞格新探

黄建滨 樊燕龙 朱桂生 陈伶俐 焦华红 编著

ZHEJIANG UNIVERSITY PRESS
浙江大学出版社
·杭州·

图书在版编目（CIP）数据

语用学视角下的英语修辞格新探 / 黄建滨等编著. —杭州：浙江大学出版社，2024.1（2025.2 重印）
ISBN 978-7-308-24444-2

Ⅰ. ①语… Ⅱ. ①黄… Ⅲ. ①英语—修辞—研究 Ⅳ. ①H315

中国国家版本馆 CIP 数据核字（2023）第 224063 号

语用学视角下的英语修辞格新探
黄建滨 樊燕龙 朱桂生 陈伶俐 焦华红 编著

责任编辑 诸葛勤
责任校对 宁 檬
封面设计 周 灵
出版发行 浙江大学出版社
（杭州市天目山路 148 号 邮政编码 310007）
（网址: http://www.zjupress.com）
排 版 浙江大千时代文化传媒有限公司
印 刷 广东虎彩云印刷有限公司绍兴分公司
开 本 710mm×1000mm 1/16
印 张 20.25
字 数 486 千
版 印 次 2024 年 1 月第 1 版 2025 年 2 月第 2 次印刷
书 号 ISBN 978-7-308-24444-2
定 价 88.00 元

前言

Preface

修辞格（figure of speech，简称辞格）是用来产生特殊文体效果的单词、短语或句子。修辞格是语言的组成部分，不仅出现在优美的文学作品和人们的日常言语活动中，在严谨的学术作品中也广泛使用。Baldick（2001）指出，修辞格是一种背离惯常的字面意思或正常的单词顺序的表达形式。Lanham（1968）将修辞格定义为任何显著或不寻常的词或短语的配置，或任何偏离正常用法的词或短语。Corbett 和 Coonors（1999）认为，修辞是话语策略的输出，是对正常的说话模式或写作模式在语音、形态、句法、语义等层面的巧妙的偏离现象，以达到特殊的交际目的。陈望道（1976）指出，辞格是为了发扬光大语词运用的可能性而造成的超脱寻常文字、寻常文法，以及寻常逻辑的新形式。王希杰（2014）给修辞格下了如下定义：修辞格是为了提高表达效果而有意识地偏离语言和语用常规之后逐渐形成的固定格式、特定格式。也就是说，修辞格具有提高语言表达效果的作用；修辞格是对语言和语用的常规的一种偏离；修辞格是一种格式，有它自己的结构模式。骆小所（1994）认为，修辞格是为了增加语言的表达效果，借助特定的语境对语言进行特殊运用并具有一定格式的言语形式。从这些定义可知，修辞格以其故意偏离字面意义的方式，加强了口头语言和书面语言的表达力度，使其或生动形象，或幽默风趣，或短小精悍，或富有韵律，或色彩鲜明，或优美精妙，或联想丰富，使语言更富有感染力，更耐人寻味，更令人难忘，更引人深思。

作为一门新兴的学科，语用学在最近几十年中发展非常迅速，学者们的语用研究领域也在不断扩大。钱冠连（1997）指出，语用学是一种语言功能理论，它研究语言使用人是如何在附着于人的符号束、语境和智力的参与和干涉下对多于话面（字面）的含义做出解释的，以及他们是如何理解并运用话语的。语用学的实质就是语用功能理论系统完全建立在人对语言干涉的基础之上。具体说来，语用学研究的是在特定的交际语境中语言使用者是如何运用话语准确地表达自己的思想和感情，从而实现自己的意图的；语言受众（读者与听者）是如何准确地理解语言使用者所表达的思想和感情及其背后的意图的。因此，语用学可以广泛地应用于与言语交际有关的各个领域，指导人们正确有效地表达自己的意思，理解他人的观点。

修辞是言语表情达意中追求最佳效果的言语实践。语用学是研究得体有效的语言交际的学问。修辞学与语用学关系密切，它们都以语言应用作为自己的研究对象，研究语言在实际中的使用。修辞可以丰富人类的语言表达，使人们的言语交际变得生动活泼、丰富多彩。从修辞学角度看，语用学理论对修辞学理论及修辞实践具有一定的作用，语用学理论可以指导人们利用语境组织最佳的言语表达方式，可以揭示各种修辞格的语用特征，可以解释修辞格在各种不同的言语活动中的使用情况。

和其他语言一样，英语中也有各种各样的修辞格。本书在修辞理论和语用学理论的指导下，通过收集大量英语修辞格实例，经过分析对比、归纳总结、分类整理，探讨英语修辞格的应用，加强读者对英语修辞格的感性认识，提高其鉴赏能力，进而使其产生模仿和运用这些修辞格手段的强烈愿望并掌握英语修辞格的构成手段和方法，从而提高其英语写作水平。

本书首先梳理了国内外知名学者关于修辞格的定义，指出修辞理论和修辞格的关系、英语修辞格的使用规律，然后探讨英语修辞格的功能、作用和特点等，并从多角度探讨英语修辞格的重要性。修辞格是修辞学中的一个范畴，但与语言学的其他学科如语音学、词汇学、句法学、语义学等有密切的关系。由此，本书将英语修辞格分为语音修辞格、句法修辞格、语义修辞格和逻辑修辞格。

在语音修辞格中，本书分别探讨了头韵、元韵、辅韵、谐缀、拟声、顿绝、顿呼和双关共八个修辞格。在句法修辞格中，本书分别探讨了反复、排比、对偶、交错配置、层进、突降、轭式搭配、一语双叙、回文、连词省略、词序倒装、省略、同位、插入和设问共十五个修辞格。其中，在反复修辞格中，还细分出了首语反复、尾语反复、首语反复＋尾语反复、尾首反复、首尾反复、连词反复和同根词反复等修辞格。在语义修辞格中，本书分别探讨了隐喻、明喻、转喻、提喻、换称、拟人、仿拟、通感、移就和类比共十个修辞格。其中，在隐喻修辞格中，又细分出了三十多种隐喻方式。在逻辑修辞格中，本书分别探讨了警句、夸张、低调陈述、反讽、委婉、悖论、矛盾修辞和典故共八个修辞格。

在以上各章所探讨的四十一类修辞格中，本书对每一个修辞格首先给出其定义和用法，然后用具体实例指出其使用目的与作用、分类及其在不同言语交际活动中的应用——这些领域涉及如诗歌、小说、戏剧、散文等文学领域的语言使用。同时，本书列举了修辞格在演讲、谚语、广告、新闻标题、学术写作等语境中的使用实例。此外，对一些修辞格，本书描述了其结构特点、构成方式等，并对一些相关的修辞格和一些易混淆的修辞格进行了辨析。对一些不易辨别其修辞格的实例，本书还提供了详尽的解说。

修辞学和语用学是两门互相关联且交叉渗透的学科，尽管它们各自有各自的研究方法、范围和任务，对研究对象的视角不同，但是它们都以语言应用作为自己的研究对象，研究语言在实际中的使用。因此本书重点从语用角度考察英语修辞格的运用。每一个修辞格都有各自的特点，有不同的使用目的和作用，分类也有各自的方式，使用范围也不尽相同。因此本书对所探讨的每一个修辞格都从三个方面分别进行论述，即目的、分类、实际应用。对有特色的修辞格，本书还单独加以说明。

同一个词语和句子，不同的人从不同的角度看，可能得出不同的归类，因此修辞格的综合运用往往困扰着一些读者。为了解决这个问题，本书单列一章“修辞格（综合）运用”，专门探讨了修辞格（综合）运用的几种方式：修辞格的连用、修辞格的兼用、修辞格的套用、修辞格的承接和修辞格的综合运用。对这些现象，我们均给出了实例及解说，以帮助中国的英语读者从多角度理解这一修辞现象，提高对修辞格的识别能力，更好地欣赏英语语言的美，更从容地从语境中理解作者所表达的意思。

本书的创新特色体现在以下几个方面：

第一，修辞理论与语用学理论结合，对英语修辞格进行专门研究。前人对修辞格的语用有一定的研究，但并不具体，也不涉及其所研究的所有的修辞格。本书的一个创新点在于，将英语修辞格的语用现象具体到每一个修辞格，对其目的、作用及在具体的言语活动中的运用进行了分别的介绍。

第二，就分类而言，本书对所探讨的四十一个英语修辞格均至少给出三个方面的内容：目的、分类、实际应用。以“夸张”为例，本书指出了“夸张”这一修辞格具有夸大、赞扬、讽刺、惊奇、幽默、加强印象、对照等目的或作用。在“分类”中，本书将“夸张”细分为十七种情况，如使用数词、名词、形容词、副词、最高级、比较级、介词、动词、非真实条件句等构成的夸张。在实际应用中，本书指出，“夸张”这一修辞格经常出现在谚语、小说、戏剧、诗歌、散文、广告、新闻标题、日常交际、学术写作中。这一做法是本书相较于之前的英语修辞格专著的创新。

第三，就修辞格的综合运用而言，本书将中国修辞学者的研究方法运用到英语修辞格的研究中，并且有所拓展。这在有关修辞格综合运用的章节中体现最为明显。修辞格的“连用”“兼用”和“套用”为中国学者（刘焕辉，1990；骆小所，1994）首次提出。本书根据他们的观点和分类，收集到大量的英语实例并对之进行了具体的分析和解说，并在他们研究的基础上，用实例指出了这几种现象综合使用的情况，从而进一步完善了他们的方法。这一做法，有助于中国英语读者了解英语修辞格综合应用的现象。

本书主要采用了如下几种方法。分类归纳法：本书对所选例句按照其修辞格属性进行归纳整理，分别置于目的与作用、类别和使用领域中。在第二章到第四十二章的四十一个章节中，只考虑所选例句在其所在章节中的修辞格属性。文本解读法：本书对所选例句中一些不易辨别的例句进行了具体的解读和分析，尤其对综合运用一章中的例句，采取尽量穷尽其所使用的修辞手段的方式。对比分析法：本书对一些相关的修辞格和一些易混淆的修辞格进行了对比和辨析。例如：头韵、元韵和辅韵的区别，隐喻和明喻的区别，转喻和提喻的区别，轭式搭配和一语双叙的区别，等等。

本书是我们多年从事英语修辞教学和研究的经验积累。在写作过程中，我们参考了大量的相关文献，对这些文献的作者，在此表示最诚挚的感谢。由于在多年的教学中对教学材料的不断增删，尽管我们在参考文献中已经列出了很多的文献，但是一定还有漏列，对此我们深表歉意。本书用英语写成，书内的汉字仅限于相关修辞格名称的汉语表达，目标读者主要是英语专业的教师、研究人员和学生。同时，我们希望这有助于本书的国际推广，向世界展示中国修辞学研究的现状和创新之处。

最后，我还要特别向本书的责任编辑诸葛勤先生表示诚挚的感谢，我们是多年的朋友和同事（他曾在浙江大学外国语学院工作多年）。二十多年来，他参与了我几十本教材、教学参考书和专著的编辑及策划工作。他的真知灼见和辛勤而细致的工作为这些书著增添了魅力。

黄建滨

2024 年于杭州

Contents

Part One

Introduction

Chapter One Figures of Speech

A knowledge of figures of speech in English, and of how they are best used will be of help to us not only in deepening our understanding of what we read, but also in appreciating more fully the finer points of the writer's or speaker's style. In the process, we can learn to write and speak more vividly, meaningfully and expressively ourselves by using some figures of speech, and progress from mere grammatical competence to rhetorical competence.

1.1 Definition of figures of speech

Different scholars have different definitions of a figure of speech.

A figure of speech is an expression that departs from the accepted literal sense or from the normal order of words, or in which an emphasis is produced by patterns of sound. Such figurative language is an especially important resource of poetry, although not every poem will use it; it is also constantly present in all other kinds of speech and writing, even though it usually passes unnoticed. (Baldick, 2001)

Figures of speech are the output of discourse strategies which we use to select units from linguistic paradigms of different levels (phonetics/phonology, morphology, syntax, and semantics) to create texts (in the sense of both written and spoken genres of discourse) which are adequate as far as their communicative purpose in some context is concerned. We will use "figures of speech" as the generic term for any artful deviations from the ordinary mode of speaking or writing. (Corbett & Coonors, 1999)

Dictionaries' definitions of a figure of speech are simpler as follows.

According to *Longman Dictionary of Contemporary English* (1997), a figure of speech is an example of the figurative use of words. By "figurative", it is of a word, phrase, meaning, etc. used in some way other than the main or usual meaning, to suggest a picture in the mind or make a comparison.

According to *The New Oxford Dictionary of English* (2001), a figure of speech is a word of phrase used in a non-literal sense to add rhetorical force or interest to a spoken or written passage.

According to *Collins COBUILD English Dictionary* (1998), a figure of speech is an expression or a word that is used with a figurative rather than literal meaning.

According to *Webster's Third New International Dictionary* (2002), it is an expression (as metaphor or euphemism) that substitutes a variation in point of view by which one thing or notion is referred to as if it were different in some way (as in identity, degree, shape) from what it actually is or seems to be but so related that the expression successfully implies an intended meaning of effect either slightly or greatly different from what it is literally said.

In classical rhetoric, a figure of speech was defined as a trope in Greek, meaning a turn or a conversation, in which words or phrases are used in a way that effects a conspicuous change in what we take to be their standard meaning, and figures of speech are termed as "rhetorical figures", or schemes (from the Greek word for "form"), in which the departure from standard usage is not primarily in the meaning of the words, but in the order or syntactical patterns of the words. (Abrams & Harpham, 2010)

Lanham (1968) defines a figure as a general term for any striking or unusual configuration of words or phrases, any departure from normal usage. Cicero would like trope to be for changes in meaning of one word only; for more than one word, use figure, and for Quintilian, a figure is a form or pattern of speech or writing which differs from the ordinary. Thus, it can be said that, a trope is a change in meaning, and a figure is a change in form, and so figures of speech can be divided into three types: (1) *lexeos* – or one word; (2) *logou* – or more than one word; (3) *dianoias* – of thought, in whatever form. (Lanham, 1968)

According to the ancient theory of rhetoric, named and categorized dozens of figures, drawing a rough and often disputed distinction between those (known as tropes or figures of thought) that extend the meaning of words, and those that merely affect their order or their impact upon an audience (known as figures of speech, schemes, or rhetorical figures). The most important tropes are metaphor, simile, metonymy, synecdoche, personification, and irony; others include hyperbole (overstatement), or litotes (understatement). The minor rhetorical figures can emphasize or enliven a point in several different ways: by placing words in contrast with one another (antithesis), by repeating words in various patterns (anadiplosis, anaphora, chiasmus), by changing the order of words (hyperbaton), by missing out conjunctions (asyndeton), by changing course or breaking off in mid-sentence (aposiopesis), or by assuming special modes of address (apostrophe) or inquiry (rhetorical question). A further category of figures, sometimes known as "figures of sound", achieves emphasis by the repetition of sounds, as in alliteration, assonance, and consonance. (Baldick, 2001)

Chinese scholars also have their definitions of figures of speech. Chen Wangdao (1976) points out that the figure of speech is a new form of extraordinary application of ordinary words and phrases, usual grammatical structures, and common logic in order to express in a more expressive and emphatic way.

Wang Xijie (2014) defines a figure of speech as a fixed format and a specific format gradually formed, after consciously deviating from language and pragmatic conventions in order to improve the expressive effect. ... It has the effect of improving the effect of language expressions; it is a deviation from the conventions of language and pragmatics; and it is a format with its own structural model.

Luo Xiaosuo (1994) points out that the figure of speech is a certain format of speech form to make special use of the language and to increase the expressive effect of the language with the help of a specific context.

It can be concluded that the figure of speech is an ancient term for any form of words and phrases in which the usual use of language is changed or altered for rhetorical or metaphorical effect, and it is an effective device and attractive method.

To sum up, figures of speech arise when the mind associates one thing with another – that is somewhat similar in one or more respects, or related in common experience, or opposite in one or more respects, or emphatic in sense. They are devices to make our language figurative; they lend force to an idea, heighten the effect of expression, or create suggestive imaginary, as compared with ordinary or literal ways of expression.

From ancient Greece on, many theorists have found out more figures of speech in great writings, especially in literary works by poets, novelists, playwrights, essayists, public speakers, et al., and figures of speech now may include all kinds of striking and unusual deviation, variation, or configuration at the word level, phrase level, sentence level, or even discourse level. It is difficult to be precise about how many figures existed in classical times. The numbers range from 65 to 200 or more. This book will focus on those that are of the most universal attraction, and of the greatest practical value.

There are different classifications of figures of speech. In this book, for simplicity, the figures of speech are classified into phonetic figures, syntactic figures, semantic figures, and logical figures.

1.2 Pragmatics and figures of speech

As a newly emerging discipline, pragmatics has developed rapidly in recent decades, and scholars have continuously expanded the field of pragmatic research. Qian Guanlian (1997) points out that pragmatics is a theory of language function, which studies how language users explain the meaning of a word and phrase which has some underlined implication under the participation and interference of symbols, context, and intelligence attached to people, and how they understand and use words and phrases, and the essence of pragmatics is that the theoretical system of pragmatic functions is completely based on human interference in the language.

Specifically, pragmatics studies how language users use language to accurately express their ideas, thoughts and feelings in a specific communicative context, so as to achieve their own intentions; and it also studies how the language audience (readers and listeners) accurately understand the ideas, thoughts and feelings expressed by language users and the intentions behind the words, phrases or sentences they use. Therefore, pragmatics can be widely used in various fields related to verbal communication, guiding people to express their own meanings correctly and effectively and to understand the real meanings and views of other people.

Rhetoric is the verbal practice of pursuing the best effect in the expression of verbal expressions. Pragmatics is the study of appropriate and effective language communication. Rhetoric and pragmatics are closely related as they both take language application as their research object and study the use of language in practice. Rhetoric can enrich human language and make people's verbal communication more lively, vividly and colorful. From the perspective of rhetoric, the pragmatic theory has a certain influence and effect on the rhetorical theory and rhetorical practice. The pragmatic theory can guide people, tell them how to use the context to find out the best expressions, help to reveal the pragmatic characteristics of various figures of speech, and explain the use of figures of speech in various speech activities.

Like the languages of different nationalities, there are also various figures of speech in the English language. Under the guidance of rhetoric theory and pragmatic theory, this book explores the application of English rhetoric devices through a large number of examples collected from English literature and practical writing, by the ways of analysis, comparison, induction, summary, classification and sorting, in order to strengthen readers' perceptual understanding of English figures of speech, and to enhance their appreciation of the English language, and then to have a strong desire to imitate and use these rhetorical devices, to master the constitutional methods and methods of English rhetoric devices, and thereby to improve their English writing ability.

1.3 Characteristics of figures of speech

1. Aesthetic

Sculpture is solid music. (metaphor)

2. Idiomatic

A monkey remains a monkey though dressed in a judge's gown. (proverb, repetition)

3. Unfamiliar

Quickly the trickle becomes a flood of glistening linseed oil as the beam sinks earthwards. ("The Middle Eastern Bazaar", in *Advanced English*)

Note: Here "flood" is a metaphor, and "linseed oil" is compared to flood, which is quite fresh to readers.

4. Vague

I want my fill of beauty before I go. ("No Signposts in the Sea", in *Advanced English*)

Note: Here "before I go" is a euphemism, meaning "before I die".

5. Influential

United, there is little we cannot do in a host of cooperative ventures. Divided, there is little we can do – for we dare not meet a powerful challenge at odds and split asunders. (John F. Kennedy: "Inaugural Address") (antithesis)

6. Multimodal

With orient pearl, with ruby red,
With marble white, with sapphire blue,
Her body every way is fed,
Yet soft to touch and sweet in view:
Heigh ho, fair Rosaline! (Thomas Lodge: "Rosaline")

Note: Here "sweet in view" is synaesthesia, in which there is a transfer appeal between the senses of taste and sight, that is, there is more than one mode in this short phrase.

7. Acceptable

So was it when my life began;
So is it now I am a man;
So be it when I shall grow old ...
The child is the father of man. (William Wordsworth: "My Heart Leaps Up")

Note: At first thought, the underlined sentence (metaphor) is ridiculous, but on second thought, it can be accepted because we can know a person from his / her childhood.

8. Economical

More haste, less speed. (proverb, antithesis)

9. National

If London Bridge had fewer eyes, it would see better.

Note: "London Bridge had fewer eyes" is personification, meaning that there are so many holes under the bridge that it is very difficult for ships to go under the bridge.

10. Context dependent

I shan't take on a job like that again. It's just horse work.

Note: Here "horse work" refers to hard work. This metaphor comes from life experience.

1.4 What can figures of speech do for us?

1. Figures of speech excite one's imagination and provide them with imaginative pleasure

Each purple peak, each flinty spire, was bathed in floods of living fire. (metaphor)

Note: If we use the evening sun instead of floods of living, we will only have a prosaic piece of information without stirring up a ripple in our imagination.

2. Figures of speech bring additional image

He was like a cock who thought that the sun had risen to hear him crow. (simile)

3. Figures of speech concretize the abstract

He earns his bread by writing. (synecdoche)

4. Figures of speech add emotional intensity

Life is a brief candle.

Note: From the metaphor we can feel intensely that life is such a short period of time.

5. Figures of speech make one's writing impressive

My heart is like a singing bird. (simile)

Compare: I feel very happy. (not figurative, but literal)

6. Figures of speech make one's writing vivid

The little girl is singing as merrily as a lark. (simile)

Compare: The little girl is singing merrily. (not figurative, but literal)

7. Figures of speech make one's writing interesting

The police dog and the wolf are both like two rival warriors. (simile)

Compare: Dogs and wolves are both animals. (literal)

8. Figures of speech create a colorful atmosphere

Vingo sat there stunned, looking at the oak tree. It was covered with yellow handkerchiefs – 20 of them, 30 of them, maybe hundreds, a tree that stood like a banner of welcome billowing in the wind. (*College English*, Book I, Unit 9)

9. Figures of speech express an idea in a clear and precise way

The rooms on the first floor are decorated with cold color. (synaesthesia)

10. Figures of speech express an idea in a contrastive way

The computer accomplished this task in seventy-two minutes, whereas a man or a woman working with pencil and paper would have taken more than a million years. ("The Man on the Street and the Men on the Moon", in *College English*, Book IV) (hyperbole)

Note: The contrast is shown by the comparison of the computer's working speed with that of people.

11. Figures of speech are used for emphasis

But one hundred years later, the Negro is still not free. One hundred years later, the life of the Negro is still sadly crippled by the manacles of segregation and the chains of discrimination. One hundred years later, the Negro lives on a lonely island of poverty in the midst of a vast ocean of material prosperity. One hundred years later, the Negro is still languished in the corners of American society and finds himself an exile in his own land. (Martin Luther King, Jr.: "I Have a Dream")

Note: Both repetition and parallelism are used here to emphasize the Negro's present conditions.

12. Figures of speech are used for exaggeration

If I knock over a vase and it is shattered into a thousand pieces, Fred puts it together again in such a way that only an expert would see the difference. ("The Record", in *College English*, Book I, Extensive Reading)

Note: The underlined part is hyperbole, which shows how skillful Fred is.

13. Figures of speech are used for beauty

A bad beginning makes a bad ending. (proverb)

Note: There is alliteration "b" in this proverb. English people like alliteration very much in poetry and also in their daily communication.

14. Figures of speech are used for euphemism

He was boarded at the expense of the state. (euphemism)

Note: The underlined part, which is a euphemism, shows that he was put in prison.

15. Figures of speech express one's comment in an appreciative way

His reputation as an authority on literature is recognized throughout the world. (hyperbole)

16. Figures of speech express one's comment in a pejorative way

... until we are marching backwards to the glorious age of the sixteenth century when bigots lighted faggots to burn the man who dared to bring any intelligence and enlightenment and culture to the human mind. ("The Trial That Rocked the World", in *Advanced English*)

Note: This is irony, by which the author condemns what happened in the sixteenth century in Europe.

17. Figures of speech express an idea in a grave way

The respondent shall continue to pay for the child's education unless and until the child has reached the age of 18.

Note: In legal documents parallelism like "unless and until" and repetition (here "child" is repeated) are often used to show gravity.

18. Figures of speech express an idea in an effective way

The wind is roaring through the woods. (metaphor)

Compare: The wind is blowing hard through the woods. (a literal and plain statement)

19. Figures of speech express an idea in a coherent way

From the great grief of one boy's death came a seed. And from that seed has grown a tree of understanding – a tree that now blossoms with the beauty of friendship and cooperation. (Ronald Reagan)

Note: The repetition of "a tree" makes the whole sentence coherent.

20. Figures of speech express an idea in a humorous way

A: Where have you been for the last four years?

B: At college taking medicine.

A: And did you get well? (pun)

Note: This dialogue is humorous because the second person misunderstands the meaning of "take medicine", which has two meanings: major in medicine, and eat medicine.

21. Figures of speech express an idea in an ambiguous way (pun)

Usually he doesn't sleep for two days at a time.

Note: This sentence is ambiguous as it has two meanings as follows:

a. The usual thing is for him to go without sleep for two days at a time.

b. It is not usual for him to go to sleep for two days at a time.

22. Figures of speech can make us find something similar between two different kinds of people or objects

Imperialism is a paper tiger. (= Imperialism appears to be strong but inwardly it is weak.)

The "paper tiger" is more suggestive of the outward ferocity and inner weakness of imperialism.

23. Figures of speech are a means of concentration, of speaking volumes in a few words

Life is a walking shadow.

Note: There are only two words in the metaphor "walking shadow", from which we can feel that life is just an empty dream and that this walking shadow is walking in the shadow of death. Walking implies the hustle and bustle of our daily life, yet it is much ado about nothing.

Figures of speech are a very important part of rhetorical analysis. There are many figures of speech in literature and everyday speech, which provide rich imagination, subtle suggestiveness, intense emotion, conciseness and concentration. We have to pay special attention to them when we want to understand and interpret literary works, especially works by great writers.

Part Two

Phonetic Figures of Speech

Chapter Two Alliteration

Alliteration (头韵, also known as "head rhyme" or "initial rhyme"), a word originating from the Latin language, meaning the repetition of the same sounds – usually initial consonants of words or of stressed syllables – in any sequence of neighboring words (Baldick, 2001), is one of the most commonly used phonetical devices in English figures of speech. That is, the same consonant sound is repeated at intervals in the initial position of words or a series of words that begin with the same letter or sound alike. Usually the term is applied only to consonants, and only when the recurrent sound is made emphatic because it begins a word or a stressed syllable within a word. (Abrams & Harpham, 2010) The use of alliteration can be traced back to the ancient times. As a rhetorical device, it is good for sound rhyme, musical effect and significant emphasis, and poets and writers like to use it in their writing.

2.1 Purposes of alliteration

1. For beauty

a war of wit and words

The fair breeze blew, the white foam flew,
The furrow followed free;
We were the first that ever burst
Into that silent sea. (Samuel Taylor Coleridge: "The Rime of the Ancient Mariner")

2. For musical effect

Wide will wear, tight will tear. (proverb)

Many a man, many a mind. (proverb)

Thence the welter of waters washes up
Wan to welkin when winds bestir
Evil storm ... (*Beowulf*)

3. For attraction

The Pattern of Fighting in Simple, Small-Scale, Prestate Societies (an article by A. Gat)

4. For emphasis

Fortune favors the fool. (proverb)

Let us go forth to lead the land we love. (John F. Kennedy)

Let every nation know, whether it wishes us well, or ill, that we shall pay any price, bear and burden. (John F. Kennedy)

5. For vividness

Spare the rod, spoil the child. (proverb)

It makes my blood boil to think two thugs decided to pick on an innocent young girl.

6. For contrast

It is good to have some friends both in heaven and hell. (proverb)

It is good to strike the serpent's head with your enemy's hand. (proverb)

2.2 Formation of alliteration

1. One consonant is repeated

baby's breath

His father was hopelessly hooked by cigarettes.

Master of Mystery and Murder (*Time*, September 1999)

2. Two or more consonants are repeated

a strong man struggling with the storms of state

Prevention of trouble is always preferable to trying to cure it.

For Ten Minutes Last Week, America Stood Still.

3. Two consonants of different spelling

Care kills the cat.

June, July and August offer an opportunity for reflection, research, and writing.

4. Two pairs of alliteration in the same sentence

A living dog is better than a dead lion.

Waste not, want not.

2.3 Use of alliteration

1. In idioms

as busy as a bee

as fit as a fiddle

bag and baggage

might and main

from top to toe

part and parcel

tit for tat

safe and sound

with might and main

2. In compounding words

tiptop

zigzag

ping-pong
clish-clash
tick-tock
tick-tack

3. In phrases
make money
learn one's own lessons

4. In proverbs
A word is enough to the wise.
He that trusts in a lie shall perish in truth.

5. In people's names or company's titles
Colin Creevey
Ted Tonks
William Wordsworth
United Parcel & Passenger Service

6. In titles of books and movies
The Great Gatsby (a novel by F. Scott Fitzgerald)
Man on the Moon (a movie)
The Man Who Mistook His Wife for a Cat (a book by O. Sacks)

7. In news headlines
"Too Good to Be True" (*Time*, September 1998)
"Method or Madness?" (*Time*, January 1999)
"Wheeeeeeels! A Week of Auto Debuts" (*Time*, January 1996)

Note: "Wheeeeeeels" is a newly created word in which the letter "e" is repeated several times to show how fast the new automobiles in 1996 are so as to attract consumers' attention.

8. In advertisements
Street Smart. (advertisement for cars)
BETA Builds It Better. (advertisement for furniture)
Cuts Costs Without Cutting Corners (advertisement for cars)
Be Brilliant! Be Sharp! (advertisement for Sharp)

Better life with better Roads and Rail. (advertisement for Highways Department)

9. In poetry

Over the harvest-field forsaken,
Silent, and soft, and slow
Descends the snow. (Henry Wadsworth Longfellow: "Snowflakes")

No longer mourn for me when I am dead
Than you shall hear the surly sullen bell
Give warning to the world that I am fled
From this vile world with vilest worms to dwell. (William Shakespeare: "Sonnet LXXI")

10. In dramas

The preyful princess pierc'd and prick'd a pretty pleasing pricket;
Some say a sore; but not a sore, till now made sore with shooting ... (William Shakespeare: *Love's Labour's Lost*)

Anon comes Pyramus, sweet youth and tall,
And finds his trusty Thisby's mantle slain;
Whereat, with blade, with bloody blameful blade,
He bravely broach'd his boiling bloody breast; ... (William Shakespeare: *A Midsummer Night's Dream*)

11. In novels and short stories

A speckled hen swaggered down the main street of the "settlement", cackling foolishly. (O. Henry: *The Whirligig of Life*)

The flakes were falling thick and hard now, pouring past the window, a waterfall of mystery. (Jonathan Nicholas: *First Snow*)

She went on with sudden serious sweetness. (O. Henry: *The Gift of Magi*)

12. In prose

All week I wondered why he wasn't fired. (*College English*, Book I, Unit 6)

It was difficult to stand or walk on the glassy surface and the red dog slipped and slithered and I fell twice, hard, ... (*College English*, Book III)

13. In speeches

I see a world without a slave. Man at last is free. Nature's forces have by science been enslaved. Lightning and light, wind and wave, frost and flame, and all the secret, subtle powers of earth and air are the tireless toilers for the human race. (Robert Green Ingersoll: "A Vision of War and a Vision of the Future")

In a nation founded on the promise of human dignity, our colleges, our communities, our country should challenge hatred wherever we find it. (Hillary Rodham Clinton)

14. In well-known quotations

The housewife is the most important person – she holds the world together. (Bernard M. Baruch)

Only a life lived for others is a life worthwhile. (Albert Einstein)

15. In tongue twisters

Susan sells sea-shells
She sells sea-shells by the sea-shore,
And the shells she sells are sea-shells, I'm sure;
So if she sells sea-shells by the sea-shore,
The shells she sells are sea-shells, for sure.

Note: In this tongue twister, there are two pairs of initial consonants: "s" and "sh" for children to practice these sounds.

Peter Piper picked a peck of pickled pepper;
A peck of pickled pepper Peter Piper picked;
If Peter Piper picked a peck of pickled pepper,
Where's the peck of pickled pepper Peter Piper picked?

16. In academic writing

Solar System Search from Space

Textual Typology Theory

The electronic devices are used in computers as switches that simply turn on and off.

Chapter Three Assonance

Assonance (元韵), sometimes called vocalic rhyme, is the repetition of identical or similar vowel sounds in the stressed syllables (and sometimes in the following unstressed syllables) of neighboring words. (Baldick, 2001) It involves the echoing or resemblance of vowel sounds in the stressed syllables of a sequence of rhyming words and deals with similar vowel sounds repeated in successive or proximate words containing different consonants. It gives readers / listeners a kind of sensory impressions.

3.1 Purposes of assonance

1. For beauty

Great boast, small roast.

Haste makes waste.

2. For musical effect

How sad and bad and mad it was,

But then, how sweet it was! (Robert Browning: "Confessions")

Punishing is justice for the unjust.

3. For attraction

Make this Sunday a fun day. (advertisement for tourism)

Fight for right (words on a T-shirt)

4. For emphasis

It is high time that you finished your task.

The end makes all equal.

5. For vividness

Shop till you drop.

Pain in Spain (*The Guardian*, 1991)

6. For contrast

Stability is not immobility.

It is hard to wive and thrive both in a year. (proverb)

3.2 Formation of assonance

1. Vowels

The glass hardly fell off the table when Jack grasped it.

If a man will begin with certainties, he shall end in doubts; but if he will be content to begin with doubts, he shall end in certainties.

2. Diphthongs

The kind guide said aside he would chop the way for us.

With this faith we will be able to hew out of the mountain of despair a stone of hope.

3. Vowel combination

Large factories in this country wish to be given a freer hand in the right of hire and fire.

4. The stressed second or third syllable

While the morality of our mission was clear, the legality was not.

3.3 Use of assonance

1. In compounding words

1) The same word

chin-chin

buddy-buddy

so-so

wee-wee

puff-puff

2) Different words

fuddy-duddy

pop-top

hurry-scurry
helter-skelter

2. In phrases

quite right
high time
healthy and wealthy
free as a breeze

3. In idioms

hand in hand
word for word
side by side
as snug as a bug in a rug
shoulder to shoulder
shout out

4. In proverbs

Truth sits upon the lips of a dying man.
Bitter pills may have wholesome effects.
What is worth doing is worth doing well.
Time and tide wait for no man.
Little strokes fell great oaks.
A fall into a pit, a gain in your wit.

5. In poetry

The curfew tolls the knell of parting day,
The lowing herd wind slowly o'er the lea,
The plowman homeward plods his weary way,
And leaves the world to darkness and to me. (Thomas Gray: "Elegy Written in a Country Churchyard")

Note: In this poem, there are three groups of assonance: (1) day and way; (2) lowing and slowly; (3) lea, leaves and me.

May they wander stage by stage
Of the same vain Pilgrimage,

Stumbling on, age after age,
Night and day, mile after mile,
At each and every stile, withal,
May they catch their feet and fall. (Robert Graves)

Note: There are three groups of assonance, that is, (1) may, stage, same, vain, age and day; (2) night, mile and stile; (3) withal and fall.

6. In prose

The rain in Spain falls on the plain.

American technicians living in Latin America used to complain that they felt "left out" of things.

Can defense pain be turned to gain?

7. In dramas

The employers found that extremes sweating, like killing the goose that laid the golden eggs, was not the best way to make business pay. (George Bernard Shaw: *The Intelligent Woman's Guide to Socialism*)

8. In titles of books and articles

"The Woman Who Would Not Tell" (*College English*, Book III, Unit 2)

The Meanings of Weaning (a book by P. C. Lee)

9. In news headlines

"Rotting Rockets" (*Time*, February 1996)

"What the Knees Really Need?" (*Time*, July 2002)

"The Battle of Seattle" (*Time*, May 2001)

10. In well-known quotations

Love ceases to be a pleasure, when it ceases to be a secret. (Aphra Behn)

Men mourn for what they have lost, women for what they ain't got. (Josh Billings)

11. In advertisements

Sofa-So-Good. (advertisement for sofa)

You Can't Beat the Feeling! (advertisement for Coca-Cola)

12. In nursery rhymes

Hey, diddle, diddle,
The cat and the fiddle.
The cow jumped over the moon,
The little dog laughed to see such fun and the dish ran away with the spoon.

13. In tongue twisters

Nine nice night nurses nursing nicely.
Sam's shop stocks short spotted socks.
Six sharp smart sharks.

Chapter Four Consonance

Consonance (辅韵) comes from Latin, meaning "to harmonize". It refers to the repetition of identical or similar consonants in neighboring words whose vowel sounds are different (Baldick, 2001), or the repetition of the internal of ending consonant sounds of words close together especially in poetry, or the resemblance of stressed consonant sounds where the associated vowels differ, or a kind of reverse alliteration, in which terminal rather than initial consonants are repeated. (Lanham, 1968)

4.1 Purposes of consonance

1. For musical effect

Thinking is one of the most wonderful and powerful tools we have.

2. For attraction

The path descended the hill in a series of zigzags.

The athlete is in his tip-top condition.

3. For vividness

The ousel-cock so black of hue,

With orange-tawny bill, ... (William Shakespeare: *A Midsummer Night's Dream*)

A horn spoon holds no poison. (proverb)

4. For emphasis

I'd go back to Canada if I got the chance. First and last, the ten years I spent there were the happiest days of my life.

He laughs best who laughs last. (proverb)

5. For contrast

I expect the best, not the worst. (*College English*, Book II, Unit 3)

"Farms Not Arms" (newspaper heading)

4.2 Formation of consonance

1. A stressed consonant and a vowel

"Out of this house" – said rider to reader,
"Yours never will" – said farer to fearer,
"They're looking for you" – said hearer to horror,
As he left them there, as he left them there. (W. H. Auden: "O Where Are You Going?")

Roger Ringler raised a ruckus.

2. One consonant at the end of a word

What would houses and horses be to me without him!
He had made other's words the tool of his wicked deed.

3. Two consonants at the end of a word

First and foremost
Hundreds of thousands

4. Three consonants at the end of a word

Amid the mists and coldest frosts,
With barest wrists and stoutest boasts,
He thrusts his fists against the posts,
And still insists he sees the ghosts.

4.3 Use of consonance

1. In idioms

first and last
odds and ends
short and sweet

2. In compounding words

clish-clash
snip-snap
whim-wham
tick-tock

3. In proverbs

Kill not the goose that lays golden eggs.

A hundred thieves cannot strip one naked man.

Let the devil get into the church and he'll mount the altar.

Make no fire, raise no smoke.

A man cannot do no more than he can.

He that talks to himself speaks to a fool.

4. In titles of books and articles

"Lady Hermits – Down but Not Out" (*College English*, Book III, Unit 4)

"How to Mark a Book" (*College English*, Book IV, Unit 6)

5. In news headlines

"Churn and Burn" (*Time*, April 1999)

"Street but Sweet" (*Time*, July 2001)

6. In poetry

Doubt thou the stars are fire;
Doubt that the sun doth move;
Doubt truth to be a liar;
But never doubt I love. (William Shakespeare: *Hamlet*)

I am the enemy you killed, my friend.
I know you in this dark: for so you frowned
Yesterday, through me as you jabbed and killed.
I parried, but my hands were loath and cold.
Let us sleep now ... (Wilfred Owen: "Strange Meeting")

7. In prose

What sculpture is to a block of marble, education is to the soul. (Addison)

She tipped her loyal big dog a big hug.

8. In dramas

Life's but a walking shadow; a poor player,
That struts and frets his hour upon the stage,
And then is heard no more. (William Shakespeare: *Macbeth*)

The ousel cock so black of hue,

With orange-tawny bill, ... (William Shakespeare: *A Midsummer Night's Dream*)

9. In novels and short stories

So he scraped and scratched and scrabbled and scrooged, and then he scrooged again and scrabbled and scratched and scraped, working busily with his little paws and muttering to himself, "Up we go! Up we go!" (Kenneth Grahame: *The Wind in the Willows*)

Note: There are two pairs of consonance: scraped and scratched; scrabbled and scrooged.

10. In well-known quotations

In love there are two things: bodies and words. (Joyce Carol Oates)

Civilized people cannot fully satisfy their sexual instinct without love. (Bertrand Russell)

Forbidden fruit is sweet. (Henry George Bohn)

11. In tongue twisters

A bloke's back bike brake block broke.

Chip ship trip.

Good blood, bad blood.

Rita repeated what Reardon recited when Reardon read the remarks.

I scream, you scream, we all scream for ice-cream!

4.4 Differences between alliteration, consonance, assonance and other rhymes

All of them repeat something in the word but they repeat different sounds.

great / grow	send / sit	alliteration
great / fail	send / bell	assonance
great / meat	send / hand	consonance
great / grazed	send / sell	reverse rhyme (倒尾韵)
great / groat	send / sound	pararhyme (头尾韵 / 类尾韵)
great / bait	send / end	rhyme (尾韵)

Chapter Five Homeoteleuton

Homeoteleuton (谐缀), a word coming from the Greek language, meaning similar of endings, refers to the use of identical or similar sounding suffixes on the final words of phrases or clauses.

5.1 Purposes of homeoteleuton

1. For musical effect

Success in any scientific career requires an unusual equipment of capacity, industry, and energy.

2. For attraction

Adversity leads to prosperity. (proverb)

Science is nought worth without conscience. (proverb)

3. For contrast

Speaking without thinking is shouting without aiming.

4. For vividness

One of the most picturesque and impressive parts of the bazaar is the copper-smith's market. As you approach it, a tinkling and banging and clashing begins to impinge on your ears.

5. For parallelism

There indeed, only a few paces off, stood one of them, in Panama hat and yellow boots, seriously, softly, absorbedly, for all that he was watched by ten little boy ... (Virginia Woolf: *To the Lighthouse*)

5.2 Formation of homeoteleuton

1. Adjective suffix

Impossible made possible. (advertisement for Canon xerox)

I had the "right" accent, respectable middle-class parents in court, reliable witnesses, and I could obviously afford a very good solicitor. (*College English*, Book III, Unit 1)

2. Adverbial suffix

Yet the public has every reason to be wary of professional deception, for such practices are peculiarly likely to become deeply rooted, to spread, and to erode. (*College English*, Book IV, Unit 5)

All night long he can hear Nature breathing deeply and freely.

Swiftly, cleanly, the ambulance sped to the hospital, having picked up instantly, humanely, some poor devil ... (Virginia Woolf: *Mrs. Dalloway*)

3. Noun suffix

Instead of rivets there came an invasion, an infliction, a visitation. (Joseph Conrad: *Heart of Darkness*)

Let honesty and industry be your consistent companions.

Modern technology owes ecology an apology. (Alan M. Edison)

4. Verb suffix

We integrate, you communicate. (advertisement for Mitsubishi Electric)

One is apt to forget all about life, seeing it humped and bossed and garnished and cumbered so that it has to move with the greatest circumspection and dignity. (Virginia Woolf: *Death of the Moth*)

5. -ing form as gerund

Deliberating is not delaying.

Sweeping and swerving, accurately, punctually, noiselessly, there, precisely at the right instant, the motor-car stopped at the door. (Virginia Woolf: *Mrs. Dalloway*)

6. -ing form as present participle

As it was a fine day and I was in no hurry, I was taking my time, looking in shop windows, strolling in the park, and sometimes just stopping and looking around me. ("A Brush with the Law", in *College English*, Book III, Unit 1)

Boys and girls were always there waiting for their turns, resting, trading playthings, quarrelling, fighting, footing about.

7. Comparative or superlative degree

Our sweetest songs are those that tell of saddest thought.

"Kinder, Gentler – and in the Lead" (*Time*, June 1998)

5.3 Use of homeoteleuton

1. In proverbs

Prosperity makes friends, adversity tries them.

Saving is getting.

A merry companion is a wagon in the way. (proverb)

2. In prose

Loyalty is seen largely as a relic of the 50s, replaced by a corporate Darwinism that leaves little room for commitment and none for sentiment. (J. Buckley)

Illness brought her a strange restlessness and made her all the more eager to cling to life and squeeze from it the last drop of happiness. It made her envy health, but it also made her sentimental over a leaf that the wind had blown into her room.

3. In poetry

If I can stop one heart from breaking,
I shall not live in vain;
If I can ease one life the aching,
Or cool one pain,
Or help one fainting robin
Unto his nest again,
I shall not live in vain. (*College English*, Book I, Unit 8)

Some are skinny like chicken lips.
Some are baggy like soggy Band-Aids

After you get out of the bathtub
I don't care what kind I get,
Just as long as I get hips. (Sandra Cisneros: "The House on Mongo Street")

4. In advertisements

You can have the smoother, softer, sleeker skin you want now and forever. (advertisement for depilatory)

Safer, thriftier, cleaner. (advertisement for Chery cars)

5. In novels and short stories

All the hill was boiling with excitement. On every side there rose a continual chattering and squeaking, whispering and whistling, as the Animals discussed the great news. Through it all could be heard again and again the words, "New Folks coming." (Robert Lawson: *Rabbit Hill*)

Dalloway rowed them in. He said nothing. But somehow as they watched him start, jumping on to his bicycle to ride twenty miles through the woods, wobbling off down the drive, waving his hand and disappearing, he obviously did feel, instinctively, tremendously, strongly, all that; the night; the romance; Clarissa. He deserved to have her. (Virginia Woolf: *Mrs. Dalloway*)

6. In speeches

But in a larger sense, we cannot dedicate – we cannot consecrate – we cannot hallow – this ground. (Abraham Lincoln: "Gettysburg Address")

7. In well-known quotations

Getting married is easy. Staying married is more difficult. Staying happily married for a lifetime should rank among the fine arts. (Robert Flack)

There is less joy in being loved than in loving. (John Train)

Fools are never uneasy. Stupidity is without anxiety. (Johann Wolfgang von Goethe)

8. In academic writing

It is not only his enormous numbers that take up room; more so, it is all the structure he builds to house himself and his machines, to make possible his transportation and communication, to offer him rest and recreation. (*College English*, Book IV, Unit 8)

The substitution of rolling friction for sliding friction results in a considerable reduction in friction.

9. In riddles

– What keys are too big to carry in your pocket?

– A donkey, a monkey, and a turkey.

10. In tongue twisters

Double bubble gum bubbles double.

Betty beat a bit of butter to make a better butter.

"The Battle of Seattle" (*Time*, May 2001)

Chapter Six Onomatopoeia

Onomatopoeia (拟声), a word coming from Greek, meaning name-making, refers to the use of words that seem to imitate the sounds they refer to; or any combination of words in which the sound gives the impression of echoing the sense, and relies more on conventional associations between verbal and non-verbal sounds than on the direct duplication of one by the other. (Baldick, 2001) There is no exact duplication of nonverbal by verbal sounds; the perceived similarity is due as much to the meaning, and to the sensation of articulating the words, as to their sounds. (Abrams & Harpham, 2010) Simply put, onomatopoeia refers to the formation of a word in imitation of the natural sound associated with the object or action involved, and is often found in poetry and prose for vividness and vitality.

6.1 Purposes of onomatopoeia

1. For beauty

I chatter over stony ways,
In little sharps and trebles,
I bubble into eddying bays,
I babble on the pebbles. (Alfred Tennyson: "The Brook")

The moan of doves in immemorial elms,
And murmuring of innumerable bees. (Alfred Tennyson: "The Princess")

2. For musical effect

Suddenly he heard the ticktack of her high heels in the corridor.

Lulled by the gentle motion and soothed by the rippling music of the waves, the babies soon fell asleep.

3. For vividness

Love pitapatted in their hearts.

The swish of them (her skirts) was enough to set him a – bristle with suspicion ... (Jack London: *Animals of Feeling*)

Mrs. Darling consulted Mr. Darling, but he smiled pooh-pooh. (James Matthew Barrie: *Peter Pan in Kensington Gardens*)

4. For attraction

His car screeched to a halt.

He cracked his fingers nervously.

Judge Scott pooh-poohed and laughed, but not with reason, for it was in his last days on the bench that Jim Hall had stood before him and received sentence. (Jack London: *White Fang*)

5. For emphasis

We ached and oched at the exhibits.

The express train whistled by the station.

6. For description

While he thus spoke, the growling noise became a prolonged roar, and then died away.

Over the cobbles he clattered and clashed in the dark inn-yard,

And he tapped with his whip on the shutters, but all was locked and barred. (Alfred Noyes: "The Highwayman")

Whip danced in the air – pa pa pa – as he sang out, haw haw haw. (Mo Yan)

6.2 Classification of onomatopoeia

1. Echoic words in connection with the sounds made by people

murmur – to make a soft sound, especially to speak or say in a quiet voice, and a soft low sound

whistle – to make the sound of whistle, especially with the mouth, to make music or as a signal to draw attention

hurrah / hurray – a shout of joy or approval

Some sounds produced by people or parts of people's body are: aha, ahem, bang, boo, cackle, clap, chuckle, crack, gabble, ge, giggle, ha, hey, hiss, huff, hurrah, mm, mumble, murmur, oh, ouch, ow, patter, pit-a-pat, pooh, rattle, sh, splutter, stumble, ugh, whimper, whisper, etc.

His throat rattled.

The girls giggled at his hair.

I stumbled my way down the stairs.

Sometimes it was a palpitation, sometimes a flutter; sometimes it was a sort of gasp or gurgle.

The crowd hissed the speaker when he said taxes should be increased.

2. Echoic words in connection with the sounds made by animals

cuckoo – a bird whose sound is like its name, and the call of this bird

buzz – to make a low hum, as bees do, or the sound made by bees

mew or purr – to make sounds by cats

neigh or whinny – to make sounds by horses

And cuckoo-buds of yellow hue, do paint the meadow with delight. (William Shakespeare: "Spring")

A voice so thrilling ne'er was heard, in spring time from the cuckoo bird. (William Wordsworth: "The Solitary Reaper")

Different animals and birds produce different sounds as follows.

An ape gibbers.

An ass brays.

A bear growls.

A beetle drones.

A bird twitters / trills.

A bull lows (bellows).

A calf bleats.

A camel grunts.

A cat mews (meows, purrs).

A chick(en) cheeps (pips, peeps).

A cicada chirps (chirrups).

A cock crows.

A cow moos (boos, lows, bellows).

A cricket chirps (chirrups).

A crow croaks.

A dog bow-wows (yaps, yelps, bays, barks, snarls, growls, howls).
A donkey brays.
A dove coos.
A duck quacks.
A duckling cheeps.
An eagle screams.
An elephant trumpets (bellows).
A fly hums (buzzes, drones).
A fox yelps.
A frog croaks.
A goat bleats.
A goose cackles (gabbles, gaggles).
A hen clucks (cackles, chucks, chuckles).
A horse neighs (nickers, snorts, whinnies).
A hound bays.
A kitten mews.
A lamb bleats (baas).
A lark warbles.
A lion roars.
A magpie chatters.
A mosquito hums (buzzes, drones).
A monkey chatters (gibbers).
A mouse squeaks.
A nightingale jugs (jug-jugs).
An owl hoots (screeches, whoops).
An ox lows (bellows).
A parrot squawks.
A pigeon coos.
A pig squeals (grunts).
A pigeon coos.
A puppy yelps.
A raven croaks.
A sheep baas (bleats).
A snake hisses.

A sparrow twitters (chirps, chirrups).

A swan chants.

A tiger growls (roars).

A thrush whistles.

A turkey gobbles.

A wild goose honks.

A wolf howls (growls).

3. Echoic words in connection with the sounds made by things / objects / machines / metals

bang – to strike sharply, and a sudden loud noise

crash – a sudden loud noise as made by a violent blow, fall, break, etc.

She banged the door behind her.

Andrew had only a pence jingle in his pocket. (A. Cronin)

The train whistle tooted.

Then the miner set off to the pit, his heavy boots scraping the yard.

The bus came rumbling up. Withdrawing my hand from his, I answered at the top of my voice.

Different things and objects produce different sounds as follows.

Artillery booms.

A bell jingles / tinkles.

A bike jangles.

A brake screeches.

A camera ka-doks.

A car screeches.

A cart rumbles.

A clock ticks.

A door creaks / bangs.

An engine chugs.

A gong clangs.

A hammer clangs.

A hoot horns.

A machine whirs / chugs.

A piano tinkles.

A pump thumps.

A radio squeaks.

A subway train hums.

A train puffs.

A train whistle toots.

A tram clangs.

A trumpet toots.

A valve clacks.

A van bumps.

A wheel whirs.

4. Echoic words in connection with the sounds made by nature

sound of ice: crack, growl, howl

sound of flowing water: babble

sound of rain or snow: spatter

sound of thunder: crack, rumble

sound of wave: swish, murmur

sound of wind: whisper, whirl, roar

Different natural things produce different sounds as follows.

A branch cracks.

A breeze whispers.

A brook murmurs.

The moonlight drips.

The rain pit-a-pats.

A storm roars.

A thunder rolls.

A wave swishes.

A weed rustles.

Water splashes / bubbles.

The rain <u>pattered</u> all night.

I listened to the <u>rumbling</u> of thunder.

The north wind is <u>whistling</u>.

5. Interjections produced by people

<u>O</u> destiny, you cannot be eschewed! (Geoffrey Chaucer)

I could scale the blue air,
I could plough the high hills
O, I could kneel all night in prayer,
To heal your many ills!
And one beamy smile from you
Would float like light between
My toils and me, my own, my true,
My dark Rosaleen!
My fond Rosaleen!
Would give me life and soul anew,
A second life, a soul anew,
My dark Rosaleen! (James Clarence Mangan: "My Dark Rosaleen")

"Hoosh!" said Wildeve; and the forty or fifty animals at once turned and galloped away.

It was like a fly settling whenever the hand ceased to shoo it away.

6.3 Grammatical functions of echoic or onomatopoeic words

1. Echoic words used as verbs

My heart is banging in my ears.

He cracked his whip and galloped away.

But as the door banged, she seemed to come to life again.

Jesse went out. The whole world seemed to have turned golden. He limped slowly, with the blood pounding his temples, and a wild incommunicable joy in his heart. "I'm the happiest man in the world," he whispered to himself, "I'm the happiest man in the world." (Albert Maltz: *The Happiest Man on Earth*)

Toto (a dog) did not like the addition to the party, at first. He smelled around the stuffed man as if he suspected there might be a nest of rats in the straw, and he often growled in an unfriendly way at the Scarecrow. (L. Frank Baum: *The Wizard of Oz*)

2. Echoic words used as nouns

The angry husband shut the door with a bang.

The next day was broiling, almost the last, certainly the warmest, of the summer. As my train emerged from the tunnel into sunlight, only the hot whistles of the National Biscuit Company broke the simmering hush at noon. The straw seats of the car hovered on the edge of combustion, the woman next to me perspired delicately for a while into her white shirtwaist, and then, as her newspaper dampened under her fingers, lapsed despairing into deep heat with a desolate cry. Her pocket-book slapped to the floor. (F. Scott Fitzgerald: *The Great Gatsby*)

3. Echoic words used as adverbs

Jack hit John crack on the back.

The drunken driver drove bang into the store window.

4. Echoic words used as adjectives

There were leaky roofs and cracked walls, making the miserable dwellings even more unfit to live in.

The squeaky wheel gets the oil.

5. Echoic words of -ing form used as adjectives

The scudding clouds and whistling wind speak of rain.

At the low hissing sound of the last sentence there was a swift screaming along the shadows of the porch, and a door near the kitchen snapped shut.

6. Echoic words of -ing form used as nouns

The creaking of the brakes got on my nerves.

Harry's brain filled with a sort of blank buzzing, which didn't seem to allow room for concentration.

7. Echoic words used as interjections

"Bang! Bang!" shouted the boys in imitation of gunfire.

"A – OK, what you do is the best," he said.

"Ho! ho! He! he! he!" the crowd fairly roared, ... (Jack London: *Anecdotes in the Boat*)

6.4 Use of onomatopoeia

1. In poetry

The cock is cowing,
The stream is flowing,
The small birds twitter,

The lake doth glitter. (William Wordsworth: "Written in Mach at Brother's Water")

What is translation? On a platter,
A poet's pale and glaring head,
A parrot's screech, a monkey's chatter,
And profanation of the dead.
Reflected words can only shiver,
Like elongated lights that twist,
In the black mirror of a river,
Between the city and the mist. (Vladimir Vladimirovich Nabokov: "On Translating Eugene Onegin")

2. In prose

It cracks beneath your feet. (*Advanced English*)

And then I like all the small noise of a ship: the faint creaking, as of the saddle-leather to a horseman riding across turf, the slap of a rope, the hiss of sudden pray. (*Advanced English*)

3. In novels and short stories

There was a small click, and the ball of light from the lamp flew back to the ceiling and illuminated all once more. (Joanne Kathleen Rowling: *Harry Potter and the Deathly Hallows*)

Not the shy ice cream bell's giggle of Rachel and Lucy's family, but all of a sudden and surprised like a pile of dishes breaking. (Sandra Cisneros: *The House on Mango Street*)

Wilbur grunted. He gulped and sucked, and sucked and gulped, making swishing and swooshing noises, anxious to get everything at once. (E. B. White: *Charlotte's Web*)

There was a rustle behind them, proceeding from a hedge where last year's leaves still clung thick, and a stripy head, with high shoulders behind it, peered forth on them. (Kenneth Grahame: *The Wind in the Willows*)

4. In speeches

There is no retreat but in submission and slavery! Our chains are forged! Their clanking may be heard on the plains of Boston! (Patrick Henry: "Give Me Liberty or

Give Me Death")

In my dreams I hear again the crash of guns, the rattle of musketry, the strange, mournful mutter of the battlefield. (General Douglas MacArthur: Sylvanus Thayer Award Acceptance Address, "Duty, Honor, Country")

5. In dramas and movies

For a charm of pow'rful trouble,
Like a hell-broth boil and bubble.
All, double, double toil and trouble;
Fire burn and cauldron bubble. (William Shakespeare: *Macbeth*)

Gollum: Voiceless is cries; wingless flutters; toothless hates; mouthless mutters. (*The Hobbit 1*)

6. In advertisements

PK chewing gum, penny for a packet,
First you chew it, and then you crack it.
Then you stick it to your jacket,
PK chewing gum, penny for a packet. (advertisement for chewing gum)

7. In news headlines

"The Tao of Pow!" (*Time*, June 1997)
"How Will the Universe End? (With a Bang or a Whimper?)" (*Time*, April 2000)

8. In nursery rhymes

Bow-wow, says the dog,
Mew, mew, says the cat,
Grunt, grunt, says the hug,
And squeak goes the bat.
Tu-whu, says the owl,
Caw, caw, says the crow,
Quack, quack, says the duck,
And what cuckoos say you know.

Baa, baa, black sheep,
Have you any wool?
Yes, sir, yes, sir,

Three bags full.

6.5 Secondary onomatopoeia

The above-mentioned echoic words refer to sounds of some words that suggest their meanings as they are created by imitating natural sounds or noises, and this kind of echoic words can be called primary onomatopoeia. There is another kind of onomatopoeia, which can be considered as secondary onomatopoeia.

There are some sounds or combinations of sounds in English that are associated with some symbolic meanings as follows:

"fl" means light or movement as in flame, flare, flash, flicker;

"gl" means light or movement as in glare, gleam, glint, glimmer, glisten, glitter, glow;

"gr" means dull and unpleasant as in groan, grouse, growl, grunt, grudge, grumble;

"m" means low voice as in hum, hummer, moan, mumble;

"sk" means touching a surface, as in skate, skid, skim, skimp skin;

"sl" means "slippery", as in slide, slip, slither, sludge, sluice, slush, and it also has some pejorative sense, as in slang, slattern, sloppy, sloven, slut, sly;

"sn" has three symbolic meanings – (1) it means breath noise as in sniff, snore, snort, snuff, etc., (2) it means quick separation or movement as in snap, snatch, snip, etc. and (3) it means creeping as in snail, snake, sneak, snoop.

In some words, the last part may have some symbolic meanings:

"-are" refers to strong light or sound, as in blare, flare, glare, stare;

"-ump" refers to something round, as in chump, dump, hump, mump, plump, rump, stump;

"-ump" also refers to heavy strike as in bump, clump, dump, lump, plump, stump, thump.

Second onomatopoeia also includes reduplicated words or reduplicated phrases such as chin-chin, dumdum, pop-top, puff-puff, ram-jam, wee-wee, yo-yo, etc.

Chapter Seven Aposiopesis

Aposiopesis (顿绝), a word from Greek, means becoming silent. It is a rhetorical device in which the speaker suddenly breaks off in the middle of a sentence, leaving the sense unfinished. The device usually suggests strong emotion that makes the speaker unwilling or unable to continue. (Baldick, 2001) If one wants to draw more attention from the audience, it is sometimes more effective for him or her to break off halfway in a sentence, and leave the rest unsaid.

7.1 Classification of aposiopesis

1. The speaker pauses in a sudden halfway when speaking (急收)

The speaker pauses in a sudden halfway when speaking, because he or she is very excited to go on speaking or to attempt to impress the listener with a vague hint of an idea.

"Your grammar is excellent," Professor Hilton informed him, staring at him through heavy spectacles; "but you know nothing, positive nothing, in the other branches, and your United States history is abominable – there is no other word for it, abominable. I should advise you ..." (Jack London: *Martin Eden*)

"There goes your dinner, I'm afraid," said the man from the zoo. "But better that than ...

Crofts: (starting, with a suppressed oath) Who told you?

Vivie: Your partner. My mother.

Crofts: (black with rage) The old – (George Bernard Shaw: *Mrs. Warren's Profession*)

2. The speaker leaves the rest of a sentence unsaid on purpose (蕴胁)

The speaker leaves the rest of a sentence unsaid on purpose, implying a strong sense of threat or menace. In such a context, it is easy for the listener to figure out what the speaker means.

It's a lie! You done it, and you got to say you done it, or … (Mark Twain: *Huckleberry Finn*)

All of them, dear lady, all of them, believe me. It is our duty to live as long as we can. Now, if you raise an alarm – (George Bernard Shaw: *Arms and the Man*)

3. The speaker does not finish his or her words on purpose (留疑)

The speaker does not finish his or her words on purpose, leaving some suspense on the listener.

Good morning. I must apologize for not having met you at breakfast. I have a touch of ... of ...

Crofts: [stopping short, amazed] Wound up! Wind up a business that's paying 35 percent in the worst year! Not likely. Who told you that?

Vivie: [her color quite gone] Do you mean that it is still – (George Bernard Shaw: *Mrs. Warren's Profession*)

4. The speaker pauses for some reason for a moment and goes on speaking (突接)

He said, "I'll look after him now. We couldn't have your assistants clattering around the ward" – he took a look at my leggings – "in your hobnail boots." (A. Cronin: *My Dear Aunt*)

"I know that big guy that called us a –," said the first. "I'll get him yet for that." "I thought we were in for it sure, once there," said the second. (Theodore Dreiser: *Sister Carrie*)

5. The speaker is interrupted by another speaker or by something (岔断)

Nicola: I know things about Raina that would break off her match with Sergius if …

Louka: (turning on him quickly) How do you know? I never told you! (George Bernard Shaw: *Arms and the Man*)

"... Never before in my house –"

"What room?" cried the doctor in a terrible voice, to which Mrs. Parker was a stranger. (O. Henry: *The Skylight Room*)

7.2 Use of aposiopesis

1. In novels and short stories

"You will come down tomorrow?" she urged, she interrupted. "The Prime Minster – His Royal Highness ..." she stopped. "And Dianna ..." she added.

Oliver took his hand off the bell. (Virginia Woolf: *The Duchess and the Jeweller*)

That was a pretty bit muslin hanging on your arm – who is she? (William Makepeace Thackeray: *Pendennis*)

Marry, come up – are you there with your bears? (Walter Scott: *The Abbot*)

When I consider how little of a rarity children are – how often they turn ill, and defeat the fond hopes of their parents – I can not for my life tell what cause for pride there can possibly be in having them. If they were young phoenixes, indeed, that were born but once in a year, there might be a pretext. But when they are so common ... (Charles Lamb: *A Bachelor's Complaint*)

2. In dramas

I will have revenges on you both.

That all the world shall – I will do such things – (William Shakespeare: *King Lear*)

The man [apologetic, but still greatly tickled] I didn't laugh, I assure you. At least I didn't mean to. But when I think of him charging the windmills and imagining he was doing the finest thing – (George Bernard Shaw: *Arms and the Man*)

Barne (goes back to his seat, blows his nose in silence): I have said my piece, Benjamin.

Benjamin: Lots of things I wasn't certain of, many things these radicals say ... you don't believe theories until they happen to you. (Clifford Odets: *Episodes from Waiting for Lefty*)

3. In movies and TV plays

Mother: Hello, it's good to see you.

Man: Well, was the traffic bad or ...

Mother: OK. I know you like my ...

Aunt: Hey, oh, Rachel, honey, you look great.

Daughter: Oh, thank you. (American movie: *Thanksgiving Feast*)

Becky: What was that about up there?

Annie: What was that?

Becky: What' with you?

Annie: Nothing's with me.

Becky: Something's with you.

Annie: No, no ... what are you saying?

Becky: Whatever it is you can tell me ... *Sleepless in Seattle*?

Annie: That's what she called him on the show because he couldn't sleep. (American TV play: *Sweet November*)

4. In daily communication

Get out, or else –

You'd better finish your exercise, or ...

– That's why we're having everyone write out a job description mapping out in detail how they contribute. That way management can assess who's valuable and ...

– Who's expendable?

– It's just business.

Chapter Eight Apostrophe

Apostrophe (顿呼), coming from a Greek word, *apostrephein*, means turning away. It is a direct and explicit address either to an absent person or to an abstract or nonhuman entity. The effect is of high formality, else of a sudden emotional impetus. (Abrams & Harpham, 2010) Apostrophe is usually used in poetry and speeches to impress the person or thing either present or absent with the same feeling to people, animals or even things. The purpose is to attract the audience.

8.1 Classification of apostrophe

In many cases apostrophe imply a personification of the nonhuman object that is addressed. This way apostrophe can be classified to whom to speak as follows.

1. To abstract things

Return, return, eager Hope,
And face man's latter fall. (Herman Melville: "Battle-Pieces and the Aspects of War")

And chiefly Thou, O Spirit, that dost prefer
Before all Temples th' upright heart and pure,
Instruct me. ... (John Milton: *Paradise Lost*)

2. To concrete things

O, wild West Wind, thou breath of Autumn's being ...

O, wind, if winter comes, can spring be far behind? (Percy Bysshe Shelley: "Ode to the West Wind")

Tell me, thou star, whose wings of light
Speed thee in thy fiery flight ... (Percy Bysshe Shelley: "The World's Wanderers")

3. To countries and nations

England! Awake! Awake! Awake!

Jerusalem thy Sister calls! (William Blake: "England! Awake! Awake! Awake!")

Sparta, Sparta, why in slumbers lethargic dost thou lie? (George Gordon Byron "The Famous Greek War Song")

4. To animals

"Cheer up, old girl," said Tom, patting the bay mare on the neck. (Charles Dickens: *The Pickwick Papers*)

Note: Here "old girl" refers to a horse.

O Cuckoo! Shall I call thee bird,
Or but a wandering Voice? (William Wordsworth: "To the Cuckoo")

5. To plants

O rose, thou art sick!
The invisible worm
That flies in the night,
In the howling storm,

Has found out thy bed
Of crimson joy,
And his dark secret love
Does thy life destroy. (William Blake: "The Black Rose")

Fair daffodils, we weep to see you haste away so soon. (Robert Herrick: "To Daffodils")

6. To people

Milton! Thou should'st be living at this hour,
England hath need of thee … (William Wordsworth: "London")

O Captain! My Captain! Rise up and hear the bell.
Rise up – for you the flag is flung – for you the bulge trills,
For you bouquets and ribbon'd wreaths – for you the shores a-crowding,
For you they call, the swaying mass, their eager faces turning;
Hear Captain! Dear father!
This arm beneath your head;
It is some dream that on the deck,

You've fallen cold and dead. (Walt Whitman: "O Captain! My Captain!")

8.2 Use of apostrophe

1. In poetry

Soul of the age!
The applause, delight, the wonder of our age!
My Shakespeare rise! (Ben Johnson: "Soul of the Age")

But when those meek eyes first did seem
To tell me, Love within you wrought –
O Greta, dear domestic stream!
Has not, since then, Love's prompture deep,
Has not Love's whisper evermore
Been ceaseless, as they gentle roar?
Sole voice, when other voices sleep,
Dear under-song in clamor's hour. (Samuel Taylor Coleridge: "Recollections of Love")

May, thou month of rosy beauty,
Month, when pleasure is a duty. (Henry Wadsworth Longfellow: "To May")

2. In speeches

And so, my fellow Americans: ask not what your country can do for you – ask what you can do for your country.

My fellow citizens of the world: ask not what America will do for you, but what together we can do for the freedom of man. (John F. Kennedy: "Inaugural Address")

Let us not wallow in the valley of despair, I say to you today, my friends.

And so even though we face the difficulties of today and tomorrow, I still have a dream. It is a dream deeply rooted in the American dream. (Martin Luther King, Jr.: "I Have a Dream")

3. In novels and short stories

"Dear old table," he said, "I have spent some happy hours with you, and you've been a pretty good friend, when all is said and done." (Jack London: *Martin Eden*)

Orville Mason, you deserve the thanks of this country! … Three cheers for Orville Mason. (Theodore Dreiser: *An American Tragedy*)

4. In prose

Spirit of Swift! … Your genius has prevailed. Ireland is now a nation! (Henry Grattan)

Note: Swift fought for the independence of Ireland all his life. Forty years after his death, his dream came true and so Gratten wrote the above.

Oh, Tiber! Father Tiber! You'd only be a suckling in that mighty land! And as for you, sweet Thames, flow gently till I end my song: flow gently, gentle Thames, speak softly and politely, little Thames, flow gently till I end my song. (Thomas Wolfe)

5. In dramas

Macbeth: ... fifth hag! Who do you show me this? – A fourth? – Start, eyes! (William Shakespeare: *Macbeth*)

Stars, hide your fires;
Let not light see my black and deep desire ... (William Shakespeare: *Macbeth*)

O judgement! Thou art fled to brutish beasts,
and men have lost their reason. (William Shakespeare: *Julius Caesar*)

Chapter Nine Pun

Pun (双关, which traditional rhetoricians called paranomasia) denotes a play on words that are either identical in sound (homonyms) or very similar in sound, but are sharply diverse in significance. (Abrams & Harpham, 2010) By *Webster's Third New International Dictionary* (2002), pun is the humorous use of a word, or of words which are formed or sounded alike but have different meanings, in such a way to play on two or more of the possible applications. According to *Longman Dictionary of Contemporary English* (1997), pun is an amusing use of a word or phrase that has two meanings, or of words having the same sound but different meanings.

Belgium scholar Delabastita considers pun as wordplay. "By way of a working definition of wordplay, I would suggest the following: Wordplay is the general name for the various textual phenomena in which structural features of the languages used are exploited in order to bring about a communicatively significant confrontation of two (or more) linguistic structures with more or less similar forms and more or less different meanings." (quoted from Theodore, 1975: 75)

Pun aims at building a humorous atmosphere and it can stimulate the readers' imagination. It is usually used for rhetorical effects such as for emphasis, humor, sarcasm, fun, irony and so on. In English, there are many pairs or groups of words which, though entirely different in origin and meaning, are pronounced alike or spelt alike, or both. Such words are called homonyms, which may be classified into perfect homonyms, homophones and homographs.

Homonyms are words different in meaning but either identical both in sound and spelling or identical only in sound or spelling.

9.1 Purposes of pun

Homonyms are often used to create puns for desired effect, say, sarcasm or ridicule, as they are identical in sound or spelling, particularly homophones.

1. For sarcasm

Why are parliamentary reports called "Blue Books"? – Because they are never red (read).

Note: Here, the sound [red] can be understood in two ways: a color, or a verb meaning looking at and understanding. That is why it is a kind of sarcasm because no one would like to read the parliamentary reports.

2. For double context

Why are lawyers all uneasy sleepers? Because they lie first on one side, and then on the other, and remain wide awake all the time.

Note: Here "lie" has two meanings: to be in a flat position, and say something that is not true. Lawyers could not sleep well because they tell lies to both sides.

3. For contrast

On Sunday they pray for you and on Monday they prey on you.

Note: Here "pray" means speaking to Heaven, to give thanks or ask for help, and "prey" means making use of someone or something in a dishonest way. This sentence shows the two sides of the church.

4. For humor

He is not a grave man until he is a grave man.

Note: Here "grave" has two meanings. As an adjective, it means serious, and as a noun, it means a place in the ground where a dead person is buried. So this sentence is quite humorous.

5. For emphasis

Not I, believe me. You have dancing shoes with nimble soles; I have a soul of lead, so stakes me to the ground. I cannot move. (William Shakespeare: *Romeo and Juliet*)

Note: Here "sole" and "soul" are pronounced the same but they have different meanings. "Sole" means the bottom surface of the foot, and "soul" means the spiritual part of a person. Shakespeare uses the words in the same sentence to emphasize Romeo's troubled mind.

6. For attraction

Make your every hello a real good-buy.

Note: This is an advertisement for telephone. "Good-buy" is pronounced the same as "good-bye", which is attractive to consumers.

7. For vividness

Try our sweet corn. You'll smile from ear to ear.

Note: This is an advertisement for corn. "Ear" in "from ear to ear" has two meanings: part of the body, and the top part of a grain plant. This advertisement is quite vivid to show that a person is quite happy when eating corns one after another.

9.2 Classification of puns

1. Puns with perfect homonyms

Perfect homonyms are words identical in sound and spelling but not in meaning.

She can't bear children so she never talks about them.

In this sentence, "bear" has two meanings, which should be decided by the context, and so "She can't bear children" has two meanings as follows.

(1) She cannot give birth to children (so she doesn't like to talk about the topic).

(2) She cannot tolerate children (because they are very naughty or silly).

An ambassador is an honest man who lies abroad for the good of his country.

Note: Here "lie" has two meanings, first "to live or stay", and second "to say something untrue".

2. Puns with homographs

Homographs are partial homonyms, that is, words identical in spelling but not in sound and meaning.

lead [li:d] *v.* guide somebody

lead [led] *n.* a chemical element

refuse [ri`fju:z] *v.* indicate unwillingness

refuse [`refju:s] *n.* garbage

sow [səʊ] *v.* plant seed

sow [saʊ] *n.* a female hog

tear [tɪə(r)] *n.* a single drop of fluid from the eye

tear [teə (r)] *v.* pull or come apart

Her careless spending led her into debt.

I need a soft lead pencil.

Note: "Led" and "lead" in the two sentences are pronounced the same but usually their meanings are not difficult to distinguish in the context.

The country refused to get the refuse from other countries now.

Note: Here "refuse" can be used as a verb and as a noun, and means differently.

Her tears will tear her boyfriend's heart.

Note: Here "tear" in this sentence has different grammatical functions and different meanings.

3. Puns with homophones

Homophones are partial homonyms, that is, words identical in sound but not in spelling and meaning.

wring – twist

ring – noise a bell makes

scent – smell

sent – past tense of send

see – to view something

sea – large body of salt water

tale – a story

tail – cats and dogs have them

worn – well used

warn – to give notice of potential danger

Forget hot taste. Only Kool, with pure menthol has the taster of extra coolness.

Note: "Kool" is a newly created word, which is pronounced the same as "cool". The advertiser of the cigarettes uses "Kool" to show the feature of the product and to attract the audience.

We have courses to make grown men young and young men groan. (sign on a men's gym door)

Note: "Grown" (meaning being mentally and physically an adult) and "groan" (meaning making a long deep sound because of pain, annoyance, etc.) are pronounced the same but with different spelling and meaning. It is used to attract people to go to exercise in the gym.

4. Antanaclasis (同形异义双关)

Antanaclasis is the repetition of a word in two different senses. (Corbett & Coonors, 1999)

To England will I steal, and there I'll steal. (William Shakespeare: *Henry V*)

Note: In this sentence, the first "steal" means moving secretly and quietly, and the second means taking without permission.

Although we're apart, you're still a part of me. (Lyrics of the song "On Blueberry Hill")

The long cigarette that's long on flavor. (advertisement for Pall Mall cigarettes)

Note: The first "long" refers to length in space, and the second "long" refers to length in time.

If we don't hang together, we'll hang separately. (Benjamin Franklin)

Note: The first "hang" means to be united, and the second "hang" means to kill with a rope around the neck of a person and have him dropped.

5. Paronomasia (近音双关)

Paronomasia comes from "para-", meaning "beside (expressing alteration)" and "onomasia", meaning "naming". It usually refers to a kind of partial homonym, that is, words pronounced similarly in sound but have different meanings.

If he does bleed, I'll gild the faces of the grooms withal; for it must seem their guilt.

Note: Here "guild" and "guilt" are pronounced similarly.

Civilization is syphilization.

Note: The two nouns have similar pronunciation.

What's increasingly lucrative, however, is selling naming rights. It may not make sense, but it makes some cents. Americans care about money. (*21st Century*, June 2002)

Note: Here "sense" and "cents" are pronounced similarly but have different meaning collocated with "make".

9.3 Origins of homonyms

1. Change in sound and spelling

long *a*. not short, changed from *lang* in Old English

long *v*. to want very much, changed from *langian* in Old English

2. Borrowing

fair *n.* a market, borrowed from *feria* in Latin

fair *a.* pretty, borrowed from *foeger* in Old English

3. Shortening (abbreviation, or clipping)

plane *n.* shortened from aeroplane

plain *a.* simple, honest and direct

flu *n.* shortened from influenza

flew *v.* past tense of flow

4. Differences of homonyms from polysemants

Perfect homonyms and polysemants are fully identical with regard to spelling and pronunciation, but the fundamental difference between homonyms and polysemants lies in the fact that the former refers to different words which happen to share the same form and the latter is the one and same word which has several distinguishable meanings. We can distinguish them by the following two criteria.

1) Etymology

Homonyms are from different sources whereas a polysemant is from the same source which has acquired different meanings in the course of development.

2) Semantic relatedness

The various meanings of a polysemant are correlated and connected to one central meaning to a greater or lesser degree; meanings of different homonyms have nothing to do with one another.

In most dictionaries, a polysemant has its meanings all listed under one headword whereas homonyms are listed as separate entries.

9.4 Use of pun

1. In riddles

Why is bread like the sun? – Because it rises from the yeast (east).

What's the longest sentence in the world? – Life sentence.

Why is an old man like a window? – Because he is full of pains. (panes)

When does a public speaker steal lumber? – When he takes floor.

Why did the man hit the clock and want to destroy it? – Because the clock struck first.

What grammar term do lovers dislike? – The third person.

Why are movie stars so cool? – Because they have so many fans.

2. In advertisements

Which lager can claim to be truly German? This can. (advertisement for beer)

Make Time for Time. (advertisement for the magazine *Time*)

Coke refreshes you like no other can. (advertisement for Coke)

More sun and air for your son and heir. (advertisement for tourism)

Note: There are two pairs of pun: "sun" and "son"; "air" and "heir".

The driver is safer when the road is dry;

The road is safer when the driver is dry. (public advertisement)

Note: Here "dry" in the first line means wet, while in the second line means not drunk.

You'll go nuts for the nuts you get in Nux. (advertisement for Nux, a kind of nuts)

Note: Here "go nuts" means "go crazy", and "nut" is a small hard fruit with a very hard shell.

3. In news headlines

"How to Be Guilty Parents" (*New York Times*)

"Sagging Spirits in Scotland" (*Newsweek*, 1983)

Note: "Spirits" has two meanings: alcohol, and state of mind.

"Soccer Kicks Off with Violence" (*The Times*, 1972)

Note: "Kick" collocated with different words has different meanings: "kick off" means starting the football game, and "kick with violence" means starting a fight.

4. In novels and short stories

Farewell to Arms (the title of a novel by Hemingway)

Note: "Arms" here can be understood as part of the body, and weapons.

"But they were in the well," Alice said to the Dormouse, not choosing to notice this last remark.

"Of course they were," said the Dormouse, "well in." (Lewis Carroll: *Alice in Wonderland*)

"And so these three sisters – they were learning to draw, you know –"

"What did they draw?" said Alice, quite forgetting her promise. (Lewis Carroll: *Alice in Wonderland*)

5. In poetry

The tyrant of the Chersonese
Was freedom's best and bravest friend;
That tyrant was Miltiades!
Oh! That the present hour would lend
Another despot of the kind!
Such chains as his were sure to bind. (George Gordon Byron: *Don Juan*)

Note: Here "bind" has two meanings: tie with rope, and unite.

Ben Battle was a warrior bold.
And used to war's alarms;
But a cannon-ball took off his legs,
So he laid down his arms. (Thomas Hood: *Faithless Nelly Gray*)

Note: Here "arms" has two meanings: part of the body, and weapon.

6. In dramas

King: My cousin Hamlet, and my son. How is it that the clouds still hang on you?

Hamlet: Not so, my lord, I'm too much in the sun. (William Shakespeare: *Hamlet*)

Mercutio: No, 'tis not so deep as a well, nor so wide as a church-door; but 'tis enough, 'twill serve; ask for me tomorrow, and you shall find me a grave man. I am peppered, I warrant, for this world. A plague o' both your houses! (William Shakespeare: *Romeo and Juliet*)

7. In TV plays

Sophie: I'm not buying it.

Caroline: I always knew we'd dye together. (American TV play: *Broke Girls*)

Note: Here "buy" has two meanings: purchase, and believe. And "dye" also has two meanings: change color, and die.

Mr. Brown: For the rest of this period, we are going to talk about shopping.

Giovanni: Ah, I like him, he is very good.

Mr. Brown: Pardon?

Giovanni: Shoppin! I like his *Polonaise*. (American TV play: *Mind Your Language*)

Note: "Shoppin" here is pronounced like Chopin, a well-known pianist.

Miss Courtney: I thought I'd better tell you that an inspector has arrived.

Mr. Brown: Well, my conscience is clear.

Miss Courtney: I beg your pardon?

Mr. Brown: Apart from the old parking ticket, I've never been in any trouble with the police.

Miss Courtney: An education inspector. (American TV play: *Mind Your Language*)

Note: In this dialogue, Mr. Brown thinks that the inspector refers to a policeman, while Miss Courtney means that the inspector is an education inspector.

8. In prose

Success is a relative term. It brings so many relatives. (Garfield)

– I'm happy. I've got a good job, a wonderful home, and the cleverest wife in the country.

– With your wife in the country, why shouldn't you be happy. (*Comic Book Encyclopedia*)

– Do any of you know martial art?

– I know Marshall Schwartz. (*Growing Pain*)

She guessed I'd go crazy if I didn't sail, and yet certainly I'd go crazy.

Note: Here "go crazy" has two meanings: go mad, and be very excited.

The safe way is the right way.

9. In daily communication

Mr. Black is a black ingrate.

Note: "Black" also means evil.

I am a Ford, not a Lincoln. (Ford)

Note: This was said by US Vice President Ford in 1973. Both Ford and Lincoln are presidents and brand names of cars, but the brand Ford is for ordinary people while the brand Lincoln is for rich people. President Ford said so as he wanted to be popular with ordinary people.

Part Three

Syntactic Figures of Speech

Chapter Ten　Repetition

Repetition (反复) as a rhetorical device refers to the repetition of elements of a sentence construction, sometimes in part or sometimes in whole. What are repeated can be sounds, words, phrases, or sentences. The most popular type of repetition is to repeat words in different positions in a sentence, in a line of poetry, in stanzas or in paragraphs. Repetition is often combined with parallelism, so it is also called parallel repetition. Repetition is employed for achieving rhetorical effect of emphasis, for heightening of mood, tension or atmosphere, coherence as well as aesthetic effect, especially in poetry.

Lexically, repetition can be divided into repetition of the same words, and that of synonyms. Repetition of the same words can be classified into immediate repetition and intermittent repetition, anaphora, epiphora, symploce, anadiplosis, etc.

10.1 Purposes of repetition

1. For contrast

Everything is extraordinary, everything tempts. (advertisement for Cartier)

Man is not the creature of circumstances; circumstances are the creature of men. (proverb)

2. For emphasis

Work – work – work
Till the brain begins to swim,
Work – work – work
Till the eyes are heavy and dim!

Seam, and gusset, and band,
Band, and gusset, and seam,
Till over the buttons I fall asleep,
And sew them on in a dream! (Thomas Hood: "The Song of the Shirt")

We will rally the world to this cause by our efforts, by our courage. We will not tire, we will not falter, and we will not fail. (George W. Bush)

3. For balance

And soon came a gale of wind, and carried away Curdken's hat, and away went Curdken after it, while the girl went on combing and curling her hair. (Grimm: *Grimm's Fairy Tales*)

Light come, light go.

4. For coherence

That is … the feeling conveyed by larger inland towns – walled. Walled by nothing. Nothing is plain and clay pan and dried river beds and thousands of square miles of starving sheep … (Thea Astley: *Inventing Her Own Weather*)

He gave his life; life was all he could give.

5. For rhythmic beauty

Back again! Back again! Look to the shoe!
The shoe is too small, and not made for you!
Prince! Prince! Look again for thy bride,

For she's not the true one that sits by thy side. (Grimm: *Grimm's Fairy Tales*)

This unfrequented place to find some ease,
Ease to the body some, none to the mind
From restless thoughts. (John Milton: *Samson Agonistes*)

6. For more exactness in legal documents

At termination of this lease, or of Tenant's right of possession by lapse of time or otherwise, Tenant shall yield immediate possession of the premises to Landlord, and deliver all keys to Landlord or his agent at the place where rent is payable.

7. For different feelings such as hesitation, displeasure, or satire, etc. in spoken English

"Mr. Crossett," said my father, "will you permit an old pupil to shake hands with you?"

Mr. Crossett looked at us seriously.

"An old pupil? I'm sorry but ... your name?"

"Could you wait a few days for the money! I haven't any small change about me."

The fellow looked at me coldly and said, "Oh, you haven't? Well, of course, I know that gentleman like you carry only large notes." (Mark Twain: *The Million Pound Bank-Note*)

Queen: If it be, why seems it so particular with thee?

Hamlet: Seems, madam! Nay, it is; I know not "seems". (William Shakespeare: *Hamlet*)

10.2 Classification of repetition

1. Immediate repetition / Epizeuxis

Immediate repetition (紧接反复) refers to two or more words, phrases, or sentences are repeated without intervals. It is a continuous repetition for highlighting a particular feature, to draw people's attention to it, but can be separated by conjunctions such as "and" or prepositions such as "of".

1) Repetition of a noun

There are friends and friends.

The road extends for miles and miles.

War and suffering go hand in hand.

2) Repetition of an adjective

Wonderful, wonderful, and most wonderful! And yet again wonderful! Out of all hooping! (William Shakespeare)

A strong mind is his secret, a strong watch is his choice. (advertisement for a watch)

The green green fields looked very beautiful.

3) Repetition of an adverb

Alone, alone, all, all alone,
Alone on a wide, wide sea. (Samuel Taylor Coleridge: "The Rime of the Ancient Mariner")

I like your new book very, very much.

4) Repetition of a verb

Break, break, break,
At the foot of thy crags, O sea!
But the tender grace of a day that is dead,
Will never come back to me. (Alfred Tennyson: "Break, Break, Break")

5) Repetition of a sentence

It seems so like my own
It seems so like my own
Because of the fasts I keep! (Thomas Hood: "Song of the Shirt")

6) Repetition of synonyms

She loved him heart and soul.

Each and every comrade must study hard for the revolution.

I am sure and certain that he is honest.

We are troubled on every side, yet not distressed; we are perplexed, but not in despair; persecuted, but not forsaken; cast down, but not destroyed.

A fresh supply of water is fed by pumps into the boiler to replace it. The feed-water should be pure, and free from dissolved salts which will cause deposits on the tubes and lead to overheating.

Note: Here "fresh supply of water" and "feed-water" are synonyms.

2. Intermittent repetition

Intermittent repetition (间隔反复) refers to the way the repeated words, phrases or sentences are separated by some other words, phrases or sentences, and is the most widely used type of repetition. It is used for emphasis, for expressing strong emotions or for some special purposes.

1) Repetition of a noun

Home! Home! Look to the shoes!
Princess! The shoe was made for you!
Prince! Prince! Take home thy bride,
For she is the true one that sits by thy side! (Grimm: *Grimm's Fairy Tales*)

Love built on beauty, soon as beauty, dies.

2) Repetition of an adjective

We were in the heart of Crystal Mountains! They towered round us on every side, and stretched away in interminable ranges of shining pinnacles. Such shapes! Such colors! Such flashing and blazing of gigantic rainbows and prisms! There were mountains that looked to my amazed eyes as lofty as Mont Blanc, and as massive, every solid mile of which was composed of crystalline ice, reflecting and reflecting the sunbeams with iridescent splendor. For now we could begin to see a part of the orb of the sun itself, prodigious in size, and poised on the edge of the gem-glittering horizon, where the jeweled summits split its beams into a thousand halos. (Garrett Putman Serviss: *A Columbus of Space*)

A beautiful form is better than a beautiful face; a beautiful behavior than a beautiful form.

3) Repetition of an adverb

So far, so good!

To stop too fearful, and too faint to go. (Goldsmith)

4) Repetition of a verb

Meat cooks better if it is cooked slowly.

Till the prisoner is fast,
And her doom is cast,
There stay! Oh, stay!
When the charm is around her,
And the spell has bound her,
Hie away! Away! (Grimm: *Grimm's Fairy Tales*)

5) Repetition of a preposition

It blew day and day: it blew with spite; without interval, without mercy, without rest.

The wagons creaked and the harness rattled noisily through night stillness, as slowly, one by one, they lumbered through the darkness across the river and up the bank to the village street. (Mary Shelley: *Frankenstein*)

6) Repetition of a pronoun

He mistrusted my youth, my common sense and my seamanship, and made a point of showing it in a hundred little ways.

Her style, her taste, her point of view, and her mode of thinking, are all right.

7) Repetition of a conjunction

Only the sound of the soft waves and wind which rushed and pushed pops and creaks from the house.

Is it beyond thee to be glad with the gladness of this rhythm? To be tossed and lost and broken in the whirl of this fearful joy? (Tagore: *Gitanjali*)

8) Repetition of an interjection

Early the next morning, as she and Curdken went out through the gate, she said sorrowfully:

"Falada, Falada, there thou hangest!"

And the head answered:

"Bride, bride, there thou gangest!

Alas! Alas! If thy mother knew it,

Sadly, sadly, would she rue it." (Grimm: *Grimm's Fairy Tales*)

My father was a farmer upon the Carrick border, O,

And carefully he bred me in decency and order, O;

He bade me act a manly part, though I had ne'er a-farthing, O,

For without an honest, manly heart, no man was worth regarding, O. (Robert Burns: "My Father Was a Farmer")

9) Repetition of part of a prepositional phrase

In the meanwhile I smile and I sing all alone. In the meanwhile the air is filling with the perfume of promise. (Tagore: *Gitanjali*)

So that in the end there were the trees. The boy walking through them with his head drooping as he increased in stature. Putting out shoots of green thought. So that, in the end, there was no end. (Patrick White: *The Tree of Man*)

10) Repetition of an abbreviated word

Last night I couldn't sleep
I wanted you warm against me
I wanted u on me
I wanted to feel u all over my body
But I couldn't find u ...
My pyjamas ... (advertisement for pyjamas)

I love u wen u r sad.
I love u wen u r happy.
I love u wen u r teasing.
I love u wen u r laughing.
I love u wen u r angry.
I love u wen u love love me.

11) Repetition of part of a sentence

These are good laws, these are wise provisions, these are sensible responses to social need.

Even I, depressed in mind and my spirits continually agitated by gloomy feelings, even I was pleased. (Mary Shelley: *Frankenstein*)

12) Repetition of a sentence

You are tired. Thord. You are tired. Lie down on the chest, and rest till supper. You are tired to death. (John Masefield)

If you wander off too far
My love will get you home
If you follow the wrong star
My love will get you home
If you ever find yourself
Lost and all alone
Get back on your feet and think of me
My love will get you home boy
My love will get you home
If the bright lights blind your eyes
My love will get you home

If your troubles break your stride
My love will get you home
If you ever feel ashamed
My love will get you home
If it's only you to blame
My love will get you home (Christine Glass: "My Love Will Get You Home")

10.3 Different types of intermittent repetition

Intermittent repetition can be classified into different kinds of repetition as follows.

1. Anaphora

Anaphora (首语反复) originates from Greek, meaning carrying back. It refers to the repetition of the same word or groups of words at the beginning of successive clauses, or sentences. (Corbett & Coonors, 1999)

1) Repetition of a noun

Harm set, harm get.

Children are comfort, children are amusing, and children are sometimes a nuisance.

2) Repetition of a pronoun

Nothing venture, nothing gain.

He had only to open his eyes; but a weight was on them; a fear. He strained; he pushed; he looked, he saw Regent's Park before him. (Virginia Woolf: *Mrs. Dalloway*)

3) Repetition of a preposition (phrase)

Out of debt, out of mind.

4) Repetition of an adjective

No longer pipe, no longer dance.

5) Repetition of an adverb

Lightly come, lightly go.

6) Repetition of the subject and part of the predicate

He had put on his spectacles. He had stepped back. He had raised his hand. He had slightly narrowed his clear blue eyes… (Virginia Woolf: *To the Lighthouse*)

It is a luxury, it is a privilege, it is an indulgence for those who are at their ease.

(Edmund Burke: *Letter to Noble Lord*)

7) Repetition of a short sentence

They are common just as theft, cheating, perjury, adultery have always been common. They were common, not because people did not know what was right, but because people liked to do what was wrong. They were common, though prohibited by law. They were common, though condemned by public opinion. They were common, because in that age law and public opinion united had not sufficient force to restrain the greediness of powerful and unprincipled magistrates. (Thomas Babington Macaulay: *Francis Bacon*)

2. Epistrophe

Epistrophe (尾语反复) is the opposite to anaphora, that is, the repetition of the same word or group of words at the end of successive clauses, or sentences. (Corbett & Coonors, 1999)

1) Repetition of a noun

I'll have my bond! Speak not against my bond!

I have sworn an oath that I will have my bond! (William Shakespeare: *The Merchant of Venice*)

He that desires honor, is not worthy of honor.

2) Repetition of a pronoun

He that knows nothing doubts nothing.

3) Repetition of an adjective

If slavery is not wrong, nothing is wrong. (Abraham Lincoln)

To the good American many subjects are sacred: sex is sacred, women are sacred, children are sacred, business is sacred, America is sacred, Mason lodges and college clubs are sacred. (George Santayana: *Character and Opinion in the United States*)

4) Repetition of an adverb

He's learning fast. Are you earning fast? (Aetna Life Insurance's advertisement)

Waste not, want not.

5) Repetition of a prepositional phrase

In a cake, nothing tastes like real butter, nothing moistens like real butter, nothing enriches like real butter, nothing satisfies like real butter. (Pillsbury's advertisement)

6) Repetition of a linking verb-predicative

Perhaps this is the most important thing for me to take back from beach-living; simply the memory that each cycle of the tide is valid, each cycle of the wave is valid, each cycle of a relationship is valid. (Anne Lindbergh: *Gift from the Sea*)

7) Repetition of a short sentence

As long as the white man sent you to Korea, you bled. He sent you to Germany, you bled. He sent you to the South Pacific to fight the Japanese, you bled. (Speech by Malcolm X)

8) Use of two or more modes mentioned above

But to all those who would be tempted by weakness, let us leave no doubt that we will be as strong as we need to be for as long as we need to be ... We cannot learn from on another until we stop shouting at one another. (Richard M. Nixon: "Inaugural Address")

3. Simploce

Simploce (首语反复+尾语反复) comes from Greek, meaning interweaving. It is a combination of anaphora an epistrophe, that is, the repetition of two sets of words or phrases at the beginning, and of another at the end, of successive clauses, sentences, or passages. (Lanham, 1968)

1) Repetition of a pronoun and a noun

We are the hollow men
We are the stuffed men
Learning together
Headpiece filled with straw. Alas! (T. S. Eliot)

2) Repetition of a noun and a prepositional phrase

The yellow fog that rubs its back upon the window panes;
The yellow smoke that rubs its muzzle on the window panes. (T. S. Eliot)

3) Repetition of a pronoun + verb and a verb

I am convinced that we can succeed, and I am convinced that we must succeed.

4) Repetition of a pronoun + verb and a noun

This is the dead land
This is cactus land
Here the stone images
Are raised ... (T. S. Eliot)

5) Repetition of an adjective + noun

Most true that I must fair Fidessa love,
Most true that fair Fidessa cannot love.
Most true that I do feel the pains of love,
Most true that I am captive unto love.
Most true that I deluded am with love,
Most true that I do find the sleights of love.
Most true that nothing can procure her love,
Most true that I must perish in my love.
Most true that she contemns the god of love,
Most true that he is snared with her love.
Most true that she would have me cease to love,
Most true that she herself alone is Love.
Most true that though she hated I would love,
Most true that dearest life shall end with love. (Bartholomew Griffin: "Fidessa, LXII")

6) Repetition of (part of) a sentence and a sentence

If he wishes to float into fairyland, he reads a book; if he wishes to dash into the thick of battle, he reads a book; if he wishes to soar into heaven, he reads a book. (Chesterton)

4. Anadiplosis

Anadiplosis (尾首反复) is the repetition of the last word of one clause at the beginning of the following clause. (Corbett & Coonors, 1999)

1) Most of the words repeated are nouns

It is profit now, not the product. Half the time we cheat foreman, the foreman cheats the management, the management cheats the customers. And the customers are we. (J. B. Priestly)

And it was guns and ammunition, ammunition and guns – the unceasing and eternal cry. (Jack London)

All for one, and one for all.

2) Repetition of a pronoun

Margot looked at them both and they both saw that she was going to cry. (Charles Dickens: *Hard Times*)

3) Repetition of an adjective

Aboard my ship, excellent performance is standard. Standard performance is sub-standard. Sub-standard performance is not permitted to exist. (Herman Wouk: *The Caine Mutiny*)

The crime was common, common be the pain. (Alexander Pope: *Eloisa to Abelard*)

4) Repetition of an adverb

In the base court come down: down Court, down King,

For night owls shriek, where mounting Larks should sing. (William Shakespeare: *King Lear*)

5) Repetition of a verb

The laughter had to be gross or it would turn to sobs, and to sob would be to realize, and to realize would be to despair.

6) Repetition of synonyms

Fred was wearing trousers. The pants have big patches on them.

7) Repetition of a clause

The king was bad-tempered because he was often ill. He was often ill because he ate and drank too much.

5. Epanalepsis

Epanalepsis (首尾反复) is repetition at the end of a clause of the word that occurred at the beginning of the clause. (Corbett & Coonors, 1999) Or it means that a sentence begins and ends with the same word.

1) Repetition of a noun

Year chases year, decay pursues decay. (Samuel Johnson: *The Vanity of Human Wishes*)

And when the shadow fades and is no more, the light that lingers becomes a shadow to another light. (Kahlil Gibran: *The Prophet*)

A nut nut is a person who is nuts about the fun of eating nuts. (Skippy Peanut Butter's advertisement)

2) Repetition of a verb

Possessing what we still were unpossessed by,

Possessed by what we now no more possessed. (Robert Frost: "The Gift Outright")

3) Epanalepsis usually appears in proverbs

Blood must atone for blood.

Diamond cut diamond.

Business is business.

Nothing comes of nothing.

Like cures like.

Like loves / attracts / draws like.

Boys will be boys!

6. Polysyndeton

Polysyndeton (连词反复), a word coming from Greek, *polysyndetos*, meaning much compounded, is the repetition of conjunctions. Several conjunctions are used to link up a series of things, ideas or events. The conjunctions are mainly "and" and "or".

1) Only "and" is used.

a) With nouns

Only the sound of the soft waves and wind which rushed and pushed pops and creaks from the house.

b) With verbs

We talked, and talked, and talked – at least I did, we laughed, and laughed, and laughed – at least I did. (Mark Twain)

Scrooge went to bed again, and thought and thought and thought it over and over and over. (Charles Dickens)

c) With adjectives

And they are the wisest and most honest and idealistic and decent and loving and unprejudiced and well-informed generation of Americans in history. (Gene Lees)

d) With past participles

This doctor was of a race which for nearly four hundred years had beaten and starved and robbed and despised Kino's race, and frightened it too. (Steinbeck)

e) With present participles

Whirling and boiling and roaring like thunder, the stream came down upon them.

f) With sentences

She was smartly dressed ... And her cheeks and lips were rouged a little. And her eyes sparkled. And as usual she gave herself all the airs of one very well content with herself. (Theodore Dresier)

g) With words at different levels

The tent is soaked and heavy, and it flops about, and tumbles down on you, and clings round your head, and makes you mad.

2) Only "or" is used.

Now I absolutely flatly deny that I am a soul, or a body, or a mind, or an intelligence, or a brain, or a nervous system, or a bunch of glands, or any of the rest of these bits of me. The whole is greater than the part. And therefore, I, who am a man alive, am greater than the soul, or spirit, or body, or mind, or consciousness, or anything else that is merely a part of me. I am a man, and alive. I am man alive, and as long as I can, I intend to go on being man alive.

7. Polyptoton

Polyptoton (同根词反复) is the repetition of words of the same origin or the same derivatives.

1) Repetition of the same word but of different part of speech

Let me assert my firm belief that the only thing we have to fear is fear itself. (Franklin Delano Roosevelt: "First Inaugural Address")

Note: The first "fear" is a verb, and the second "fear" is a noun.

"Please, Please Me" (title of a Beatles' song)

Note: The first "please" is an auxiliary verb, and the second "please" is an action verb.

Never trouble trouble until trouble troubles you.

Note: The first "trouble" is a verb, the second is a noun, the third is a noun, and the fourth is a verb.

2) Repetition of words of the same origin

Not as a call to battle, though embattled we are. (John F. Kennedy: "Inaugural Address")

The Greeks are strong, and skilful to their strength.

Fierce to their skill, and to their fierceness valiant; ... (William Shakespeare: *Troilus and Cressida*)

Note: There are three pairs of polyptoton in these two lines.

Their blood bleeds the nation of its sanguine assurance.

We would like to contain the uncontainable figure in a glass.

10.4 Use of repetition

1. In idioms

Day after day we pushed into the unknown wilderness. (Mary Shelley: *Frankenstein*)

By and by in came the masters of the cottage.

The story appealed to everybody and anybody.

2. In proverbs

Like begets like.

Measure for measure.

Love me love my dog.

Easy come, easy go.

Early sow, early mow.

Nothing comes from nothing.

No answer is also an answer.

3. In poetry

O Captain! My Captain! Our fearful trip is done,
The ship has weather'd every rack, the prize we sought is won,
The port is near, the bells I hear, the people all exulting,
While follow eyes the steady keel, the vessel grim and daring;
But O heart! heart! heart!
O the bleeding drops of red!
Where on the deck my Captain lies,
Fallen cold and dead.
O Captain! My Captain! Rise up and hear the bells;
Rise up – for you the flag is flung – for you the bugle trills,
For you bouquets and ribbon'd wreaths – for you the shores a-crowding,
For you they call, the swaying mass, their eager faces turning;
Here, Captain! Dear father!
This arm beneath your head;
It is some dream that on the deck

You've fallen cold and dead.
My Captain does not answer, his lips are pale and still,
My father does not feel my arm, he has no pulse nor will;
The ship is anchor'd safe and sound, its voyage closed and done;
From fearful trip the victor ship comes in with object won;
Exult, O shores! And ring, O bells!
But I, with mournful tread,
Walk the deck my Captain lies,
Fallen cold and dead. (Walt Whitman: "O Captain! My Captain!")

Back again! Back again! Look to the shoes!
The shoe is too small, and not made for you!
Prince! Prince! Look again for thy bride,
For she's not the true one that sits by thy side. (Grimm: *Grimm's Fairy Tales*)

4. In novels and short stories

He looked about him with the strangest air, – an air of wondering pleasure, as if he had some part in the things he admired – and he pulled off a rough outer coat, and his hat. (Charles Dickens: *Great Expectations*)

It was a needless question, for a new desolation in the desolate house had told me so. (Charles Dickens: *Great Expectations*)

And soon came a gale of wind, and carried away Curdken's hat, and away went Curdken after it, while the girl went on combing and curling her hair. (Grimm: *Grimm's Fairy Tales*)

Still, the sun was hot, one got over things. Still, life had a way of adding day to day. Still, he thought, yawning and beginning to take notice – Regent's Park had changed very little since he was a boy, except for the squirrels – still, presumably there were compensations... (Virginia Woolf: *Mrs. Dalloway*)

When would they all be off? She fidgeted. That man, she thought, her eager rising in her, never give; that man took. She, on the other hand, would be forced to give. Mrs. Ramsay had given. Giving, giving, giving, she had died – and had left all this. (Virginia Woolf: *To the Lighthouse*)

5. In dramas

All my poor fool is hang'd! No, no, no life!

Why should a dog, a horse, a rat, have life,
And thou no breath at all? Thou'll come no more.
Never, never, never, never, never! (William Shakespeare: *King Lear*)

Fool: ... can you make no use of nothing, uncle?

Lear: Why, no, boy; nothing can be made out of nothing. (William Shakespeare: *King Lear*)

6. In prose

Our life is an apprenticeship to the truth that around every circle another can be drawn; that there is no end in nature, but every end is a beginning. (Emerson, "Circle", in *The Essential Writings of Ralph Waldo Emerson*)

It was wretched weather, stormy and wet, stormy and wet; and mud, mud, mud, deep in all the streets.

You can fall from a mountain, you can fall from a tree, but the best way to fall, is to fall in love with me.

The two old ladies gossiped and joked and told stories to each other about their families.

The poet was born poor, and poor he remained all his life.

7. In speeches

We shall go on to the end, we shall fight in France, we shall fight on the seas and oceans, we shall defend on the beaches, we shall fight on the landing grounds, we shall fight in the fields and in the streets, we shall fight in the hills ... (Winston Churchill: *Report the Miracle of Dunkirk*)

You ask, what is our aim? I can answer in one word. It is victory. Victory at all costs – victory in spite of all terrors – victory, however long and hard the road may be, for without victory there is no survival. (Winston Churchill: *Blood, Toil, Tears and Sweat*)

8. In well-known quotations

Thunder is good; thunder is impressive. But it is lightning that does the work. (Mark Twain)

What is everybody's business is nobody's business except the journalist's. (Joseph Pulitzer)

9. In news headlines

"Guilty, Guilty, Guilty" (*Time*, June 1996)

"Millennium This, Millenium That" (*Time*, February 2000)

"When They Party, They Party Hearty" (*Time*, May 2003)

10. In advertisements

Think again. Think Canon. (advertisement for Canon)

If it's got to be clean, it's got to be Tide. If it's got to be clean, it's got to be Tide. (advertisement for Tide)

Give a Timex to all, to all a good time. (advertisement for watches)

Last night I couldn't sleep
I wanted you warm against me
I wanted u on me
I wanted to feel u all over my body
But I couldn't find u …
My pyjamas ... (advertisement for pyjamas)

11. In academic writing

The substitution of rolling friction for sliding friction results in a considerable reduction in friction.

The force upward equals the force downward so that the balloon stays at the level. (repetition)

12. In nursery rhymes

Repetition is often used in nursery rhymes for children to acquire language and aesthetic ability.

Sing, sing, what shall I sing?
Mary Ann Cotton tied up on a string.
Where? Where? Up in the air,
Selling black pudding a penny a pair.

If You Are Happy
If you are happy and you know it,
Clap your hands.
If you are happy and you know it,

Clap your hands.
If you are happy and you know it,
Clap your hands.

What Is Your House Made Of?
What is your house made of?
My house is made of bricks and stones.
What is your house made from?
My house is made from love alone.

There's No Place Like Home
There's no place like home,
Well, I say now home, home, sweet home.
There's no place like home,
Wherever you wander,
There's no place like home.

Chapter Eleven Parallelism

Parallelism (排比) comes from a Greek word, *parallismos*, meaning along one another. In classical rhetoric, this device is called parison or isocolon. Parallelism is the arrangement of similarly constructed clauses, sentences, or verse lines in a pairing or other sequence suggesting some correspondence between them. (Baldick, 2001) Parallelism is regularly employed in the listing of facts, ideas, events, etc., and the parallel elements may range from a minimum of two to any number required. To make the parallel clear, it is essential to repeat the marker of the parallelism, such as an article, preposition, infinitive, or the introductory word of a main or subordinate clause.

Parallelism involves balancing the structural elements of a sentence. The effect of parallelism is usually one of balanced arrangement achieved through repetition of the same syntactic forms. (Baldick, 2001) Parallelism can make a very formidable and forceful writing. It has rhetorical effects such as emphasizing a point, adding balance, coherence and rhythm and clarity to the sentence, keeping the trend of thought clear and so on. Parallel elements in a sentence or the parallel sentences should have the same or similar functions and grammatical forms.

I like reading, singing, and to listen to music. (not good)

→ I like reading, singing, and listening to music. (better)

They can learn cooking, canoeing, swimming, or how to make ropes. (not good)

→ They can learn cooking, canoeing, swimming, and rope-making. (better)

The hurricane not only destroyed the fishing but also the homes of the fishermen. (not good)

→ The hurricane destroyed not only the fishing but also the homes of the fishermen. (better)

The production manager was asked to write his report quickly, accurately, and in a detailed manner. (not good)

→ The production manager was asked to write his report quickly, accurately, and thoroughly. (better)

→ The production manager was asked to write his report in a quick, accurate, and a detailed manner. (better)

11.1 Purposes of parallelism

1. For emphasis

It was all so mixed up in her mind and her mind was so tired, so bewildered. (Margaret Mitchell: *Gone with the Wind*)

He stood erect, confident, masterful, and as I looked, I felt a thrill of pride in him, pride in his genius which had brought us hither, pride in our mother earth – for were we not her far-wandering children? (Garret Putman Serviss: *A Clumbus of Space*)

She's better than ninety-nine folk out of a hundred, I tell you! She's BETTER, she is! She's fair, she's honest, she's straight! There isn't anything underhand or superior about her. Don't be mean about her! (D. H. Lawrence: *Sons and Lovers*)

2. For brevity

I came, I saw, I conquered. (Julius Caesar)

I used to organize my father's tool, my mother's kitchen utensils, my sister's boyfriends. (*College English*, Book 1, Unit 6)

3. For contrast

I have a dream that my four little children will one day live in a nation where they will not be judged by the color of their skin but by the content of their character. (Martin Luther King, Jr.: "I Have a Dream")

Every text is constructed as a mosaic of citations, every text is an absorption and transformation of other texts. (Kristeva)

4. For climax in meaning

No ordinary house could have contained my feelings, but this great one in which greater longings are ever free to grow ... I am reserved for further struggles, to wrestle with rocks, to bleed if necessary, to ascend. (Patrick White: *Voss*)

The Mole had been working very hard all the morning, spring-cleaning his little home. First with brooms, then with dusters; then on ladders and steps and chairs, with a brush and a pail of whitewash; till he had dust in his throat and eyes, and splashes of whitewash all over his black fur, and an aching back and weary arms. (Kenneth Grahame: *The Wind in the Willows*)

5. For attraction

Moisture Wear Power,

It keeps your skin fresh and beautiful all day. (advertisement for Moisture Wear Power)

Not only making the whole keyboard much thinner, but also allowing for more comfortable, precise, and responsive typing that just feel right. (advertisement for keyboards)

It keeps a flower fresh and beautiful all day.

6. For listing facts

As it was a fine day and I was in no hurry, I was taking my time, looking in shop windows, strolling in the park, and sometimes just stopping and looking around me. (*College English*, Book III, Unit 1)

I shall carry with me into the darkest corners of the world knowledge, peace, freedom, religion, the hope of heaven! (Charlotte Brontë: *Jane Eyre*)

It is the study of how second languages are learned. It is the study of how learners create a new language system with only limited exposure to a second language. It is the study of what is learned of a second language and what is not learned; it is the study of why most second language learners do not achieve the same degree of proficiency in a second language as they do in their native language; it is also the study of why only some learners appear to achieve native-like proficiency in more than one language. (Gass & Selinker)

11.2 Classification of parallelism

In a parallel construction it is necessary to balance word with word, phrase with phrase, clause with clause, sentence with sentence.

1. At the word level

1) Nouns

Lumber, corn, wheat, and furs moved downtown to the delta country. (Noel

Grove: *Mark Twain – Mirror of America*)

Beauty, grace, truth

2) Verbs

He sat down and began to work.

I have always sought but seldom obtained a parking space near the door.

3) Adjectives

The child was pretty and intelligent.

The letter, short, cold, sharp-tongued, was unexpected.

I believe that every night implies a responsibility; every opportunity, an obligation, every possession, a duty.

4) Adverbs

When she came home, she found her children grown up mentally, physically and culturally.

He was exhausted physically, fiscally and mentally.

Like a ship without a rudder, like a runaway horse, like a collapsed balloon, like an iceberg in an Atlantic storm, like a boat in the Niagara rapids, she moved on sullenly, recklessly, mechanically, may hap into the very jaws of the most frightful danger, the bright intelligences within no more able to modify her motions even by a finger's breadth than they were able to affect Mercury's movements around the Sun.

5) Prepositions

We care to provide service above and beyond the call of duty. (advertisement for UPS)

Many more visitors than it can comfortably hold pour into it, off the regular steamers, off chartered boats and off yachts; all day they amble up the two-path, looking for what?

The snow falls on every wood and field, by the river and pond, on the hill and in the valley, and no crevice is forgotten.

2. At the phrase level

You can go there on foot, by bus or by train.

We can gain knowledge by reading, by reflection, by observation or by practice.

To be, or not to be, that is the question. (William Shakespeare: *Hamlet*)

3. At the clause level

When a person wants to discover and change his "losing streak", when he wants to become more like the winner he was born to be, he can use gestalt-type experiments and transactional analysis to make change happen. (Howard Kendler)

Some people think that the weather is unpleasant, the city ugly and dirty, the competition fierce and the streets unsafe.

4. At the sentence level

The man who is bored with his meals corresponds to the victim of Byronic unhappiness. The invalid who eats from sense of duty corresponds to the ascetic, the gormandizer to the voluptuary.

Moving the lamp as the man moved, I made out that he was substantially dressed, but roughly, like a voyager by sea. That he had long iron-grey hair. That his age was about sixty. That he was a muscular man, strong on his legs, and that he was browned and hardened by exposure to weather. (Charles Dickens: *Great Expectations*)

5. At the paragraph level

It is the same life that shoots in joy through the dust of the earth in numberless blades of grass and breaks into tumultuous waves of leaves and flowers.

It is the same life that is rocked in the ocean-cradle of birth and of death, in ebb and in flow. (Tagore: *Gitanjali*)

If it is not my portion to meet thee in this life then let me ever feel that I have missed they sight – let me not forget for a moment, let me carry the pangs of this sorrow in my dreams and in my wakeful hours.

As my days pass in the crowded market of this world and my hands grow full with the daily profits, let me ever feel that I have gained nothing – let me not forget for a moment, let me carry the pangs of this sorrow in my dreams and in my wakeful hours.

When I sit by the roadside, tired and panting, when I spread my bed low in the dust, let me ever feel the long journey is still before me – let me not forget for a moment, let me carry the pangs of this sorrow in my dreams and in my wakeful hours.

When my rooms have been decked out and the flutes sound and the laughter there is loud, let me ever feel that I have not invited thee to my house – let me not forget for a moment, let me carry the pangs of this sorrow in my dreams and in my wakeful hours.

I am like a remnant of a cloud of autumn uselessly roaming in the sky, O my sun ever-glorious! Thy touch has not yet melted my vapour, making me one with the light, and thus I count months and years separated from thee.

If this be thy wish and if this be they play, then take this fleeting emptiness of mine, paint it with colours, gild it with gold, float it on the wanton wind and spread it in varied wonders. (Tagore: *Gitanjali*)

11.3 Use of parallelism

1. In proverbs

Least said soonest mended.

Run with the hare and hunt with the hounds.

2. In poetry

Wherefore feed and clothe and save,
From the cradle to the grave,
Those ungrateful drones who would
Drain your sweat – nay, drink your blood! (Percy Bysshe Shelley: "Song to the Men of England")

Sow seed – but let no tyrant reap;
Find wealth, – let no imposter heap;
Weave robes, – let no idler wear;
Forge arms, – in your defense to bear. (Percy Bysshe Shelley: "Song to the Men of England")

Blow, breezes, blow!
Let Curdken's hat go!
Blow, breezes, blow!
Let him after it go!
O'er hills, dales, and rocks,
Away be it whirl'd
Till the silvery locks
Are all comb'd and curl'd! (Grimm: *Grimm's Fairy Tales*)

Day after, O lord of my life, shall I stand before thee face to face. With folded hands, O lord of all worlds, shall I stand before thee face to face.

Under thy great sky in solitude and silence, with humble heart shall I stand before thee face to face.

In this laborious world of thine, tumultuous with toil and with struggle, among hurrying crowds shall I stand before thee face to face.

And when my work shall be done in this world, O king of kings, alone and speechless shall I stand before thee face to face.

I know thee as my God and stand apart – I do not know thee as my own and come closer. I know thee as my father and bow before thy feet – I do not grasp thy hand as my friend's. (Tagore: *Gitanjali*)

3. In novels and short stories

I remember a quick snatching of precious things in boxes placed for such a moment as this, a quick snapping of halter ropes around the ponies' necks, a gleaming of gun-barrels in the hot sunlight; a solid cloud of dust rolling up behind us, bigger and nearer every second; and the urgent voice of Jondo: "Ride for your lives!" (Margaret Hill McCarter: *Vanguards of the Plains*)

Estella was always about, and always let me in and out, but never told me I might kiss her again. Sometimes, she would coldly tolerate me; sometimes, she would condescend to me; sometimes, she would be quite familiar with me; sometimes, she would tell me energetically that she hated me. (Charles Dickens: *Great Expectations*)

4. In dramas

I'll give my jewels for a set of beads,
My gorgeous palace for a hermitage,
My gay apparel for an almsman's gown,
My figured goblets for a dish of wood ... (William Shakespeare: *Richard II*)

Doubt thou the stars are fire;
Doubt that the sun doth move;
Doubt truth to be a liar;
But never doubt I love. (William Shakespeare: *Hamlet*)

5. In speeches

Now is the time to make real the promises of Democracy. Now is the time to rise from the dark and desolate valley of segregation to the sunlit path of racial justice. Now is the time to open the doors of opportunity to all of God's children. Now is the time to lift our nation from the quick sands of racial injustice to the solid rock of brotherhood. (Martin Luther King, Jr.: "I Have a Dream")

We are caught in war, wanting peace. We're torn by division, wanting unity. (Richard M. Nixon: "Inaugural Address")

6. In prose

I was neither elated by the ambition of fame, nor depressed by the apprehension of contempt. (Edward Gibbon: "Memoirs")

The traveller doesn't need to go outside Australasia for sightseeing, or to see the best, get the best or do the best this planet affords... (G. D. Meudell)

I take thee to my welded wife, to have and to hold from this day forward, for better or worse, for richer or for poorer, in health and sickness, to love and cherish till death do we part, according to God's holy ordinance; and thereto I plight thee my troth. (oath at wedding ceremony)

7. In well-known quotations

Fame and riches are fleeting. Stupidity is eternal. (Don Williams Jr.)

Most people do not really want freedom, because freedom involves responsibility, and most people are frightened of responsibility. (Sigmund Freud)

8. In news headlines

"IT'S AN AD, AD, AD AD WORLD" (*Time*, September 2002)

"Friends in Need, Friends Indeed" (*Time*, November 1997)

9. In advertisements

Deliciously simple. Simply delicious. (advertisement for food)

Marry the right person, hire the best photographer, live happily ever after. (advertisement for wedding photography)

More legroom, more elbowroom, more comfort. (advertisement for Airlines)

It's not your car;
It's not your friends;
It's not your job;
It's your watch that tells most about who you are. (advertisement for Seiko)

Best Bank
Best Trade Finance Bank
Best Bank for Payments and Collections
Best Sub-Custodian
Best Securitization House
At HSBC, we strive to do the best. (advertisement for HSBC)

I saw a city with its head in the future and its soul in the past;
I saw an ancient opera performed on the modern streets;
I saw a dozen races co-exist as one;
I didn't see an unsafe street;
Was it a dream I saw?
– Singapore! So easy to enjoy, so hard to forget. (advertisement for tourism)

10. In academic writing

The next medical revolution will change the problem, because genetic engineering has the potential to conquer cancer, grow new blood vessels in the heart, block the growth of blood vessels in tumors, create new organs from stem cells and perhaps even reset the primeval genetic coding that causes cells to age.

Burning these fuels produces many unwanted substances, such as smoke, and the gases sulphur dioxide and carbon monoxide.

First the logs are placed in the shredder. Then they are cut into small chips which are mixed with water and acid. Next they are heated and crushed to a heavy pulp which is cleaned. It is also chemically bleached to whiten it. After this, it is passed through rollers to flatten it. Then, sheets of wet paper are produced. Finally, the water is removed from the sheets which are pressed, dried and refined until the finished paper is produced.

Chapter Twelve Antithesis

Antithesis (对偶) refers to a contrast or opposition, either rhetorical or philosophical. It depends on the disposition of words that serves to emphasize a contrast or opposition of ideas, usually by the balancing of connected clauses with parallel grammatical constructions (Baldick, 2001) to achieve force and emphasis, whether for profundity of judgment, for humor or for satire. Antithesis is presented in the parallel form, but it is different from parallelism in that in parallelism, the objects are related and equally important, while antithesis focuses on the contrasting relationship between only two objects.

12.1 Purposes of antithesis

1. For contrast

To err is human; to forgive, divine. (Alexander Pope)

That's one small step for a man, one giant leap for mankind. (Neil Armstrong)

It (American imperialism) is the strongest in history and also the weakest in history. (Anna Louise Strong)

Not where one is bred, but where he is fed. (proverb)

All tragedies are finished by a death,
All comedies are ended by a marriage. (George Gordon Byron)

2. For humor

Money is a good servant but a bad master. (proverb)

Hope is a good breakfast but a bad supper. (proverb)

3. For satire

Many are harsh, but few are brave. (proverb)

A wise man thinks all that he says, a fool says all that he thinks. (proverb)

When you are present, you wish to (be) absent, and when absent, you desire to be present.

4. For emphasis

They are beautiful: they are only decorated. They are not clean: they are only shaved and starched. They are not dignified: they are only fashionably dressed. They are not educated: they are only college passmen. They are not religious: they are only few renters; they are not moral: they are only conventional ... (George Bernard Shaw)

Any man or state who fights on against Nazidom will have our aids. Any man or state who matches with Hitler is our foe. (Winston Churchill)

If we try, we might succeed; if we do not try, we cannot succeed.

5. For conveying a certain sense of complexity in a person, a situation or an idea by admitting opposite or contrasting truths

Success makes men proud; failure makes them wise.

Education makes a people easy to lead, but difficult to drive; easy to govern, but impossible to enslave.

12.2 Forms of antithesis

1. Antithesis of contrasting two kinds of people

For contemplation he and valour formed,
For softness she and sweet attractive grace;
He for God only, she for God in him. (John Milton: *Paradise Lost*)

The best woman has always somewhat of a man's strength; and the noblest man of a woman's gentleness. (Miss Mulock)

2. Antithesis of contrasting two kinds of objects things

With the sky above my head,
And the grass beneath my feet; … (Thomas Hood: "The Song of the Shirt")

Yet poor with fortune, and with learning blind,
The bad must miss; the good, untaught, will find. (Alexander Pope: "An Essay on Man")

Successful love may sometimes use the language of flattery. But hopeless love always speaks the truth. (Wilkie Collins)

3. Antithesis of contrasting two aspects of one person

They that saw tears shall reap in joy.

They were weak in number but strong in pride.

He who has never tasted what is bitter does not know what is sweet.

4. Antithesis of contrasting two aspects of one object / thing

A contemporary classic. A timeless timepiece. (advertisement for watches)

America is the paradise for the rich and the hell for the poor.

12.3 Use of antithesis

1. In proverbs

Harm set, harm get.

Man proposes, God disposes.

More haste, less speed.

Lost ounces. Save pounds.

You can take the boy out of the country, but you can't take the country out of the boy.

A friend exaggerates a man's virtue, an enemy his faults.

The best horse needs breaking, and the aptest child needs teaching.

Modesty helps one to go forward, whereas conceit makes one lag behind.

Little pigeons can carry great messages.

2. In advertisements

Tide's in, dirt's out. (advertisement for Tide)

Be Brilliant! Be Sharp! (advertisement for Sharp)

Big thrills, small bills. (advertisement for Taxi)

3. In prose

Yet poor with fortune, and with learning blind,

The bad must miss; the good, untaught, will find. (Alexander Pope: "An Essay on Man")

There is hardly any body good for every thing, and there is scarcely any body who is absolutely good for nothing. (P. D. Chesterfield)

To love is to suffer, to be loved is to cause suffering. (Comtesse Diane)

4. In speeches

On this day, we gather because we have chosen hope over fear, unity of purpose over conflict and discord. (Barack Obama)

I know not what course others may take; but as for me, give me liberty, or give me death. (Patrick Henry)

5. In news headlines

"Warm Welcome, Cold Feet" (*Time*, January 1996)

"Less Cost, More Risk" (*Time*, July 1996)

6. In well-known quotations

Wise men talk because they have something to say; fools, because they have to say something. (Plato)

Many receive advice, few profit by it. (Publilius Syrus)

7. In novels and short stories

It was the best of times, it was the worst of times, it was the age of wisdom, it was the age of foolishness, it was the epoch of belief, it was the epoch of incredulity, it was the season of light, it was the season of darkness, it was the spring of hope, it was the winter of despair. We had everything before us, we had nothing before us … (Charles Dickens: *A Tale of Two Cities*)

Her eyes were shining brilliantly, but her face lost its color within twenty seconds. (O. Henry)

A young gentleman may be over-careful of himself, or he may be under-careful of himself. He may brush his hair too regular, or too un-regular. He may wear his boots much too large for him, or much too small. That is according as the young gentleman has his original character formed. (Charles Dickens: *David Copperfield*)

8. In poetry

The night has a thousand eyes,
And the day but one;… (F. W. Bourdillon: "The Night Has a Thousand Eyes")

A honey tongue, a heart of gall,
Is fancy's spring, but sorrow's fall. (Walter Raleigh: "The Nymph's Reply to the Shepherd")

Youth is full of pressure, age is full of care,
Youth like summer morn, age like winter weather,
Youth like summer brave, age like winter bare,
Youth is full of sport, age's breath is short,
Youth is nimble, age is lame,
Youth is hot and bold, age is weak and cold,
Youth is wild, and age is tame,
Age, I do abhor thee, youth, I do adore thee,
Oh! My love, my love is young. (William Shakespeare)

Beauty, strength, youth are flowers but fading seen;
Duty, faith, love are roots, and ever green.

9. In dramas

The evil that men do lives after them.
The good is oft interred with their bones;
So let it be with Caesar. (William Shakespeare: *Julius Caesar*)
Not that I lov'd Caesar less,
But that I lov'd Rome more. (William Shakespeare: *Julius Caesar*)

10. In academic writing

Some sounds are unpleasant to our ears while others are very pleasant to hear.

Chapter Thirteen Chiasmus

Chiasmus (交错配置) (derived from the Greek term for the letter X, or for a crossover) is a sequence of two phrases or clauses which are parallel in syntax, but which reverse the order of the corresponding words. (Abrams & Harpham, 2010) Or it is a figure of speech, by which the order of the terms in the first of two parallel clauses is reversed in the second. This may involve a repetition of the same words. (Baldick, 2001) Simply put, chiasmus is the reversal of grammatical structures in successive phrases or clauses. (Corbett & Coonors, 1999)

Antimetabole, a sub-type of chiasmus, is a figure of speech in which a pair of words is repeated in reverse order. (Baldick, 2001) According to Corbett & Coonors (1999), chiasmus and antimetabole are similar in that both involve a reversal of grammatical structures in successive phrases or clauses, but chiasmus does not necessarily involve a repetition of words, and both can be used to reinforce antithesis.

13.1 Purposes of chiasmus

1. For contrast

A man may not always be what he appears to be, but what he appears to be is always a significant part of what he is. (Williard Gaylin)

2. For intensity

Let us never negotiate out of fear, but let us never fear to negotiate. (John F. Kennedy: "Inaugural Address")

3. For balance

Vigor is the way of youth; the way of age is wisdom.

4. For coherence

Mary went to London; to Paris went Peter.

5. For rhythmic beauty

Forty is the old age of youth; fifty is the youth of old age. (Victor Hugo)

13.2 Classification of chiasmus

1. Repetition of words in reverse order

1) Change of the subjects

Mankind must put an end to war, or war will put an end to mankind. (John F. Kennedy)

Pleasure's a sin, and sometimes sin's a pleasure. (George Gordon Byron)

2) Change of the objects

A pessimist is one who makes difficulties of his opportunities; an optimist is one who makes opportunities of his difficulties. (Reginald B. Mansell)

3) Change of the predictive

The real cause for dread is not a machine turned human, but a human turned machine. (Franz F. Winkler)

4) Different subjects

Live simply, so that others may simply live.

5) The same subject

Eat to live, and not live to eat.

6) Change of the order of words of the same parts

For the sky and the sea, and the sea and the sky,

Lay a load on my weary eye. (Samuel Taylor Coleridge: "The Rime of the Ancient Mariner")

7) Homonym

It is better to make fast friends than to make friends fast.

8) Homophone

We can make young people groan and grown people young.

2. Repetition of syntactic elements in reverse order

1) Change of the whole sentence in reverse order

Lack of confidence is not the result of difficulty, the difficulty comes from lack of confidence.

Pleasure's a sin, and sometimes sin's a pleasure. (George Gordon Byron)

2) Change of parts of the sentence

The reasonable man adapts himself to the world; the unreasonable one persists in trying to adapt the world to himself. Therefore all progress depends on the unreasonable man. (George Bernard Shaw: *Man and Superman*)

3) With some different words of the similar meaning

Whoever shall exalt himself shall be based; and he that shall humble himself shall be exalted. (The Bible)

3. A reversed parallel between two corresponding pairs of ideas

1) Without omission

The fool does think he is wise, but the wise man knows himself to be a fool. (proverb)

Language changes. So should your dictionary. (advertisement for *Webster's Seventh New Collegiate Dictionary*)

We have escaped as a bird
From the snare of the fowlers
The snare is broken
And we have escaped. (Psalms)

It is hard to make money, but to spend it is easy.

2) With omission

Despised, if ugly; if she's fair, betrayed. (Mary Leapor: "Essay on Woman")

Works without show, and without pomp presides. (Alexander Pope)

The years to come seemed waste of breath,
A waste of breath the years behind. (William Butler Yeats: "An Irish Airman Foresees His Death")

By day the frolic, and the dance by night. (Samuel Johnson: "The Vanity of Human Wishes")

His time a moment, and a point his space. (Alexander Pope: "Essay on Man")

13.3 Use of chiasmus

1. In poetry

Flowers are lovely; love is flower-like. (Samuel Taylor Coleridge)

Exalts his enemies, his friends destroys. (John Dryden: "Absalom and Achitophel")

The land was ours before we were the land's.
She was our land more than a hundred years
Before we were her people. (Robert Frost)

2. In prose

You cannot be truly free unless we are free too, for such is the nature of things that he who entrenches on the liberty of others is the first to lose his own and become a slave. (John Milton)

Beauty is truth, truth beauty. (John Keats)

3. In dramas

Love's fire heats water, water cools not love. (William Shakespeare)

But O, what damned minutes tell he o'er
Who dotes, yet doubts; suspects, yet strong loves. (William Shakespeare)

4. In novels and short stories

The top of mine to the foot of yours – the foot of yours to the top of mine ... (Charles Dickens)

The jail might have been the infirmary, the infirmary might have been the jail ... (Charles Dickens)

5. In speeches

And so, my fellow Americans: ask not what your country can do for you – ask what you can do for your country. (John F. Kennedy)

We cannot always build the future for our youth, but we can build our youth for the future. (Franklin Delano Roosevelt)

Whether we bring our enemies to justice or bring justice to our enemies, justice will be done. (George W. Bush: "Address on September 20, 2011")

6. In well-known quotations

A statesman is a politician who places himself at the service of the nation. A politician is a statesman who places the nation at his service. (Georges Pompidou)

You can fool all the people some of the time, and some of the people all the time, but you cannot full all the people all the time. (Abraham Lincoln)

Chapter Fourteen Climax

Climax (层进) is derived from the Greek, *klimax*, meaning ladder, which implies the progression of thought at a uniform or almost uniform rate of significance or intensity, like the steps of a ladder ascending evenly. It is a figure of speech in which a sequence of terms is linked by chain-like repetition through three or more clauses in ascending order of importance. (Baldick, 2001) It is usually put at the end of the sentence, paragraph, or a stanza of a poem. The successful construction of this device depends much on the character of the thought itself as well as a good command of vocabulary, from weak to strong, from light to weighty. Climax can be classified according to semantic intensity, degree, space order, and time order. It is used to increase importance, weight, or emphasis.

14.1 Purposes of climax

1. For semantic intensity

He who loses wealth loses much; he who loses a friend loses more; but he who loses courage loses all.

He has gone, he has escaped, he has broken away. (Marcus T. Cicero)

2. For emphasis

We strive for the good, aim for the better, and seize the best.

Reading maketh a full man; conference a ready man; and writing an exact man. (Francis Bacon)

3. For description

Rain fell on the roof of the barn and dripped steadily from the eaves. Rain fell in the barnyard and ran in crooked courses down into the lane where thistles and pigweed grew. Rain spattered against Mrs. Zuckerman's kitchen windows and came gushing out of the downspouts. Rain fell on the backs of sheep as they grazed in the meadow. When the sheep tired of standing in the rain, they walked slowly up the lane and into the fold. (E. B. White: *Charlotte's Web*)

He gazed upon the pretty houses, the green hills and the broad Pacific, his heart was filled with awe.

First the lights fused, next a water pipe burst, and then, to cap it all, part of the ceiling fell down.

14.2 Classification of climax

There are three kinds of climax according to the parallel components.

1. Parallel words

1) Nouns

Social position, friends, reputation, life itself, had no longer any attraction for him.

2) Adjectives

I am alone now, quite alone, and my heart is broken. (H. Haggard: *Stella Fregelius*)

3) Verbs

They talked and laughed and shouted, and there was the clatter of knives and forks, and strange sounds of eating. (W. S. Maugham: *Of Human Bondage*)

4) Adverbs

The prisoner was first questioned, then tortured, and finally shot.

5) Numerals

The nurse came back with a bunch of keys, and led me up one, two, three, four, five flights of stairs, all muffled in crimson carpet, the walls thick with large brownish pictures. (Doris Lessing: *In Pursuit of the English*)

2. Parallel phrases

It was the ruin of the family, the uprooting of morals, the destruction of Germany. (W. S. Maugham: *Of Human Bondage*)

3. Parallel sentences

Lincoln recognized worth in the common people; he loved the common people; he fought for the common people; and he died for the common people.

When wealth is lost, nothing is lost; when health is lost, something is lost; when character is lost, all is lost!

14.3 Use of climax

1. In proverbs

One boy is a boy, two boys half a boy, three boys no boy.

Early to bed, early to rise, makes a man healthy, wealthy and wise.

2. In prose

For want of a nail, the shoe was lost; for want of a shoe the horse was lost; for want of a horse the rider was lost. (Benjamin Franklin)

I'm firm, you are stubborn, he is pigheaded. (P. D. Chesterfield)

He who loses money loses much; he who loses a friend loses more; and he who loses his mind loses all.

3. In speeches

These are not dark days; these are great days – the greatest days our country has ever lived. (Winston Churchill)

But, in a large sense, we cannot dedicate, we cannot consecrate, we cannot hallow this ground. The brave men, who struggled here have consecrated it far above our power to add or detract. (Abraham Lincoln)

4. In novels and short stories

The Mole had been working very hard all the morning, spring-cleaning his little home. First with brooms, then with dusters; then on ladders and steps and chairs, with a brush and a pail of whitewash; till he had dust in his throat and eyes, and splashes of whitewash all over his black fur, and an aching back and weary arms. (Kenneth Grahame: *The Wind in the Willows*)

She had discussed the possibility of Dogs, Cats, and Ferrets; of shotguns, rifles, and explosives; of traps and snares; of poisons and poison gases. There might even be Boys! (Robert Lawson: *Rabbit Hill*)

The springtime came, first to the plains and foothills and then up to the mountain snows. (Agnes Smedley)

5. In dramas

As Caesar loved me, I weep for him; as he was fortunate, I rejoice at it; as he was valiant, I honour him; but he was ambitious, I slew him. There is tears for his love; joy for his fortune; humour for his valour; and death for his ambition. (William Shakespeare: *Julius Caesar*)

Doubt thou the stars are fire;
Doubt that the sun doth move;
Doubt truth to be a liar;
But never doubt I love. (William Shakespeare: *Hamlet*)

Your brother and my sister no sooner met but they looked, no sooner looked but they loved, no sooner loved but they sighed, no sooner sighed but they asked one another the reason, no sooner knew the reason but they sought the remedy; and in these degrees they have made a pair of stairs to marriage. (William Shakespeare: *As You Like It*)

6. In poetry

Say I'm weary, say I'm sad,
Say that health and wealth have missed me,
Say I'm growing old, but add,
Jenny kiss'd me. (Leigh Hunt: *Rondeau*)

Tomorrow, and tomorrow, and tomorrow,
Creeps in this petty pace from day to day,
To the last syllable of recorded time.
And all our yesterdays have lighted fools.
The way to dusty death, out, out, brief candle.
Life's but a walking shadow, a poor player,
That struts and frets his hour upon the stage,
And then is heard no more: it is a tale,
Told by an idiot, full of sound and fury,
Signifying nothing. (William Shakespeare: *Macbeth*)

7. In advertisements

Less space. Less noise. Less expense. (advertisement for an apartment)

One drop makes beauty; two drops make lovers; three drops make a love affair.

(advertisement for perfume)

To laugh, to love, to understand each other. (advertisement for a magazine)

8. In news headlines

"Drugs, Money and a President's Ruin" (*Time*, February 1996)

"Point, Click, Win!" (*Time*, January 2000)

9. In university slogans

The Way, The Truth, The Life (University of Glasgow)

Knowledge, Wisdom, Humanity (University of Manchester)

10. In well-known quotations

Renounce my love, my life, myself – and you. (Alexander Pope)

I think we've reached a point of great decision, not just for our nation, not only for all humanity, but for life upon the earth. (George Wald)

Chapter Fifteen Anticlimax

Anticlimax (突降), or bathos, the opposite of climax, refers to an abrupt lapse from growing intensity to triviality in any passage of dramatic, narrative, or descriptive writing, with the effect of disappointed expectation or deflated suspense. (Baldick, 2001) It involves stating one's thoughts in a descending order of significance or intensity, from strong to weak, from weighty to light. It is based on the principle that the more power the thought decreases in importance, the higher the force of the ridicule or satire would be. Its effects are of being ironic, sarcastic, humorous, funny, laughable, devastating or dramatic. It is usually put at the end of a sentence / paragraph, or a stanza of a poem.

15.1 Purposes of anticlimax

1. For fun

We had plenty of company in the way of wagon-loads and mule-loads of tourists – and the dust. (Mark Twain: *A Tramp Abroad*)

I came, I saw, I was conquered.

There are three kinds of lies: lies, damned lies, and statistics. (Benjamin Disraeli)

2. For satire

In our country we have those three unspeakably precious things: freedom of speech, freedom of conscience, and the prudence never to practice either of them. (Mark Twain)

A woman who could face the very devil himself – or a mouse – loses her grip and goes all to pieces in front of a flash of lightning. (Mark Twain)

3. For surprise

A woman with fair opportunities, and without an absolute hump may marry

WHOM SHE LIKES. (William Makepeace Thackeray: *Vanity Fair*)

He sprang to his feet, flung off his boat, drew his sword, jumped upon the enemy, and burped.

15.2 Levels of anticlimax

1. At the word level

He lost his empire, his family, and his fountain pen.

The explosion completely destroyed a church, two houses, and a flowerpot.

A family is a unit composed not only of children, but of men, women, an occasional animal, and the common cold. (Ogden Nash)

2. At the sentence level

I love my motherland, I love my people, I love my wife and my son and my daughter, I also love my pretty little dog.

He has been a doctor a year now and has had two patients – no three, I think – yes, it was three; I attended their funerals. (Mark Twain)

One speaks the glory of the British Queen.

And one describes a charming Indian screen. (Alexander Pope: *Rape of the Lock*)

3. At the discourse level

"Gentlemen, it is a very great honor to have you here in Hiroshima."

There were fresh bows, and the faces grew more and more serious each time the name Hiroshima was repeated.

"Hiroshima, as you know, is a city familiar to everyone," continued the mayor.

"Yes, yes, of course," murmured the company, more and more agitated.

"Seldom has a city gained such world renown, and I am proud and happy to welcome you to Hiroshima, a town known throughout the world for its – oysters." (Jacques Danvoir)

15.3 Use of anticlimax

1. In proverbs

Religion, credit and the eye are not to be touched.

The big fish eat the little ones, the little ones eat the shrimps, and the shrimps are forced to eat mud.

2. In novels and short stories

"Who is he?" "Why, he has gone the vole – has been soldier, ballad-singer, travelling tinker and is now a beggar. (Walter Scott)

It is a truth universally acknowledged that a single man in possession of a fortune must be in want of a wife. (Jane Austin: *Pride and Prejudice*)

3. In poetry

How haughtily he cocks his nose,
To tell what every schoolboy knows. (Jonathan Swift)

But thousands die, without this or that,
die, and endow a college or a cat. (Alexander Pope)

A Book of Verses underneath the Bough,
A Jug of Wine, a Loaf of Bread – and Thou,
Beside me singing in the Wilderness,
Oh, Wilderness were Paradise enow! (Omar Khayyam: *The Rubaiyat*)

4. In dramas and movies

There may be some doubt as to who are the best people to have charge of children, but there can be no doubt that parents are the worst. (George Bernard Shaw)

Forrest: Now because I'd been a football star, and a war hero, and a national celebrity, and a shrimping boat captain, and a college graduate, the city fathers of Greenbow, Alabama decided to get together and offered me a fine job – a gardener. (*Forrest Gump*)

5. In prose

When George the Fourth was still reigning over the privacies of Windsor, when the Duke of Wellington was Prime Minister, and Mr. Vincy was major of the old corporation in Middlemarch, Mrs. Cassaubon, born Dorothea Brooke, had taken her wedding journey to Rome. (George Eliot)

Waggish non-Yale men never seem weary of calling "For God, for Country, for Yale!" the outstanding single anticlimax in the English language. (*The Times*)

In Italy for thirty years under the Borgias, they had warfare, terror, murder and bloodshed, but they produced Michelangelo, Leonardo da Vinci and the Renaissance. In Switzerland, they had brotherly love; they had five hundred years of democracy and peace, and what did they produce? The cuckoo clock. (Orson Welles)

6. In well-known quotations

Men will confess to treason, murder, arson, false teeth, or a wig. How many of them will own up to a lack of humor. (Frank Moore Colby)

At twenty man is a peacock, at thirty a lion, at forty a camel, at fifty a serpent, at sixty a dog, at seventy an ape, at eighty nothing at all. (Boltasar Gracián)

7. In daily conversations

Father: What a bad boy! If you steal the neighbor's apple again, I'll give you a good beating! How many apples have you stolen?

Son: Two.

Father: Give me one to eat.

Chapter Sixteen Zeugma

Zeugma (轭式搭配), from Greek word *zeugnynai* which literally means a "yoking", is a kind of rhetorical device by which one word refers to two others in the same sentence. Zeugma may be achieved by a verb or preposition with two objects or it may employ a verb with two subjects (Baldick, 2010), that is, a single word is made to modify or to govern two or more words in the same sentence, either properly applying in sense to only one of them, or applying to them in different sense. Simply put, the use of a verb with two subjects or objects, or of an adjective with two nouns, although appropriate to only one of the two. It also indicates humor and emphasis. According to *The American Heritage Dictionary of the English Language*, zeugma makes a word modify or govern two or more words although its use is grammatically or logically correct with only one.

16.1 Purposes of zeugma

1. For humor

And the waves oozing through the port-hole made
His berth a little damp, and him afraid. (George Gordon Byron: *Don Juan*)

The loud tempests raise
The waters, and repentance for past sinning. (George Gordon Byron: *Don Juan*)

Mr. Camfield's most sanguine estimate of his finances could not raise them within full five pounds of the desired amount; and in a species of arithmetical desperation, he was alternately cudgeling his brains and his donkey. (Charles Dickens: *David Copperfield*)

2. For emphasis

The wolf may lose his teeth, but never his nature.

I would rather be clothed in rags than be clothed with shame.

3. For parallelism

The freshman excelled in calculus; the sophomore, in music; the senior, in drama.

Glass, china and reputation are easily cracked and never well mended. (proverb)

4. For surprise

He halted in the district where by night are found the lightest street, hearts, vows, and librettos. (O. Henry: *The Cop and the Anthem*)

At noon Mrs. Turpin would get out of bed and humor, put on kimono, airs, and the water to boil for coffee. (O. Henry)

16.2 Classification of zeugma

1. One verb + two or more nouns

They planted a rosebush outside John's bedroom and they planted a bomb inside it.

She washed the baby and the floor.

2. One adjective + two or more nouns

He will be released because he keeps a clean record and appearance, too.

When commemorating the great soul, the friends of his went to the graveyard with weeping eyes and hearts.

3. One preposition + two or more nouns

We found them in funny clothes and astonishment.

They gathered in the hall for friendship and a hot lunch.

4. One verb + two or more adverbials

As I left home after breakfast, I shivered inwardly as well as outwardly.

5. Two or more nouns + one verb

This kind of zeugma is called hypozeugma, that is, a zeugma where a verb falls at the end of a sentence and governs several parallel clauses that precedes it.

Ten minutes later, the coffee and the commander arrived simultaneously.

6. One noun + many verbs

This kind of zeugma is called diazeugma, that is, a zeugma where a noun as the subject of a sentence is followed by many verbs.

"Dear!" said Clarissa, and Lucy shared as she meant her to her disappointment (but not the pang); felt the concord between them; took the hint; thought how the gentry love; gilded her own future with calm; and taking Mrs. Dallowy's parasol, handled it like a sacred weapon which a goddess, having acquitted herself honourably in the field of battle, sheds, and placed it in the umbrella stand. (Virginia Woolf: *Mrs. Dalloway*)

7. One verb + two or more nouns, but the verb is elided in the latter clause(s)

This kind of zeugma is called prozeugma, that is, a zeugma where a verb in the first part of a sentence governs several later clauses in a series.

I speak sense, you nonsense.

He runs for pleasure, I for fear.

16.3 Use of zeugma

1. In novels and short stories

At noon, Mrs. Turpin would get out of bed and humor, put on kimono, airs and the water to boil for coffee. (O. Henry)

There he stood in the parlour ... waiting for her, while she went upstairs a moment to see a woman. He heard her quick step above; heard her voice cheerful, then low; looked at the mats, tea-caddies, glass shades; waited quite impatiently; looked forward eagerly to the walk home; determined to carry her bag; then heard her come out; shut a door; say they must keep the windows open and the doors shut, ask at the house for anything they wanted (she must be talking to a child), when suddenly, in she came, stood for a moment silent (as if she had been pretending up there), and for a moment let herself be now, stood quite motionless for a moment against a picture of Queen Victoria wearing the blue ribbon of the Garter; when all at once he realized that it was this: – she was the most beautiful person he had ever seen. (Virginia Woolf: *To the Lighthouse*)

Slowly and painfully, with broom and pail, mopping, scouring, Mrs. McNab, Mrs. Bast, stayed the corruption and the rot; rescued from the pool of Time that was fast closing over them now a basin, now a cupboard; fetched up from oblivion all the

Waverly novels and a tea-set one morning; in the afternoon restored to sun and air a brass fender and a set of steel fire-iron. (Virginia Woolf: *To the Lighthouse*)

2. In prose

Yesterday Mrs. Grey had a blue heart and coat.

A politician is a man who shakes your hand before election and your confidence afterwards.

Millie put out her cigarette and her cat.

3. In dramas

He bites his lips, and starts;
Stops on a sudden, looks upon the ground,
Then lays his finger on his temple; straight
Springs out into fast gait, then stops again ... (William Shakespeare: *Henry VIII*)

She is too low for a high praise, too brown for a fair praise, and too little for a great praise. (William Shakespeare: *Much Ado about Nothing*)

4. In proverbs

Lawsuit consumes time, and money, and rest, and friends.

It is better to have a patched jacket than to have a patched character.

5. In advertisements

We'll see to it that the blouses appeal to the eye as well as to the purse. (advertisement for blouses)

Chapter Seventeen Syllepsis

Syllepsis (一语双叙), a word from Greek meaning taking together, refers to a construction in which one word (usually a verb or preposition) is applied to two other words or phrases, either ungrammatically or in two differing senses. In the first case, the verb or preposition agrees grammatically with only one of the two elements which it governs. In the second case, the word also appears only once but is applied twice in differing senses (often an abstract sense and a concrete sense). (Baldick, 2001) That is, a figure of speech, by which a word may refer to two or more words in the same sentence, applies to one literally and to the other figuratively.

17.1 Purposes of syllepsis

1. For humor

He uses it once, when Mistress Quickly in "The Merry Wives of Windsor" says of the master coming home in a rage, "... here will be an old abusing of God's patience and the King's English." (*Advanced English*)

The young officer has lost his fine hat, and a great deal of his vanity.

2. For parallelism

Here thou, great Anna! whom three realms obey

Dost sometimes counsel take – and sometimes tea. (Alexander Pope: *The Rape of the Lock*)

Travelers and poets have leave to lie. (proverb)

3. For contrast

I never loved them that find fault with my shoes, and give me no leather. (proverb)

Maids want nothing but husbands, and when they have them they want everything. (proverb)

4. For emphasis

Nobody don't ever get nothing for nothing, nowhere, no time, nohow. (proverb)

17.2 Classification of syllepsis

1. One verb + two or more nouns

He lost his coat and his temper.

They couldn't keep a cook and a secret.

He lost limbs and mind in the war.

2. One adjective + two or more nouns

She returned with a young handsome man and a handsome sum of money.

His temper was as short as his coat-tails.

3. One preposition + two or more noun phrases

She went home in a huff and a taxi.

I live in shame and the suburbs.

He fought with desperation and a stout club.

Take heed of foul dirty ways and long sickness. (proverb)

4. two nouns + one verb

By the time I reached my home, the sun and my father had risen.

She was dressed in a maid's cap, a pinafore, and a bright smile.

5. One verb + two or more adverbials

He took her to dinner and seriously.

Hi, George. What a nice surprise! Come on in.

6. Two verbs + one adverbial

He took the call himself and came right out.

The old man dozed right off when he went home.

7. One verb + two or more object complements

The headmaster instructed us to keep our public image intact and our students in their seats.

17.3 Use of syllepsis

1. In proverbs

Never show the bottom of your purse and your mind.

The only real voyage of discovery consists not in seeking new landscapes but in having new eyes.

2. In prose

When the Vietnam vet was fighting, and losing limbs and mind, and dying, others stayed behind to pursue education and career. (*The Atlantic*, June 1980)

You can fall from a mountain, you can fall from a tree, but the best way to fall, is to fall in love with me.

In Crissscrossing Island, it is the landscape that sticks in the mind, that comes back in memory long after you have departed ... A landscape like this, which stretches not only the eye but the soul can be marked ... (*National Geographic*, April 1981)

3. In novels and short stories

On the opposite side of the street was a restaurant of no great pretensions. It catered to large appetites and modest purses. Its crockery and atmosphere were thick; its soup and napery thin. (O. Henry: *The Cop and the Anthem*)

I bounced out of bed at her call this morning, and bounced my breakfast into a healthy, good-natured stomach. (Mary Shelley)

4. In poetry

He works his work, I mine. (Alfred Tennyson)

Here, thou, great Anna! whom three realms obey.

Whether the Nymph shall break Diana's Law,
Or some frail china jar receive a flaw,
Or stain her Honour, or her new Brocade,
Forget her prayers, or miss a Masquerade,
Or lose her Heart, or Necklace, at a Ball. (Alexander Pope: *The Rape of the Lock*)

5. In advertisements

There is a certain type of woman who'd rather press grapes than clothes. (advertisement for Peck & Peck suits)

Who was the first to wrap up a case: Scotland Yard or Alexander Gordon? (advertisement for Gordon's Whiskey)

17.4 Differences between zeugma and syllepsis

Sometimes it is difficult to distinguish zeugma and syllepsis. As Nicholas (2016) says, a zeugma (or syllepsis) is a linguistic construction where a single constituent is related to two different semantic interpretations, in a way that give rise to a semantic anomaly. Syllepsis has one verb lacking congruence with at least one subject that it governs: "The Nobles and the King were taken." And zeugma has no faulty congruence. (Lanham, 1968)

According to Corbett & Coonors (1999), in syllepsis the single word is grammatically and idiomatically compatible with both of the other words that it governs, while in a zeugma the single word does not fit grammatically or idiomatically with one member of the pair.

Simply put, syllepsis is a figure of speech in which one verb or verbal phrase is used to govern two or more words, phrases or clauses, the meaning changing with each expression. One is to be understood literally, while the other may be used figuratively.

e.g. While he was fighting, and losing limbs and mind, and dying, others stayed behind to pursue education and career.

Here, "losing one's limbs" is used literally, but "losing one's mind" is figurative, which means to go mad. So this is syllepsis.

e.g. I left my heart and my wallet in San Francisco.

"Leave my wallet" is literal, but what does "leave my heart" mean? So this is syllepsis.

e.g. He grabbed his hat from the rack by the stairs and a kiss from the lips of his wife.

In "grab his hat" and "grab a kiss", the verb "grab" is interpreted differently, the former is literal while the latter is metaphorical. So this is syllepsis.

e.g. He grabbed his hat from the rack in the closet, his gloves from the table near the door, and his car keys from the punchbowl.

The verb "grab" appears only in the first part and is omitted in the latter parts. The meaning of grab remains the same in the three expressions. So this is zeugma.

e.g. He took his time and the floor.

"Take" can be used with the two objects. So it is syllepsis.

e.g. We ate a bun and a glass of milk.

"Eat a glass of milk" is unusual. So it is zeugma.

e.g. He lost his coat and his temper.

"Lose" can be used with both objects. So it is syllepsis.

e.g. That murderer killed the boy and the luggage.

"Kill the luggage" is unusual. So it is zeugma.

e.g. Alison bumped her head against that of the bed.

As "head" ("that" is used in the second part instead of "head") in this sentence refers to two different things, it is zeugma.

e.g. Alison bumped her head against that of her brother.

Because "head" is used in the same "body-part" sense in reference to both Alison and her brother, this is neither zeugma nor syllepsis but a simple collocation.

The following three examples are neither zeugma nor syllepsis but mere collocations.

Commodity and cultural exchanges may be encouraged or discouraged as circumstances warrant.

Because Einstein was a Jew, his property and German citizenship were taken away by the Nazi government in 1933.

People need time to deepen their affection, to appreciate one another's differences, to share one another's joys and griefs.

It can be concluded that in both form and meaning, there is not much difference between syllepsis and zeugma. Therefore, syllepsis can be considered as a special type of zeugma which makes use of polysemy and idiomatic usage of words. In comparison, zeugma does not necessarily use the same word in different meanings.

Chapter Eighteen Palindrome

Palindrome (回文) comes from the Greek word *palindromos*, meaning running back again. A palindrome is a word or sentence, or string of them which can be read either forwards or backwards with the same meaning.

18.1 Purposes of palindrome

1. For fun

Stella won no wallets.

Name no one man.

No x in Nixon.

God! a dog!

2. For vividness

Ten animals I slam in a net.

Ooh, a yahoo!

Rise to vote sir. (slogan for election)

3. For emphasis

Live, O devil! Revel ever! Live! Do evil!

Do, O God, no evil deed, live on, do good!

This rhetorical device is not for a serious purpose but usually for fun. The only exception is: A man, a plan, a canal, Panama! It was created to hail the work of Goethals, the US army engineer who completed the canal's construction in 1914, after many years of setbacks.

18.2 Classification of palindrome

1. Reverse letters in words

Reverse words with the same meaning:

Three-letter words: Bob; dad; did; eye; mam, pop

Four-letter words: deed; noon; peep; toot

Five-letter words: civic; kayak, level; madam; minim; radar; refer; rotor; solos

Seven-letter words: Glenelg (a place name in South Australia); racecar; repaper; reviver; rotator

Eight-or-more-letter words: evitative; kinnikinnik (Indian tobacco leaf); redivider; rotavator (brand name)

2. Reverse letters in words with a different meaning each way

dam / mad; devil / lived; regal / lager; stressed / desserts

3. Reverse letters in sentences with the same meaning

The following are examples with two-to-fourteen-word sentences.

Tie it.

Revolt lover! (goodbye to romance and all that)

Borrow or rob?

Don't nod! (injunction to bored audience)

I prefer pi.

Too hot to hoot.

Niagara, O, roar again!

Step on no pets! (warning as you enter the premises of an incorrigible cat breeder)

Won't lovers revolt now?

Poor Dan is in a droop.

Red rum sir is murder. (I'd settle for a red-label beer)

Pull up if I pull up.

Ma is as selfish as I am.

Able was I ere I saw Elba. (Napoleon)

Red lost case, Ma. Jesse James acts older.

Unremarkable was I ere I saw Elba Kramer, nu?

Cigar? Toss it in a can. It is so tragic.

Evil is a name of a foreman, as I live.

Gert, I saw Ron avoid a radio-van – or was it Reg?
You bat one in, resign in evening. Is Ernie not a buoy?
Did I strap red nude, red rump, also slap murdered underparts? I did!
Doc Note: I dissent. A fast never prevents a fatness. I diet on cod.

4. Reverse words in sentences with the same meaning
So patient a doctor to doctor a patient so.
Girl, bathing on bikini, eyeing boy, finds boy eyeing bikini on bathing girl.

18.3 Use of palindrome

1. In prose
Pa's a sap. (*Reader's Digest*)
Live not on evil.

2. In daily conversations
Evade me, Dave!
Madam, I'm Adam.
'Tis Ivan, on a visit.

– Was it a cat I saw?
– No, Miss, it is Simon.

3. In business
YREKA BAKERY (a slogan for a bakery)
KLIM (brand name for milk powder)

4. Use of figures of speech in palindrome
Mad as it is it is Adam. (repetition)
No melons, no melon. (repetition; assonance)
Ma's story rots Sam. (alliteration)
Zeus sees Suez. (allusion)
Was it felt? I had a hit left, I saw. (rhetorical question)
Oh, who was it I saw? Oh, who? (apostrophe; rhetorical question)
Panic in a *Titanic*, I nap. (allusion)
No pet so tragic as a cigar to step on. (simile)
Must sell at tallest sum. (assonance)

Late Bill is ill, I bet, Al. (two pairs of consonance)

No garden, one dragon. (antithesis; consonance)

Now eve, we’re here; we’ve won. (parallelism)

A Toyota’s a Toyota. (repetition; alliteration)

A Dan acts Niagara war against Canada. (assonance)

Boston did not sob. (personification)

I made us sit tissued, Ami! (metaphor)

Don did nod. (assonance; consonance)

God, a wasp saw a dog! (apostrophe; assonance)

Chapter Nineteen Asyndeton

Asyndeton (连词省略), also parataxis, comes from Greek, meaning unconnected. It is a form of verbal compression which consists of the deliberate omission of connecting words (usually conjunctions) between words, phrases, or clauses. The most common form is the omission of "and", leaving only a sequence of phrases linked by commas. (Baldick, 2001) Asyndeton is opposite of polysyndeton, and is used to relate a series of facts, events, ideas, etc., or to show that a series of actions, events, etc. occur in a rapid succession.

19.1 Purposes of asyndeton

1. For parallelism

A number of White House staff people – stunned, silent, stumbling along as if dazed – walked with it. Mrs. Kennedy walked down the coffin, her hand on it, her head down, her hat gone, her dress and stockings spattered. She got into the hearse with the coffin. The staff men crowded into cars and followed. (Tom Wicker: *The Assassination*)

They smiled, shook hands, parted.

2. For brevity

Better come join us. (= Better come and join us.)

Her husband doesn't want to help take care of the children.

I've heard say he is a miser.

3. For emphasis

A sculptor must perceive an egg as a simple single solid shape, quite apart from its significance as food, or from the literary idea that it will become a bird. And so with solids such as a shell, a nut, a plum, a pear, a tadpole, a mushroom, a mountain peak, a kidney, a carrot, a tree-trunk, a bird, a bud, a lark, a ladybird, a bulrush, a bone. (Henry Moore)

The difference between the qualities of intelligence and intellect is more often assumed than defined. Whereas intelligence seeks to grasp, manipulate, reorder, adjust, intellect examines, ponders, wonders, theorizes, criticizes, imagines. (Richard Hofstadter)

Note: Grammatically, this sentence should be as follows:

The difference between the qualities of intelligence and intellect is more often assumed than defined. Whereas intelligence seeks to grasp, manipulate, reorder, and adjust, and intellect examines, ponders, wonders, theorizes, criticizes, and imagines.

4. For attraction

Looks like a pump, feels like a sneaker. (advertisement for the shoes, Easy Spirit)

Go well, go shell. (advertisement for airlines)

19.2 Classification of asyndeton

1. Parallel of words

1) Nouns

I have found the warm caves in the woods,
filled them with skillets, carvings, shelves,
Closets, silks, innumerable goods. (Anne Sexton: "Her Kind")

2) Verbs

I've heard tell of such happiness.

Come say good night.

Run get the ball for me, Jami.

I will just go see.

Tests will help make your new knowledge permanent.

They are not rich, but they make do on what they have.

On your mark, get set, go!

Of course, you have to let go some of the things that are currently filling up the schedule to make room for the new priorities.

Chinese often shake my hand and don't let go. (*New College English*)

3) Adjectives

An empty stream, a great silence, an impenetrable forest. The air was thick, warm, heavy, sluggish. (Conrad: *Heart of Darkness*)

2. Parallel of phrases

1) Noun phrases

When the miscarriages point to is the need of reforming the jury system, the rules of evidence, the customs of prosecution, the machinery of appeal.

2) Prepositional phrases

He has provided the poor with jobs, with opportunity, with self-respect.

3. Parallel of sentences

Lisa chose French, May chose accounting, Mary chose computer, Alice chose history.

The wind blew, the clouds gathered, the rain fell. I looked, called, no one answered.

Note: Most of the examples in this figure of speech are grammatically wrong, and the word "and" should be used before the listing of the last item. For example,

Lisa chose French, May chose accounting, Mary chose computer, Alice chose history. (grammatically wrong)

Lisa chose French, May chose accounting, Mary chose computer, and Alice chose history. (correct)

He has provided the poor with jobs, with opportunity, with self-respect. (grammatically wrong)

He has provided the poor with jobs, with opportunity, and with self-respect. (correct)

But the "verb + and + verb" pattern with the first verb such as "go", "come" and "run" now are accepted in spoken English as follows.

Come say good night.

He left his grandmother's house to go live in Chicago.

19.3 Use of asyndeton

1. In poetry

Faynt, wearie, sore, employed, grieved, brent

With heat, toil, wounds, armes, smart, and inward fire. (Edmund Spenser: *The Faerie Queene*)

Two there were
Cleaned out a damaged shaft by hand. (W. H. Auden: *The Watershed*)
Note: "Who" is omitted between "were" and "cleaned").

The first sort by their own suggestion fell,
Self-tempted, self-depraved; man falls, deceived
By the other first; man therefore shall find grace,
The other none. (John Milton: *Paradise Lost*)

2. In novels and short stories

He paused and swayed, the heat, the drink, the nervousness, the guilt at last joined force in him ... (Kingsley Amis: *Lucky Jim*)

People move slowly. They ambled across the square, shuffled in and out of the stores around it, took their time about everything. (H. Lee: *To Kill a Mockingbird*)

3. In prose

On forty rules Manya Sldodowska lives, studies, learns. Solitude, near-starvation, an unheated garret – none of these things matter, as long as at least a part of her day is spent in the laboratory. Marie, doing the work of four strong men, pounds away at her chemical masses, boils, separates, refines, stirs, strains. (*The New Yorker*, No. 27, 1937)

The high stern castle of Vasa was a riot of carved gods, demons, knights, kings, warriors, mermaids, cherubs ...

4. In speeches

Let every nation know, whether it wishes us well or ill, that we shall pay any price, bear any burden, meet any hardship, support any friend, oppose any foe to assure the survival and the success of liberty. (John F. Kennedy: "Inaugural Address")

Confidence ... thrives only on honesty, on honour, on the sacredness of obligations, on faithful protections, on unselfish performance; without them it cannot live. (Franklin Delano Roosevelt)

5. In well-known quotations

There is not much harm in a lion; he has no ideals, no religion, no politics, no chivalry, no gentility. (George Bernard Shaw)

The unreal is more powerful than the real. Because nothing is as perfect as you can imagine it. Because it's only intangibles, ideas, concepts, beliefs, fantasies that last. Stone crumbles. Wood rots. People, well, they die. But things as fragile as a thought, a dream, a legend, they can go on and on. (Chuck Palahniuk)

You can't wait for inspiration, you have to go after it with a club. (Jack London)

6. In advertisements

The sun is out, the moisture is in. (advertisement for suncream)

Double delicious, double your pleasure. (advertisement for food)

7. In news headlines

"No Bill, No Bibi, No Deal" (*Time*, July 1996)

Note: "Bill" refers to American president Bill Clinton then, and "Bibi" refers to Israel's prime minister Benjamin Netanyahu.

"New Woman, New Charges" (*Time*, April 1999)

8. In academic writing

To do so, all we need to do is lower the cost of converting seas water into fresh water.

What we need are the time and money to make the technology available to everyone.

9. In daily communication

Run get the ball for me, Jami.

Both of you go stand in the back of the line and wait your turn.

19.4 Appendix: Syndeton

There are several figures of speech that have the same morpheme "syndeton" such as asyndeton, polysyndeton. In fact, syndeton (连词单用) alone is also a word, meaning a coordination with only one conjunction. It is appropriate to use one conjunction in front of the last part of a series of words, phrases, clauses or sentences as follows.

1. Parallel of words with one "and"

I crawled back under the cover of the boat and huddled there, wet, cold and sobbing. (Sam McKinney: *Sailing Uphill*)

2. Parallel of phrases with one "and"

You are talking to a man who has laughed in the face of death, sneered at doom, and chuckled at catastrophe. (L. Frank Baum: *The Wizard of Oz*)

3. Parallel of clauses with one "and"

However, those of us who are parents of children in this age group know that such offers are relatively rare and that many liberal-arts students graduate with the belief that the prospective workplace may not have a place for them. (*New College English*)

4. Parallel of sentences with one "and"

John likes English, Peter likes mathematics, Jack likes chemistry, and Michael likes physics.

5. Use of "or"

I'd like it to be black, white or grey.

If we don't use the conjunctions in the above examples, grammatically we are wrong, but the sentences without the conjunction(s) can be considered as asyndeton, and rhetorically we are right. As language learners, it is not appropriate for us to use asyndeton in English writing.

Chapter Twenty Anastrophe

Anastrophe (词序倒装) comes from a Greek word, *anastrephein*, in which *ana* means "back" and *strephein* means "to turn", and thus anastrophe means "turning back". As a figure of speech, it involves the unusual arrangement of words or clauses within a sentence (Lanham, 1968), in which the normal word order, often involving an adjective and a noun, is reversed or inverted with the intention, or at least the effect, of emphasizing a certain word.

A related figure of speech is hyperbaton (倒置法), a word from Greek, with hyper (meaning over) and baton (meaning step), thus meaning an overstepping. According to Baldick (2001), hyperbaton is a figure of speech by which the normal order of words in a sentence is significantly altered. These two similar figures refer more generally to the inverted order or inversion grammatically, that is, words normally grouped together are separated.

The ordinary sentence order in English is as follows: subject + predicate, and adjective + noun. If the normal order is altered, then inversion occurs.

20.1 Purposes of anastrophe

1. For emphasis

Rare indeed is the individual who does not belong to one of these groups.

Only later did they realize what a terrible thing had happened.

Not only do we need heroes to guide us and give us unity, but we need them to help us become great.

Not only did we lose all our money, but we also came close to losing our lives.

Seldom had I seen such confusion.

This I must see.

2. For balance

Also included are many business executive jobs, making speeches, running for an elected office, heading a fund-raising campaign and many other jobs of leadership. (the subject part is too long compared with the predicate)

Enclosed is a sample of a similar cloth, of exactly the same color, which we have in stock.

Thus began an intricate minuet between us and the Chinese.

3. For closer connection

For a long time, he refused to talk to his wife, and kept her in ignorance of his troubles. Equally strange was his behaviour to his son.

Ed passed the exam and so did Mary.

The door burst open and in rushed a troop of children in all sorts of fancy dresses.

Hard by a great forest dwelt a poor wood-cutter with his wife and his two children. The boy was called Hansel and the girl Gretel.

20.2 Classification of anastrophe

1. Complete inversion

When the whole predicate is put before the subject it is complete inversion.

Up went the flag.

Down came the rain.

Up above is our Father Sun.

Came the dawn.

Here comes the bus!

There goes my last dollar.

Now comes your turn.

Out into the fields ran the frightened villagers.

Crack went the gun and the hawk crumpled out of the sky.

On the hill stands a castle.

Beyond them lay the fields.

Up shot the rocket into the sky.

Away ran Catherine, and away ran the dog across the field.

Great was the excitement as procession poured its eager masses into the town.

2. Part of the predicate at the beginning of the sentence

May you succeed!

Was my face red!

So absurd was his manner that everyone stared.

3. The predicative at the beginning of the sentence

How delightful her manners are!

Here he is.

So depressed did he feel that nothing would cheer him up.

4. The adverbial at the beginning of the sentence

Not only is there wisdom in knowing when to keep your mouth shut; there are practical advantages as well.

To such lengths did he go with his risqué stories that everybody began to be disgusted.

Many a summer have I spent in my aunt's home.

Never in his career as postman had he known that address.

I didn't care; neither did my friends, whose marks were equally bad.

Only then is it time to reduce costs and grow more efficient.

5. The object at the beginning of the sentence

Many a letter did he write yesterday.

Such a bad time did we have that we'll never forget it.

Many a time has Mike given me good advice.

6. The predicative before the conjunction

Important as they are, genes alone are never absolutely responsible for any trait.

Unarmed though he was, he bravely went forward to meet his enemies.

7. In "the more ... the more" structure

The more parents talk with their young children, the more good things happen intellectually for those kids later on.

The more powerful one's car is, the more dangerously one tends to drive.

8. Inverted order in subjunctive mood

Inverted order is used in subjunctive mood when "were", "had", "should" in the conditional clause are put at the beginning with "if" omitted.

Had I been more motivated, I might have passed those courses.

Should ministers decide to instigate an inquiry, we would welcome it.

Were he alive today, he would be horrified.

Were one to stroll down Broadway with a Numidian lion at his heels the effect would be somewhat similar to that which I should have produced had I entered Zodanga with Woola. (*A Princess of Mars*)

20.3 Use of anastrophe

1. In proverbs

By and by in came the masters of the cottage.

Not such a fool as he looks.

Not what is she but what has she.

So goth the world; now woe, now weal.

2. In poetry

Then am I
A happy fly,
If I live
Or if I die. (*College English*, Book V)

A Dungeon horrible, on all sides round
As one great Furnace flam'd, yet from those flames
No light, but rather darkness visible
Serv'd only to discover sights of woe (John Milton: *Paradise Lost*)

3. In prose

Two years ago that was, and since Myra had been to see her mother three times, but her husband never. (*College English*, Book I)

Written on the card was a message under the printed Happy Birthday (*College English*, Book I)

Up comes the cotton, down goes the woven cloth; up comes the silk, down goes the woolen; up comes the book, but down goes the wit that writes them. (Henry David Thoreau: *Walden*)

It is really from the union of Hellenism, in its breadth, its beauty of purpose, its calm possession of beauty, with the adventure, the intensified individualism, the passionate colour of the romantic spirit, that springs the art of nineteenth century in England, as from the marriage of Faust ans Helen of Troy sprang the beautiful boy Euphorion. (Oscar Wilde)

Note: In the emphatic sentence, "the art" is the subject, "from the union" is the adverbial, and "springs" is the predicate.

4. In novels and short stories

Sweet was her smile, swift her submission; … (Virginia Woolf: *Mrs. Dalloway*)

Insoluble questions they were, it seemed to her, standing there, holding James by the hand. (Virginia Woolf: *To the Lighthouse*)

Peter Walsh had got up and crossed to the window and stood with his back to her, flicking a bandanna handkerchief from side to side. Masterly and dry and desolate he looked, his thin shoulder-blades lifting his coat slightly; blowing his nose violently. (Virginia Woolf: *Mrs. Dalloway*)

Around his neck was slung a tin bottle, as I had often seen his meat and drink slung about him in other days. (Charles Dickens: *Great Expectations*)

There, smoking his pipe in the old place by the kitchen firelight, as hale as strong as ever, though a little grey, sat Joe; and there, fenced into the corner with Joe's leg, and sitting on my own little stool looking at the fire, was – I again! (Charles Dickens: *Great Expectations*)

5. In academic writing

There will one day spring from the brain of science a machine of force so fearful in its potentialities, so absolutely terrifying, that even man, the fighter who will dare torture and death in order to inflict torture and death, will be appalled, and so will abandon war forever. (Thomas Edison)

Philosophy is like trying to open a safe with a combination lock; each little adjustment of the dials seems to achieve nothing, only when everything is in place does the door open. (Ludwig Wittgenstein)

6. In speeches

Those of us who manage the public's dollars will be held to account – to spend wisely, reform bad habits, and do our business in the light of day – because only then can we restore the vital trust between a people and their government. (Barack Obama: "President's Inaugural Address in 2009")

Nor is the question before us whether the market is a force for good or ill. (Barack Obama: "President's Inaugural Address in 2009")

7. In the use with direct quotation

Says she: "More and more women are coming into the profession and doing well, but there aren't a whole lot at the top. I'm a rarity."

Snapped back the 18-year-old princess: "No comment."

Chapter Twenty-one Ellipsis

Ellipsis (省略) refers to the omission from a sentence of a word or words or phrases under the context of the passage, which would be required for complete clarity but which can usually be understood from the context. (Baldick, 2001) Or ellipsis is the deliberate omission of a word or words which are readily implied by the context. (Corbett & Coonors, 1999) As a kind of rhetorical device, ellipsis is used to achieve emphasis, compactness and brevity, sometimes also for dramatic effect in conveying mood or atmosphere.

Ellipsis is used in English as well as in Chinese to be effective and economical. As the two languages have different structures and ways of thinking, their omission is different. In Chinese, we can omit whatever we think are redundant in the context. In English, we can only omit something, the omission of which will not affect the integrity of the structure and meaning. We should not use ellipsis if we are not sure what should be omitted.

21.1 Purposes of ellipsis

1. For brevity

People with good manners do better in most situations than those without (good manners do).

I fixed things (in) the way (that) he wanted.

The questioning impulse in us is our deepest instinct. It is deeper even than the hunger for food. (It is) Deeper than the drive to sleep.

2. For emphasis

I knew that the combination of these things reminded me of something, and soon enough I realized what that something was. (It was) Final Exams.

Down with your gun!

3. For attraction

Good taste. Kent Style. (advertisement for Kent, a kind of cigarette)

Note: The complete sentence may be "It has a Good taste. Kent Style."

Wow, would (that) I love to do that!

4. For balance

Histories make men wise; poems witty; mathematics subtle; natural philosophy deep; moral grave; logic and rhetoric able to contend. (Francis Bacon)

The more you study, the more you will find yourself ignorant. (Rene Descartes)

5. For contrast

It takes your enemy and your friend, working together, to hurt you: the one to slander you, and the other to bring you the news. (Mark Twain)

It is better to suffer wrong than to do it, and happier to be sometimes cheated than not to trust. (Samuel Johnson)

Nothing is so mild and gentle as courage, nothing so cruel and pitiless as cowardice.

21.2 Classification of ellipsis

1. Omission of preposition

In the following structures, "in" can be omitted: It is no use (in) doing sth., It is no use/good (in) doing sth.; be busy (late, weary) (in) doing sth.; There is no point (in) doing sth.; be employed, engaged, occupied (in) doing sth.; spend time (in) doing sth.

There's no point (in) talking about it again.

There's no use complaining; they won't do anything about it.

2. Prepositions "for", "in" and "by"

Prepositions "for", "in" and "by" can be omitted when they refer to time, distance, manner, or frequency, but in negative sentences or at the beginning of a sentence, the prepositions can't be omitted:

The war lasted (for) five years.

To put it (in) another way, you will never find what you don't look for.

3. Omission of relative adjectives and adverbs

No offence intended, but the things (that) you think are important probably aren't even relevant at all.

Kate, could it be (that) you miss your good-night kiss?

Charles loves golf so much (that) he would play at halftime if he could.

4. Omission of some determiners

Determiners such as the definite article and possessive pronouns can be omitted in coordinate or parenthesis structures.

My mother and (my) father worked hard.

His grandpa and (his) grandma will attend his graduation ceremony.

5. Omission in sentence structures

(You) Think about it another way.

(You are) Getting in trouble in school, eh?

(Would) You rather I waited?

6. Omission of the predicates

The master's degree is awarded by 70 departments, and the Ph. D. (is awarded) by forty.

Cowards die daily, the brave (die) but once. (proverb)

7. Omission in adverbial clauses

When (they are) drawing their conclusions about men and women, observers do not focus on individual differences.

When (it is) possible, it is best to deal with dating expenses in the beginning.

8. Omission in the discourse

Government workers in Washington D. C., for example, frequently work sixty to seventy hours a week. They don't do this because they have to (work sixty to seventy hours a week); they do it because they want to (work sixty to seventy hours a week).

– Bob's very angry.

– Why (is he very angry)?

9. Omission of the core word(s)

He would say that a thing must be done in this way, and I (would say) that it must be done in that (way).

Of the five candidates, the first (one) was the best.

10. Omission in some particular structures

In English, sometimes it is difficult to find out the omitted part in the context in the following structures: what if, what though, what say, why not, how come, if only.

If only I had taken her advice!

Why not take a chance on it?

11. Omission in imperative sentences

Out of my room!

Down with smoking!

12. Omission of "to" between to verbs

Harry was tired of John's advice and told him to go fly a kite!

Why would a mental vision of success help produce real success?

21.3 Use of ellipsis

1. In proverbs

Keep still at home, never knowledge have.

Judge not a book by its cover.

Don't swap horses when crossing a stream.

Like father, like son.

2. In prose

(Being) A career journalist whose wit, talent and savior vivre became personal trademarks, Bauby saw his fast-paced life come to an abrupt end on Dec. 8, 1995, with the stroke that left him paralyzed.

We hold the truth to be self-evident: that all men are created equal; that they are endowed by their creator with certain unalienable rights; that among these are life, liberty, and the pursuit of happiness. (Thomas Jefferson)

When talking, they (actors) are servants of the dramatist. It is what they can show the audience when they are not talking that reveals the fine actor. (Cedric Hardwicke)

3. In speeches

This is the journey we continue today. We remain the most prosperous, powerful nation on Earth. Our workers are no less productive than when this crisis began. Our minds are no less inventive, our goods and services no less needed than they were last week or last month or last year. Our capacity remains undiminished. (Barack Obama: "President's Inaugural Address in 2009")

4. In novels and short stories

The figures were before them: a somewhat colourless show, appearing to disclose a state of things which would pass muster, if within the next six months there were no further violent disturbances of currency exchange. (John Galsworthy: *The White Monkey*)

"How now!" he cried ... "Why, where have you been hiding?" (Charles Dickens: *Barnaby Rudge*)

"Beautiful?" cried Skene with emotion. "Beautiful! There ain't but me and my boy in the world can give the upper cut like that! I wish I could see my old missus's face now! This is nuts to her." (George Bernard Shaw: *Cashel Byron's Profession*)

5. In dramas

Lady Capulet: Why, how now, Juliet?

Juliet: Madam, I am not well. (William Shakespeare: *Romeo and Juliet*)

Page: Sir, I thank you.

Shallow: Sir, I thank you; by yea and no, I do. (William Shakespeare: *The Merry Wives of Windsor*)

6. In poetry

My face in thine eye, thine in mine appears,
And true plain hearts do in the faces rest;
Where can we find two better hemispheres,
Without sharp north, without declining west?
If your two loves be one, or thou and I,
Whatever dies, was not mix'd equally;
Love so alike that none can slacken, none can die. (John Donne: "The Good-Morrow")

On this wondrous sea
Sailing silently,
Ho! Pilot, ho!
Knowest thou the shore
Where no breakers roar –
Where the storm is o'er?

In the peaceful west
Many the sails at rest –
The anchors fast –
Thither I pilot thee –
Land Ho! Eternity!
Ashore at last! (Emily Dickinson: "On This Wondrous Sea")

7. In academic writing

The greater the power, the more dangerous the abuse. (Edmund Burke)

Science is nothing but developed perception, interpreted intent, common sense rounded out and minutely articulated. (George Santayana)

Science is built of facts the way a house is built of bricks; but an accumulation of facts is no more science than a pile of bricks is a house. (Henri Poincaré)

8. In well-known quotations

Wise men are instructed by reason; men of less understanding by experience; the most ignorant by necessity; and beasts by nature. (Marcus T. Cicero)

Reform is affirmative, conservatism negative. Conservatism goes for comfort, reform for truth. (Herbert Spencer)

9. In daily communication

– To whom did you give the book?
– (I gave the book) To John.
(Is there) Any coffee left?

Chapter Twenty-two Apposition

Apposition (同位) refers to the placing side by side of two coordinate elements, the second of which serves as an explanation or modification of the first. (Corbett & Coonors, 1999) Usually, the use of a noun phrase immediately after another noun phrase which refers to the same person of thing. The functions of apposition are to explain or describe.

22.1 Purposes of apposition

1. To provide more information

This is the source of our confidence – the knowledge that God calls on us to shape an uncertain destiny. (Barack Obama: "President's Inaugural Address in 2009")

2. For description

We must build a new world, a far better world, – one in which the eternal dignity of man is respected. (Harry S. Truman)

Venus, a beautiful good-natured lady, is the goddess of love; Juno, a terrible shrew, the goddess of marriage; and they are always mortal enemies. (Jonathan Swift)

3. To explain in greater details

And yet, at this moment – a moment that will define a generation – it is precisely this spirit that must inhabit us all. (Barack Obama: "President's Inaugural Address in 2009")

Mathematics possesses not only truth, but supreme beauty – a beauty cold and austere, like that of sculpture. (Bertrand Russell)

4. For emphasis

In science, the important is something that has been researched out, not the researcher himself. (Marie Curie)

22.2 Classification of apposition

1. Reflective pronoun

He will do it himself.

They themselves had a similar experience.

The world owes all its onward impulses to men ill at ease; the happy man inevitably confines himself to ancient limits. (Nathaniel Hawthorne)

2. Indefinite pronoun

We each have a plan for the coming holiday.

They each have their own e-mail address.

3. Demonstrative pronoun

With only one dissenting voice in the executive, that of Rev. I. G. Perkins, Dr Jesse Arnup, as moderator, set forth the church's position in February 1948, in a document entitled "Dr J. G. Endicott and the Board of Foreign Missions". (Stephen Endicott: *James G. Endicott: Rebel Out of China*)

4. Noun phrase

Jeff, a 27-year-old hacker, has a different point of view.

The leader of the opposition, George Drew, like most of the newspaper editors, was not satisfied with the government's position. (Stephen Endicott: *James G. Endicott: Rebel Out of China*)

5. The infinitive

The need to take charge of our fleeting lives – to decide who we will be and what we will try to do – is just as pressing as it ever was for Socrates and for all those others who have preceded us.

6. -ing phrase

These are jobs where people work with people – healing them, teaching them, helping them.

7. Appositive clause

A year later, the father received a letter that one of his lost ships had been found and had arrived filled with merchandise for him.

This reinforced the idea that anything was possible, that I could do anything I wanted.

8. Separated from the first noun by comma

Joanna, Faber's teenage daughter, came home one day looking distressed.

Mr. Budd told himself hurriedly – there was his friend, Bert Webber, who had sliced the top of his thumb right off in a motor-cycle chain – his nail looked very much like that.

9. Separated from the first noun by dash(es)

Nouns are definite, the names of persons or things, but verbs cause all the trouble in the world. All lawsuits are about something coming between two nouns – those verbs. (Carl Sandburg)

But first of all, I want to say this – that there are two things which stand out to everybody. One is that he was received and welcomed – an enthusiastic welcome – during the past few months, by the people of China of all classes – a welcome such as has never been granted before to any Canadian. (Stephen Endicott: *James G. Endicott: Rebel Out of China*)

22.3 Use of apposition

1. In prose

John Morgan, the president of the Sons of the Republic, could not be reached by phone.

Men of this kind – soldiers of fortune, pool-hall habitues, gigolos, beachcombers – expend their talents on trivialities.

2. In speeches

Our challenges may be new. The instruments with which we meet them may be new. But those values upon which our success depends – hard work and honesty, courage and fair play, tolerance and curiosity, loyalty and patriotism – these things are old. These things are true. They have been the quiet force of progress throughout our history. What is demanded then is a return to these truths. What is required of us now is a new era of responsibility – a recognition, on the part of every American, that we have duties to ourselves, our nation, and the world, duties that we do not grudgingly accept but rather seize gladly, firm in the knowledge that there is nothing so satisfying to the spirit, so defining of our character, than giving our all to a difficult task. (Barack Obama: "President's Inaugural Address in 2009")

These are the indicators of crisis, subject to data and statistics. Less measurable but no less profound is a sapping of confidence across our land – a nagging fear that America's decline is inevitable, and that the next generation must lower its sights. (Barack Obama: "President's Inaugural Address in 2009")

3. In poetry

If there be two, they are two so,
As stiff twin compasses are two,
Thy soul, the fixed foot, makes no show,
To move, but doth, if the other do. (John Donne: "A Valediction: Forbidding Mourning")

As if the Sea should part –
And show a further Sea –
And that – a further – and the Three
But a presumption be –

Of periods of Seas –
Unvisited of Shores –
Themselves the Verge of Seas to be –
Eternity – is Those – (Emily Dickinson: "As If the Sea Should Part")

4. In novels and short stories

Still discomposed with the idea that his brother, so much injured, and to whom he was so much indebted, had suddenly arrived in his native kingdom, even the distinctions pointed out by Fitzurse did not altogether remove the Prince's apprehensions; and while, with a short and embarrassed eulogy upon his valour, he caused to be delivered to him the war-horse assigned as the prize, he trembled lest from the barred visor of the mailed form before him, an answer might be returned, in the deep and awful accents of Richard the Lion-hearted. (Walter Scott: *Ivanhoe*)

Go ye now to rest, full to your heart's desire of meat and wine, wherein courage is and strength; but when fair rosy-fingered Dawn appeareth, array thou with all speed before the ships thy folk and horsemen, and urge them on; and fight thyself amid the foremost. (Homer: *Iliad*)

While the students at the convention showed considerable willingness to ask "what can I do?" they did not give evidence that they held any common basis for action or belief in the practicability of the Kingdom of God. (Stephen Endicott: *James G. Endicott: Rebel Out of China*)

5. In dramas

Therefore our sometime sister, now our queen,
Th's imperial jointress to this warlike state,
Have we, as 'twere with a defeated joy, –
With an auspicious and a dropping eye,
With mirth in funeral and with dirge in marriage,
In equal scale weighing delight and dole, – Taken to wife: (William Shakespeare: *Hamlet*)

O God, I could be bounded i a nutshell and count myself a king of infinite space, were it not that I have bad dreams. (William Shakespeare: *Hamlet*)

6. In well-known quotations

Every person has two educations, one which he receives from others, and one, more important, which he gives himself. (Edward Gibbon)

A woman is not a whole woman without the experience of marriage. In the case of a bad marriage, you win if you lose. Of the two alternatives – bad marriage or none – I believe bad marriage would be better. It is a bitter experience and a high price to pay for fulfillment, but it is the better alternative. (Fannie Hurst)

7. In academic writing

Apart from the association of Latin with rhetoric as an art, this last mentioned fact, that Latin was totally controlled by writing no matter how much it was used for speech, produced other special kinds of drives toward the oral within the academic world. (Walter J. Ong)

What is an artist? A provincial who finds himself somewhere between a physical reality and a metaphorical one ... It's this in-between that I'm calling a province, this frontier country between the tangible world and the intangible one – which is really the realm of the artist. (Federico Fellini)

The creative person wants to be a know-it-all. He wants to know about all kinds of things – ancient history, nineteenth century mathematics, current manufacturing techniques, hog futures. Because he never knows when these ideas might come together to form a new idea. It may happen six minutes later, or six months, or six years. But he has faith that it will happen. (Carl Ally)

Note: Here "ancient history, nineteenth century mathematics, current manufacturing techniques, hog futures" is the apposition of "all kinds of things", and "that it will happen" is the apposition of "faith".

Chapter Twenty-three　Parenthesis

Parenthesis (插入) is a word, phrase, or sentence inserted as an explanation or afterthought into a passage which is grammatically complete without it, in writing usually marked off by brackets, dashes, or commas. (Pearsall, 2001) Parenthesis usually adds something significant, forceful or elucidating to what is being said. Short sentences, adverb phrases, adjective phrases, prepositional phrases, participle phrases, and infinitive phrases can be used as parentheses.

23.1　Purposes of parenthesis

1. To provide more information

Jeff, a 27-year-old hacker, has a different point of view.

Joanna, Faber's teenage daughter, came home one day looking distressed.

2. To explain in greater details

The vibrations are fed into a tiny "chip" – little bigger than the end of a match – which is crammed with more than a thousand transistors and other components. (*The Observer Magazine*)

It is convenient because it permits the models in question to use isolated examples closer to the norms of formal, published written mode and ignore deviant, ill-formed and difficult to parse forms which might come under debate if real-world examples of speech (and, indeed, writing) were the basis for the model. (Rebecca Hughes: "Teaching and Researching Speaking")

3. To indicate the speaker's or writer's opinion, comment, or idea

Hopefully, we'll arrive before dark.

Judging from what I've heard about my grandfather, I think it is impossible that I inherited my curiosity from him.

I've Seen a Dying Eye
Run round and round a Room –
In search of Something – as it seemed –
Then Cloudier become –
And then – obscure with Fog –
And then – be soldered down
Without disclosing what it be
'Twere blessed to have seen – (Emily Dickinson: "I've Seen a Dying Eye")

4. To indicate contrast

The courageous man is the man who forces himself, in spite of his fear, to carry on. (George S. Patton)

Men have a much better time of it than women: for one thing, they marry later; for another thing, they die earlier. (H. L. Mencken)

23.2 Classification of parenthesis

1. Short affirmative sentences, usually with two or a few words

These affirmative sentences include: I know, I presume, I think, I wonder, I admit, I hope, I believe, I am afraid, you know, you see, a study shows, it is understood, it is needless to say, it is true, it turns out, that is, it seems, it was hoped, he thinks, she asks, some say, they claim, they say, what's more.

When I was asked to come and speak to you, your secretary made the suggestion that she thought I must be interested in the feminist movement. I replied – a little irritably, I am afraid, – that I was not sure I wanted to "identify myself," as the phrase goes, with feminism, and that the time for "feminism," in the old-fashioned sense of the word, had gone past. (Dorothy Sayers: *Are Women Human*)

The first group were told by a doctor that they had been given a new drug which, it was hoped, would give them some relief.

A woman, I always say, should be like a good suspense movie: the more left to the imagination, the more excitement there is. (Alfred Hitchcock)

2. Clauses with "as"

These clauses include: as I see it, as is generally known, as (it) often happens, as (it) was pointed out, as it appears to me, as it is, as the name indicates, as things are, as this is the case, as you have heard, as you know, as you say.

As the Bible tells us, worrying about money won't do us any good.

"Merry", as you may know, has two meanings: happy and drunk.

3. Clauses with "if"

We can't make it, sir. It's spoiling for a hurricane, if you ask me.

It is wise to get insurance cover for this kind of care, if at all possible.

4. Infinitive phrases

These phrases include: let alone, not to mention, not to say, not to speak of, so to speak, to be frank, to be honest, to be sure, to begin with, to put it another way, to put it briefly, to sum up, to tell you the truth.

But at the very last minute – before the ax falls, so to speak – they will hit the books.

It is amazing to watch a crammer trying to avoid doing homework. Cleaning the room even takes precedence over homework – not to mention sleep.

5. Participles or participle phrases

These phrases include: according to, admitting that, coming to, concerning, considering, considering the circumstances, generally speaking, granting that, including, judging from/by, provided that, providing that, putting this and that together, regarding, respecting, seeing that, speaking of, strictly speaking, supposing/ suppose that, talking of.

Strictly speaking, the seller should accept the thing you reject.

Judging from what you say, he could have done his work still better.

6. Prepositional phrases

These phrases include: by my estimate, by the way, for example, for instance, in a few words, in fact, in general, in my opinion, in other words, in short, of course, to one's amazement, to one's regret, to one's surprise.

One can, for instance, give them a choice of verbs which would be grammatically and semantically acceptable in the sentence, although only one allows them to form a sentence in keeping with the meaning of the text. (Françoise Grellet: *Developing Reading Skills*)

What, besides their name, do all these people have in common?

7. Adjective phrases

These phrases include: curious enough, least possible, most important, strange enough, worst still.

More important, there was a 45% reduction in the rates of mortality and recurrent heart problems among those who modified their behavior.

To be a real failure you first have to have a job. Better yet, have a series of them.

8. Adverbs or adverbial phrases

These phrases include: admittedly, amazingly, apparently, basically, certainly, clearly, evidently, fortunately, frankly, generally, happily, normally, oddly enough, probably, reportedly, seriously, surely.

When parents bring home a pet, their child gladly grooms it. Within a short time, however, the burden of caring for the animal is shifted to the parents.

A few people consider me egotistical. Actually, I am humble.

9. With brackets

It is extremely difficult exercise, highly specialized (very few people need to read aloud in their profession) and it would tend to give the impression that all texts are to be read at the same speed. (Françoise Grellet: *Developing Reading Skills*)

Others (for example, Rutherford, 1987) believe that a linguistic focus, in the form of grammatical consciousness-raising activities, should be incorporated into task design. (David Nunan: "Design Tasks for the Communicative Classroom")

10. With dash(es)

All services in business – such as gift wrapping, delivery, and credit – have some amount of costs associated with them, and these costs must be covered by higher prices.

Youth is not a time of life – it is a state of mind ... Youth means a temperamental predominance of courage over timidity, of the appetite for adventure over a life of ease. (Samuel Ullman)

23.3 The position of parenthesis

1. At the beginning of a sentence

Fortunately, I found the book I'd lost.

On the other hand, the streets of many suburban communities are lined with trees and each house has its own grassy yard.

2. In the middle of a sentence

One day, it is said, Newton saw an apple fall from a tree.

The following procedure, for instance, is very helpful with most texts. (Françoise Grellet: *Developing Reading Skills*)

The greatest thing to be achieved in advertising, in my opinion, is believability, and nothing is more believable than the product itself. (Leo Burnett)

3. At the end of a sentence

She knows much more about computer science than the other students do, for example.

Is college not preparing us for real life, as Neusner puts it?

23.4 Use of parenthesis

1. In speeches

Yet, if God wills that it continue until all the wealth piled by the bondsman's two hundred and fifty years of unrequited toil shall be sunk, and until every drop of blood drawn with the lash shall be paid by another drawn with the sword, as was said three thousand years ago, so still it must be said, "The judgments of the Lord are true and righteous altogether." (Abraham Lincoln: "Second Inaugural Address")

America, in the face of our common dangers, in this winter of our hardship, let us remember these timeless words. With hope and virtue, let us brave once more the icy currents, and endure what storms may come. Let it be said by our children's children that when we were tested we refused to let this journey end, that we did not turn back nor did we falter; and with eyes fixed on the horizon and God's grace upon us, we carried forth that great gift of freedom and delivered it safely to future generations. (Barack Obama: "President's Inaugural Address in 2009")

2. In novels and short stories

We can scarcely pack in as it is, and the dear knows what will happen when Paul (younger son) arrives tomorrow. (E. M. Foster: *Howards End*)

They are wonderful when they are good, he thought. There is no people like them when they are good and when they go bad there is no people that is worse.

(Ernest Hemingway: *For Whom the Bell Tolls*)

Soon after his arrival, however, there grew up an undercurrent of resentments. (Stephen Endicott: *James G. Endicott: Rebel Out of China*)

3. In dramas

... Heaven and earth!
Must I remember: why, she would hang on him,
As if increase of appetite had grown
By what it fed on: and yet, within a month –
Let me not think on't – Frailty, thy name is woman! (William Shakespeare: *Hamlet*)

Nay, indeed, if you had your eyes, you might fail of knowing me; it is a wise father that knows his own child. (William Shakespeare: *The Merchant of Venice*)

4. In prose

Quartz, one of the world's most common minerals, lies at the heart of every digital watch. (*The Observer Magazine*)

All of us have read thrilling stories in which the hero had only a limited and specified time to live. Sometimes it was as long as a year, sometimes as short as 24 hours. But always we were interested in discovering just how the doomed hero chose to spend his last days or his last hours. I speak, of course, of free men who have a choice, not condemned criminals whose sphere of activities is strictly delimited. (Helen Keller: "Three Days to See")

5. In poetry

The mountains they are silent folk;
  They stand afar – alone,
And the clouds that kiss their brows at night
  Hear neither sigh nor groan.
Each bears him in his ordered place
  As soldiers do, and bold and high
They fold their forests round their feet
  And bolster up the sky. (Hamlin Garland: "The Mountains Are a Lonely Folk")

Frequently are brown.

Frequently the hills undress
Behind my native town.
Oft a head is crested
I was wont to see –
And as oft a cranny
Where it used to be –
And the Earth – they tell me –
On its Axis turned!
Wonderful Rotation!
By but twelve performed! (Emily Dickinson: "Frequently the Woods Are Pink")

6. In well-known quotations

Life, after all, is not as good or as bad as we believe it to be. (Guy de Maupassant)

It takes immense genius to represent, simply and sincerely, what we see in front of us. (Edmund Menotti)

Sooner or later – and I think I should be sooner – women have to face the question of who they are besides their children's mother. (Alice S. Rossi)

No situation, however, wretched it seems, but has some sort of comfort attending it. (Oliver Goldsmith)

7. In academic writing

Reading can be done as a class activity (see above) but reading activities can also be devised to individualize students' work at home. (Françoise Grellet: *Developing Reading Skills*)

Hand baton usually employ all the digits working together, but there is one common baton posture in which a single digit – the forefinger – plays a dominant role. This is the extended-forefinger posture. (Desmond Morris: *Manwatching*)

As a result, 70 percent of the people in the first group got much better.

Chapter Twenty-four Rhetorical Question

A rhetorical question (设问) is a sentence in the grammatical form of a question that is not asked to request information or to invite a reply, but to achieve a greater expressive force than a direct assertion (Abrams & Harpham, 2010) or to assert something or to impart an oratorical tone to an utterance. It is often used in argument or persuasive discourse, for effect, emphasis, provocation, or for drawing a conclusive statement from the facts at hand, or for making the language more vivid and convincing, so as to attract listeners' / readers' attention and encourage them to think.

24.1 Purposes of rhetorical questions

1. To emphasize

Catching me going to the concert with Mary? (= I shall definitely not go to the concert with Mary.)

2. To attract the audience

Are you going grey too early? (advertisement for hair-darkening cream)

Isn't it a peculiar name for a journal that also discusses America, Britain, Europe, science and technology, world politics, books plus rats, current affairs ... along with business, finance and economics? (advertisement for the journal *The Economist*)

3. To show one's emotion

Do you think I am a fool?

Am I a free man in England and do I become a slave in six hours by crossing the Channels? (Jonathan Swift)

4. To satirize

Why don't you go and pick someone else's pocket?
You also have two hands, have you?

5. To give advice or order

Can't you hold your tongue for a little while?
Why don't you go and see the doctor?

6. To negate

Is Jack a gentleman? (The implied meaning: Jack is not a gentleman.)
Who knows? (The implied meaning: No one knows.)

7. To question

What difference does it make?
Can't you answer even such a simple question? (surprise)

24.2 Classification of rhetorical questions

1. Without answer

How can we expect another to keep our secret if we cannot keep to others?
Who wouldn't have dreamed of becoming rich overnight?
Is it live, or is it Memorex? (advertisement for the video recorder Memorex)
Is her skin really this beautiful? (advertisement for Max Factor)

2. Answer by the writer or speaker

Do you love life? Then do not squander time; for that's the stuff life is made of. (Benjamin Franklin)

When you were growing up,
Did you know what you wanted to be?
A mother?
A dancer?
A glittering success?
And did you know that whatever your path,
Something inside you would always shine through?
Ghost Myth, the new fragrance by Coty.
You can't see it, but you know it's there. (advertisement for the perfume Ghost

Myth)

Popularity? It's glory's small change. (Victor Hugo)

3. Unreasonable questions are used to refer to something else

Mother to her son: You have two hands, don't you? (The implied meaning: You should do it with your hands.)

Is this a place to adjust clothing? (The implied meaning: This is not the toilet.)

4. Negative for affirmative

Why don't we borrow a camera from Mary?

Wouldn't it be better for us to set off a little earlier?

5. Affirmative for negative

Am I a fool?

Why should I do such a thing? (= I shall not do such a thing.)

What's the use of crying?

24.3 Use of rhetorical questions

1. In poetry

Shall I compare thee to a summer's day?
Thou art more lovely and more temperate. (William Shakespeare: "Sonnet 18")

"You are old, Father William," the young man said,
"And your hair has become very white:
And yet you incessantly stand on your head –
Do you think, at your age, it is right?" (Lewis Carroll: "Father William")

The turmoil from war and opium and poverty
made you leave your country.
Exposed now to lands that will restrict your
entry, you had travelled long and far to be
subject to another's language,
another's syntax.
Right away, those rules of grammar were the
forgetting of yourself.
Those letters never pronounced before

became the subject of your ridicule.
The bitterness on your tongue became hidden
in need for survival
a proof of assimilation,
the invisibility of yourself.
Now you are here
do you remember your syntax, your language
that which would be remembering of yourself? (Laiwan: "The Imperialism of Syntax")

2. In novels and short stories

Can a man be too cruel to his mother's enemy? (Thomas Hardy)

With its untold depths, couldn't the sea keep alive such huge specimens of life from another age, this sea that never changes while the land masses undergo almost continuous alteration? Couldn't the heart of the ocean hide the last-remaining varieties of these titanic species, for whom years are centuries and centuries millennia? (Jules Verne: *Twenty Thousand Leagues under the Sea*)

3. In dramas

Honour pricks me on. Yea, but how if honour prick me off when I come on, – how then? Can honour set to a leg? Or an arm? No; or to take away the grief of a wound? No. Honour hath no skill in surgery, then? No. What is honour? A word. What is in that word honour? What is that honour? Air. A trim reckoning! Who hath it? He that died o' Wednesday. Doth he feel it? No. Doth he hear it? No. It is insensible, then? Yea, to the dead. But will it not live with the living? No. Why? Detraction will not suffer it. Therefore I'll have none of it. Honour is a mere scutcheon. And so ends my catechism. (William Shakespeare: *Henry IV*)

Brutus: Not that I loved Caesar less, but that I love Rome more. Had you rather Caesar were living, and die all slaves, than that would Caesar were dead, to live all free men? ... Who is here so base that would be a bond man? If any, speak; for him have I offended. Who is here so rude that would not be a Roman? If any, speak; for him have I offended. Who is here so vile that will not love his country? If any speak; for him have I offended. I pause for a reply.

All: None, Brutus, none. (William Shakespeare: *Julius Caesar*)

4. In prose

If your riches are yours, why don't you take them with you to the other world? (Benjamin Franklin)

Free? Why, I have never been in any country where the individual has such an adject fear of his fellow-countrymen. Because, as I say, they are free to lynch him the moment he shows he is not one of them. (D. H. Lawrence: *Studies in Classic American Literature*)

5. In speeches

Fellow citizens, pardon me, allow me to ask, why am I called upon to speak here today? What have I, or those I represent, to do with your national independence? Are the great principles of political freedom and of natural justice, embodied in that Declaration of Independence, extended to us? (Frederick Douglass)

Why stand we here idle? What is it that gentlemen wish? What would they have? Is life so dear or peace so sweet, as to be purchased at the price of chains and slavery? (Patrick Henry)

Such stories set us thinking, wondering what we should do under similar circumstances. What events, what associations should we crowd into those last hours as mortal beings? What happiness should we find in reviewing the past? What regrets? (Helen Keller: "Three Days to See")

6. In well-known quotations

In fact, is there anyone in the world who does secretly feel that he is worthy of a biography? (Colin Wilson)

As man increases his knowledge of the heavens, why should he fear the unknown on earth? As man draws nearer to the stars, why should he not also draw nearer to his neighbor? (Lyndon B. Johnson)

7. In news headlines

"Psst! Wanna Buy an Illegal Toilet?" (*Time*, April 2000)

"Time to Jump Ship?" (*Time*, May 1997)

8. In advertisements

Do you have it today? (advertisement for health product)

Asia is changing. Shouldn't its magazines? (advertisement for the magazine *Asia Week*)

Was there engineering genius involved? Yes, there was. For example, when you're putting the block right at the top, how are you going to lug a block of stone that weighs several tons 480 feet up a structure? How are you going to do it, and how are you going to do it without leaving scratches on all the rest of the structure? And how many people does it take to drag a block weighing several tons 480 feet up into the sky? Approximately, 2.3 million blocks of stone were cut, transported and assembled to create the Great Pyramid. (advertisement for tourism)

I came back.
I came back to softness and comfort.
I came back to Dr. White's.
And I wonder why I ever went away.
Because only Dr. White's gives me two kinds of comfort.
The super-comfort of their cotton-wool content.
That makes them so much softer.
And the comfort of a safer, more absorbent towel,
With a flush-away design, too,
For even more convenience.
I tried the best, but I came back.
Isn't it time you came back to Dr. White's?
Dr. White's
Two kinds of comfort. (advertisement for towels made by Dr. White's)

9. In daily communication

Are you in your sense?
Haven't you got anything better to do?
Didn't I tell you he would forget?

10. In academic writing

What's life? Two crucial traits are that life produces (autopoietically self-maintains) and reproduces itself. Then there is inherited change: DNA and chromosome mutations, symbiosis, and sexual fusion of growing life. When combined with natural selection, it means evolutionary change. Nonetheless, autopoiesis, reproduction, and evolution only begin to encompass the fullness of life. (*What's Life?*)

People don't want to work at home, even if they could. Look at all the women struggling to get out of the home and into a job.

How can you get any work done with kids running around?

People won't be motivated unless there's a boss watching them.

People need face-to-face contact with each other to develop the trust and confidence necessary to work together. (Alvin Toffler: *Future Shock*)

What is the role of clones in society? Can they become human's slaves or organ donors? Who are their parents? Who is their family?

How does it happen that children learn their mother tongue so well? Let us compare them with adults learning a foreign language for the comparison is both interesting and instructive.

Part Four

Semantic Figures of Speech

Chapter Twenty-five　Metaphor

Metaphor (隐喻), a word coming from Greek, *metaphora*, meaning transference, carrying over, is the most important and widespread figure of speech, in which one thing, idea, or action is referred to by a word or expression normally denoting another thing, idea, or action, so as to suggest some common quality shared by the two. In metaphor, this resemblance is assumed as an imaginary identity rather than directly stated as a comparison. (Baldick, 2001)

As Lakoff & Johnson (1980) point out, metaphor is pervasive in everyday life, not just in language but in thought and action. Our ordinary conceptual system, in terms of which we both think and act, is fundamentally metaphorical in nature. As Minsky (1986) says, "All thoughts are metaphorical to some extent." So metaphor is not only a figure of speech, but also a way of thinking and cognition. It plays an important role in daily life, scientific research, social management, etc., that is, everywhere we are. That's why Lakoff and Johnson use *Metaphors We Live By* as the title of their great book.

According to Mohanty (2009), metaphor directly compares seemingly unrelated subjects in the form: "The first subject is a second subject" describing the first as being or equal to the second in some way, and thus the first can be economically described because implicit and explicit attributes from the second are used to enhance the description of the first. Metaphor differs from a simile in that the comparison is only implied, instead of being formally expressed, and so a metaphor is in a sense a condensed simile. Traditionally, metaphor is based on similarity between different things, but now metaphor is considered to be based on all the experiences of human beings, including all the experiential relatedness, all non-objective similarity, the same biological and cultural roots, etc.

The use of metaphor is arbitrary. We use metaphor based on our own experience, knowledge, culture, environment, etc. So different people have different metaphor and different people understand metaphor in different ways. For example, German scientists say that light is a wave, while English scientists say that light is a particle.

Richards (1936) introduces the terms "tenor" and "vehicle: to refer to the subject and the metaphorical term respectively. He considers tenor as an idea or subject, while vehicle is an image. The vehicle (the thing compared to) must be set out explicitly while the tenor (the thing described) may be only implied.

e.g. Imperialism is a paper tiger. ("Imperialism" is the tenor, while "paper tiger" is the vehicle)

e.g. He has been revered by generations of teachers inspired by the belief that children are not empty vessels. to be filled with knowledge (as traditional pedagogical theory had it) but active builders of knowledge and little scientists who are constantly creating and testing their own theories of the world. ("Children" is the tenor while "empty vessels" is the vehicle)

25.1 Purposes of metaphor

1. For comparison

His mind is a meadow in winter. (Metaphor. He is compared to a meadow in winter.)

Compare: His mind is barren. (Not metaphor)

He is a mushroom of opulence. (Metaphor. He is compared to a mushroom.)

2. For relatedness

What do you think of Ms. Thatcher?

She is made of iron. (Metaphor, more difficult to understand, but contains more implication)

Compare: She is a tough lady. (Clear, direct reply, but not metaphor)

3. For brevity or economy

This room is a pigsty. (Metaphor, brief and vivid)

Compare: This room is filthy and untidy. (Not metaphor)

4. For emphasis

The tree of liberty must be refreshed from time to time with the blood of patriots and tyrants. It is its natural manure. (Thomas Jefferson)

Note: From the comparison of blood to manure, we can feel how difficult the struggle would be between patriots and tyrants.

5. For description

Campaign posters sprouted across the land like wild flowers after a spring rain.

Note: Here, "campaign posters" are described as wild flowers after a spring rain, and we can sense how many they are.

6. For novelty

What will parents do without the electronic baby-sitter?

Note: The use of "electronic baby-sitter" as TV set is quite fresh and strange.

7. For attraction

One look at his face and we realized that a thunderstorm was about to break.

8. For praise

He shows a lot of strength for such a peanut.

Note: Praise is shown by using peanut with a lot of strength.

9. For contempt or criticism

"You chicken!" He cried, looking at Mark with contempt.

Note: Mark is compared to a chicken, which is a coward.

10. For humor

Last night, I heard him driving his pigs to the market.

Note: His snore is humorously compared to the noise of driving pigs to the market.

11. For euphemism

I haven't had time to clear up, so I am all at sixes and sevens.

Note: Here, "at sixes and sevens" shows how dirty the place is.

12. For exaggeration

He hogged down his dinner and rushed out.

13. For vividness

The crowd seemed to feel that their champion had not scorched the infidels with the hot breath of his oratory as he should have. ("The Trial That Rocked the World", in *Advanced English*)

14. For suggestion

Oak may bend but will not break.

Note: The proverb indicates that one can be tenacious like the oak.

15. For wordplay

Doe, a deer, a female deer.
Ray, a drop of golden sun.
Me, a name I call myself.
Far, a long, long way to run.
Sew, a needle pulling thread.
La, a note to follow Sew.
Tea, a drink with jam and bread. (*The Sound of Music*)

25.2 How to recognize metaphor

1. From one register to another

The Prime Minister cannot claim immunity from criticism.

Note: "Immunity" is originally used in medicine, meaning the ability not to be affected, but here it is used politically, meaning the state of being protected.

2. Conversion

Every one of her words hammered its way into my heart.

Note: Here "hammer", a noun, is used as a verb, thus providing a vivid image in readers' mind.

3. Conflict in the context

His words whetted my curiosity.

Note: "Whet", originally meaning grind, here means stimulate, as it is used with curiosity, which is not usually used in collocation.

25.3 Structural features of metaphor

1. Noun metaphor

1) Noun as the subject

The human tide was rolling westwards. (Charles Dickens)

War clouds were still hanging over the Middle East.

2) Noun as the predictive

Life is not a "brief candle". It is a splendid torch that I want to make burn as brightly as possible before handing it on to future generations. (George Bernard Shaw)

Books – the best antidote against the marsh-gas of boredom and vacuity. (George Steiner)

Praise is not pudding.

If the fatherland is sound, my personal troubles are only a flea bite.

In their glory days, these corporate champions were magnets for the best and brightest people.

3) Noun as the complement

The loss of jobs is regarded by some as a necessary evil in the fight against inflation.

2. Verb metaphor

I was snowed under by work.

He wolfed down his supper.

During the 1980s, a new drug called crack began to flood the street.

He stories about his academic career and his professional career.

He is dressed to kill.

I'm reading this book just to kill time.

She kills her child with kindness.

3. Adjectival metaphor

A heavy purse makes a light heart.

We regard it as a burning shame to have lagged behind.

It was a conference fruitful of results.

4. Adverbial metaphor

He flatly refused me.

They smashed the plot at one blow.

A right extremis group is suspected of being behind the killing.

5. Phrase as metaphor

His criticisms were enough to make anyone see red.

It is reported that the robber armed with a pistol kills in cold blood.

6. Noun's + noun as metaphor

In his mind's eye he was passing the Clearys in review, as he had first seen them from the station yard. (*The Thorn Bird*)

As I listened to those songs [of the glee club], in memory's eye I could see those staggering columns of the First World War, ... (General Douglas MacArthur: "Thayer Award Acceptance")

7. Sentence as metaphor

Many proverbs can be metaphorically used as follows:

Every dog has his day.

Every cloud has a silver lining.

Two of a trade never agree.

If you run after two hares, you will catch neither.

Ignorance is the parent of fear.

The burnt child dreads the fire.

25.4 Classification of metaphor

1. Sustained metaphor

A sustained metaphor (博喻，并列隐喻) refers to a metaphor in which the tenor is compared to two or more things in succession.

Beauty is but a vain and doubtful good;

A shining gloss that vadeth suddenly;

A flower that dies when first it begins to bud;

A brittle glass that's broken presently … (William Shakespeare: *The Passionate Pilgrim*)

Note: In this poem, "beauty" is compared to god, gloss, flower and glass.

Macbeth doth murder sleep, the innocent sleep,
Sleep that knits up the ravell'd sleave of care,
The Death of each day's life, sore labour's bath,
Balm of hurt minds, great nature's second course,
Chief nourisher in life's feast. (William Shakespeare: *Macbeth*)

2. Extended metaphor

An extended metaphor (延伸隐喻) sets up a principal subject with several subsidiary subjects or comparisons (Mohanty, 2009), that is, a metaphor in which there is a basic comparison that is then developed in such a way that every new stage of its elaboration throws new light on the subject. Thus, in an extended metaphor several comparisons are used and they are related in one way or another.

Unchecked violence has already dulled the luster of the Big Apple. The daunting task before its leaders is to prevent it from rotting to the core.

Note: "The Big Apple" refers to New York; "luster", originally meaning light, implies here glory of the city; "rot", meaning bad, implies here the institution of the city has become corrupted; and "core", originally meaning the center of the apple, metaphorically means the central part of the city's government. These points are closely associated with each other to show that the leaders of New York have been faced with a very difficult task of preventing the city from becoming worse and worse.

3. Mixed metaphor

A mixed metaphor (混合喻) is one that leaps from one identification to a second identification that is inconsistent with the first one. (Mohanty, 2009) Put in another way, it is a metaphor in which the combination of qualities suggested is illogical or ridiculous, usually as a result of trying to apply two metaphors to one thing (Baldick, 2001), or one in which two or more incongruous comparisons are made together and thus incongruous images come into being. Different from extended metaphor, a mixed metaphor contains several, but completely unrelated comparisons. Mixed metaphor can produce very amusing imagery.

The seeds of rebellion were kindled in secret.

Note: Seeds cannot be kindled and so the metaphors in this sentence are incongruous.

The bad news congealed into a block of ice.

4. Dead metaphor

A dead metaphor (死隐喻) is one in which the sense of a transferred image is not present (Mohanty, 2009), or a metaphor in which there is no freshness in it as it has existed so long that it has lost its metaphorical strength and vividness.

At last they reached the river mouth.

Note: We are so familiar with the expression "river mouth" that we don't think it is a metaphor, but when it was first created, it was a metaphor. This way we can say it is a kind of dead metaphor.

More examples of dead metaphor:

He's a dirty rat.

Correct principles are lighthouses.

The world is but a little place, after all.

5. Quasi-metaphor

A quasi-metaphor (半隐喻) is a metaphor in which the metaphorical meaning is indicated by the word with some suffixes such as -y, -ly, -ish, and -ic.

He was accompanied by his mousy little wife.

Don't be so beastly to him!

There's something fishy going on.

His suggestion was received with frosty disapproval.

6. Alphabetic metaphor

An alphabetic metaphor (字母隐喻) refers to a metaphor in which a letter of the alphabet serves as vehicle.

He wore a T-shirt.

I went out and bought a V-neck sweater in the evening.

Long lines of women, bent double like inverted capital Ls, working their way slowly across the field ... (George Orwell)

7. Orientational / Spatializational metaphor

An orientational / spatializational metaphor (方向隐喻 / 空间隐喻) is one produced by reference of space or direction.

One harsh word would send her into the depths of despair.

He pondered, as if over some deep philosophical point.

Feelings ran high as the election approached.

8. Active metaphor

An active metaphor (活隐喻) is a metaphor which, by contrast to a dead metaphor, is not part of daily language and is noticeable as a metaphor.

You are my sunshine.

Light is the music of glass for makers of fine crystal.

Life is an isthmus between two eternities.

9. Absolute metaphor

An absolute metaphor (绝对隐喻), or called paralogical metaphor (sometimes called an anti-metaphor), is a metaphor in which there is no discernible point of resemblance between the idea and the image.

The couch is the autobahn (a German word meaning highway) of the living room.

10. Complex metaphor

A complex metaphor (复杂隐喻) is a metaphor which mounts one identification on another.

That throws some light on the question.

Note: "Throwing light" is a metaphor and there is no actual light.

11. Compound metaphor

A compound or loose metaphor (复合隐喻) is one that catches the mind with several points of similarity.

He has the wild stag's foot.

Note: This suggests grace and speed as well as daring.

The bloodhounds of the Wiki's Ban Patrol can sniff this out.

Note: This suggests tenacity and determination as well as something doglike.

12. Implicit metaphor

An implicit metaphor (内隐隐喻) is one in which the tenor is not specified but implied.

Shut your trap!

Note: Here, the mouth of the listener is the unspecified tenor.

13. Submerged metaphor

A submerged metaphor (潜隐喻) is one in which the vehicle is implied, or indicated by one aspect.

My winged thought.

Note: Here, the audience must apply the image of the bird.

14. Simple or tight metaphor

A simple metaphor (简单隐喻) is two in which there is but one point of resemblance between the tenor and the vehicle.

Cool it.

Note: Here, the vehicle, "I'm" is a temperature and nothing else, so the tenor, "HOT!!!!!!!", can only be grounded to the vehicle by one attribute.

15. Conceptual metaphor

A conceptual metaphor (概念隐喻) is an underlying association that is systematic in both language and thought.

A lifetime is a day. (Dylan Thomas: "Do Not Go Gentle into That Good Night")

A nation is a family.

Our relationship has hit a dead-end street. It's stalled; we can't keep going the way we've been going. Look how far we've come. It's been a long, bumpy road. We can't turn back now. We're at a crossroads. We may have to go our separate ways. The relationship isn't going anywhere. We're spinning our wheels. Our relationship is off the track. Our marriage is on the rocks. I'm thinking of bailing out.

16. Dying metaphor

A dying metaphor (垂死隐喻) is a derogatory term coined by George Orwell in his essay "Politics and the English Language". He defines it as a metaphor that isn't dead, but has been worn out and is used because it saves people the trouble of inventing an original phrase for themselves.

You're just a good for nothing bum!

Jack is the apple of Mary's eye.

Once again, the Achilles heel of the Eagles' defense has reared its ugly head.

17. Animal metaphor

An animal metaphor (动物隐喻) is one produced by reference of an animal.

The hallway was zebra-striped with darkness and moonlight.

He had been a pig about money.

He's such a mouse; he never dares to complain about anything.

My father will have a cow when I tell him the news.

Don't believe him. He often talks horse.

Enrico was too good, an old fox, cunning. He was giving nothing away.

He apes their walk and mannerisms behind their backs with hilarious results.

18. Plant metaphor

A plant metaphor (植物隐喻) is one produced by reference of a plant.

He is a peach to work with.

While it may seem to be painting the lily, I should like to add somewhat to Mr. Alistair Cook's excellent article.

He is practically off his onion about her.

Deeds are fruits, words are leaves.

19. Numerical metaphor

A numerical metaphor (数字隐喻) is one produced by reference of a number.

The bride was welcomed by the family, one and all.

He arrived at the eleventh hour.

The teacher could not decide who started the fight. It seemed to be six of one and half a dozen of the other.

20. Color metaphor

A color metaphor (颜色隐喻) is one produced by reference of a color.

Mr. Brown is a very white man. He was looking rather green the other day. He has been feeling blue lately. When I saw him, he was in a brown study. I hope he'll soon be in the pink again.

It's ironic that he should criticize such conduct – he's not exactly lily-white himself.

So that in the end there were the trees. The boy walking through them with his head drooping as he increased in stature. Putting out shoots of green thought. So that, in the end, there was no end.

21. Food metaphor

A food metaphor (食物隐喻) is one produced by reference of things and action related with food and eating.

This is the meaty part of the paper.

What he said left a bad taste in my mouth.

There are too many facts for me to digest them all.

Your sister is such a dish.

22. Body metaphor

A body metaphor (身体隐喻) is one produced by reference of part of the body.

The airlines are being asked to shoulder a disproportionate share of the tax.

It is likely that the Government will bury its head in the sand and drive a bulldozer through the educational system.

How to bargain with the seller is at her finger tips.

The little boat nosed carefully between rocks.

23. Disease metaphor

A disease metaphor (疾病隐喻) is one produced by reference of disease and medicine.

He has been at the centre of politics for too long to escape responsibility for the state's deeper sickness.

I don't expect men to join the guilt-driven overwork syndrome we career women somehow accept.

Diffidence is the poison of true friendship.

24. Building metaphor

A building metaphor (建筑隐喻) is one produced by reference of things and action related with building and building materials.

The police team has cemented close ties with the hospital staff.

The middle class tend to work for someone else. They have a job. A career. Upper middle class tend to be self-employed. They own a job. The rich tend to own the business. They own that corporate ladder that the middle class are busy working up.

Having now seen their schooling systems, it has been brought home to me just how far we lag behind.

25. Machine metaphor

A machine metaphor (机器隐喻) is one produced by reference of a machine or a machine part.

The private sector is also an engine of innovation.

For decades it was these people who kept the wheels of the British economy turning.

In its tough, often remorseless way, New York is a crucible for every manner of talent.

26. Game metaphor

A game metaphor (游戏 / 运动隐喻) is one produced by reference of game and sports.

It was a dangerous game his friend had been playing.

Computers have become household toys.

The operation may not succeed; it's a gamble whether he lives or dies.

27. Weather metaphor

A weather metaphor (天气隐喻) is one produced by reference of weather and climate.

Peter was really snowed under with work.

At one point during Richard's reading, I looked over at Linda, and saw tears sliding down her cheeks, Steve was holding her hand, and his eyes, too, were clouded. (Budd Hopkins: *Witnessed: Brooklyn UFO Abductions*)

A whirlwind Asian tour that took her to Japan, Indonesia, and R. O. Korea, as well as China, appeared to have served its purpose "to introduce America to the world and to bring a message … about how we are going to work with people to find common ground," as Secretary Clinton put it.

Nature prescribes snow as an occasional antidote to the gasoline habit.

28. Money metaphor

A money metaphor (金钱隐喻) is one produced by reference of money and things related.

But the truth is that it is energy that makes the world go round. Energy is the currency of the ecological system and life becomes possible only when food is converted into energy, which in turn is used to seek more food to grow, to reproduce and to survive. (*College English*)

Plain dealing is a jewel.

29. Time metaphor

A time metaphor (时间隐喻) is one produced by reference of money and things related.

Truth is the daughter of time.

There are seasons of the heart. There are seasons in our lives, just as there are seasons to all of nature. These seasons cannot be forced any more than one can force the coming of spring by pulling at tender blades of grass to make them grow. It took me a while to understand.

Time is money.

30. Clothing metaphor

A clothing metaphor (衣物隐喻) is one produced by reference of clothing.

They cap when they pass the dean.

He pocketed all the profits.

The whole family were dressed up to the nines when they left for the wedding. ("Up to the nines" is used for exaggeration)

31. Weapon metaphor

A weapon metaphor (武器隐喻) is one produced by reference of weapons or things and actions related.

He took a snack to kill his hunger.

The reporters torpedoed difficult questions at the president.

It's also aging, leaving her looking more like Coronation Street's Bet Lynch than a blonde bombshell.

32. Metaphor of natural phenomena

A metaphor of natural phenomena (自然现象隐喻) is one produced by reference of natural phenomena or things related.

Jadd remained, besides, intensely interested in natural forms. For instance, he would pick at the black fruit of trees to release the seed ... Jadd, it would sometimes appear, was himself an element.

The police who patrolled the big city slum area that summer were sitting on a volcano.

Some of the talented young are swiftly defeated, and retreat into more ordinary lives. Others are shooting stars, here and gone.

25.5 Uses of metaphor

1. In prose

Youth is not a time of life; it is a state of mind; it is not a matter of rosy cheeks, red lips and supple knees; it is a matter of the will, a quality of the imagination, a vigor of the emotions; it is the freshness of the deep springs of life. Youth means a temperamental predominance of courage over timidity of the appetite, of the craving for adventure over the love of ease. (Samuel Ullman: *Youth*)

Now that the war is over – the real war – your war ... and you will return to what belongs to you. And Gil to London? To the bomb craters and his mother's coffin, and his friend Nigel Brown's ghost. Gil himself is a ghost haunting the garden on the precipice in Cameron Street, as you are haunting this mouldy back yard. Twin ghosts in the one haunting. Is this where we belong to? (Hannah Arendt: *The Human Condition*)

Our life is an apprenticeship to the truth that around every circle another can be drawn; that there is no end in nature, but every end is a beginning. (Emerson: *Circle in the Essential Writings of Ralph Waldo Emerson*)

Every man has in himself a continent of undiscovered character. Happy is he who acts the Columbus to his own soul.

But without Adolf Hitler, who was possessed of a demoniac personality, a granite will, uncanny instincts, a cold remarkable intellect, a soaring imagination and – until toward the end, when drunk with power and success, he overreached himself – an amazing capacity to size up people and situations, there almost certainly would never have been a Third Reich.

2. In poetry

Beauty is but a flower
Which winkles will devour;
Brightness falls from the air;
Queens have died young and fair,
Dust hath closed Helen's eye,
I am sick, I must die,

Lords, have mercy on us! (Thomas Campion)

I would be tickled by the rub that is:
Man be my metaphor. (Dylan Marlais Thomas)

All the world's a stage,
And all the men and women merely players:
They have their exits and their entrances;
And one man in his time plays many parts,
His acts being seven ages. At first the infant,
Mewling and puking in the nurse's arms.
Then the whining school-boy, with his satchel
And shining morning face, creeping like snail
Unwillingly to school. And then the lover,
Sighing like furnace, with a woeful ballad
Made to his mistress' eyebrow. Then a soldier,
Full of strange oaths, and bearded like the pard,
Jealous in honour, sudden and quick in quarrel,
Seeking the bubble reputation,
Even in the cannon's mouth. And then the justice,
In fair round belly with a good capon lin'd,
With eyes severe and beard of formal cut,
Full of wise saws, and modern instances;
And so he plays his part. The sixth age shifts
Into the lean and slippered pantaloon,
With spectacles on nose and pouch on side,
His youthful hose, well sav'd, a world too wide
For his shrunk shank; and his big manly voice,
Turning again toward childish treble, pipes,
And whistles in his sound. Last scene of all,
That ends this strange eventful history,
Is second childishness, and mere oblivion,
Sans teeth, sans eyes, sans taste, sans everything. (William Shakespeare: *As You Like It*)

3. In novels and short stories

His eyes were blazing with anger.

Inside, the crimson room bloomed with light.

It seemed to be the entrance to a vast hive of six or seven floors.

4. In dramas

If music be the food of love, play on;
Give me excess of it, that, surfeiting,
The appetite may sicken, and so die. (William Shakespeare: *The Twelfth Night*)

Good name in man and woman, dear my lord,
Is the immediate jewel of their souls;
Who steals my purse steals trash; 'tis something, nothing;
'Twas mine, 'tis his, and has been slave to thousands:
But he that filches from me my good name
Robs me of that which not enriches him
And makes me poor indeed.
…
O, beware, my lord, of jealousy;
It is the green-eyed monster which doth mock
The meat it feeds on;
…
Poor and content is rich and rich enough,
But riches fineless is as poor as winter
To him that ever fears he shall be poor.
Good heaven, the souls of all my tribe defend
From jealousy! (William Shakespeare: *Othello*)

5. In speeches

Independence would not be a trial separation; it would be a painful divorce. (David Cameron: "Address before the Vote for Scotland's Independence")

I have a dream that one day even in the state of Mississippi, a state sweltering with the heat of injustice, sweltering with the heat of oppression, will be transformed into an oasis of freedom and justice. (Martin Luther King, Jr.: "I Have a Dream")

6. In advertisements

You're better off under the Umbrella.

We're rolling out the red carpet for Asia's elite travelers. (advertisement for DRAGONAIR)

It cleans your hair gently without harshly stripping off all the essential oilskin or leaving anything strange ones behind. So all the health and beauty of your hair shines through. (advertisement for shampoo)

Elegance is attitude. (advertisement for the watch Longines)

Then came the twilight colors of sea and heaven, the wine-pink width merging into lawns of aquamarines, the sky a tender palette of pink and blue. (advertisement for tourism)

The hotel has a beautiful garden, a paradise of birds and flowers. (advertisement for a hotel)

7. In proverbs

Birds of a feather flock together.

Patience is the best remedy.

If wishes are horses, beggars would ride.

Better be the head of a dog than the tail of a lion.

An old fox is not easily snared.

Gold is the devil's hook.

Law is a pickpurse.

8. In news headlines

"Zipped Lips" (*Time*, February 1996)

"Wars of Words" (*Time*, July 1997)

9. In well-known quotations

Speech is a mirror of the soul; as a man speaks, so is he. (Ephraem Syru)

Without education, you're not going anywhere in this world. Education is our passport to the future, for tomorrow belongs to the people who prepare for it today. (Malcolm X)

Love is the star a man look up to and marriage is the hole he falls into. (Frank Ward O'Malley)

Life is an opportunity, benefit from it.

Life is beauty, admire it.

Life is bliss, taste it.

Life is a dream, realize it.
Life is a challenge, meet it.
Life is duty, complete it.
…
Life is love, enjoy it.
Life is mystery, know it.
Life is a promise, fulfill it.
Life is a sorrow, overcome it.
Life is a song, sing it.
Life is a struggle, accept it.
Life is a tragedy, confront it.
Life is an adventure, dare it.
Life is luck, make it.
Life is too precious, do not destroy it.
Life is life, fight for it. (Mother Teresa)

9. In academic writing

More often, the heart disease, process progresses silently until symptoms occur because the pump is not supplying blood in sufficient quantity to other organs.

Note: Here "pump" refers to heart.

Einstein took a huge conceptual leap.

The British thrusted their language down the linguistic throats of the conquered peoples.

Those slick operators, with their patent leather souls!

Before the electronic brain solved this problem, a number of engineers having the same information had worked for a year to produce only three designs, none of which was as efficient as the computer's.

Note: Different peoples have different understanding and expression of metaphor. Even the same people but in different areas have different understanding and expression of metaphor. The following are life metaphors for Americans and Hungarians.

American	**Hungarian**
Life is a precious possession.	Life is a struggle / war.
Life is a game.	Life is a compromise.

Life is a journey.	Life is a journey.
Life is a container.	Life is a gift.
Life is a gamble.	Life is a possibility.
Life is a compromise.	Life is a puzzle.
Life is an experiment.	Life is a labyrinth.
Life is a test.	Life is a game.
Life is war.	Life is freedom.
Life is play.	Life is a challenge.

Chapter Twenty-six Simile

Simile (明喻), from a Latin word *similis*, meaning like, refers to an explicit comparison between two different things, actions, or feelings, using the words "as" or "like" (Baldick, 2001), or a juxtaposed comparison of two or more objects to draw attention to their similarities (Mohanty, 2009). Simply put, simile is a figure of speech in which one thing is likened to another, in such a way as to clarify and enhance an image. It is a clear comparison that can be recognized by the use of the words: like, just like, as, just as, more than, as if, as though, resemble, resemblance, not unlike, as it were, as comparable to, be compared to, similar to, akin to, be analogous to, be something of, etc. But not all sentences with these words can be considered as simile.

For example:

Mary is as beautiful as Jane. (Not simile, as they are like elements)

Mary is as beautiful as a rose. (Simile, as Mary, a human being, and a rose, a flower, are two different elements)

Jack is like his father. (Not simile, as they just look alike)

She resembles her mother. (Not simile, as it is a comparison of the same kind of people)

Her face resembled a silver moon. (Simile, as it is a comparison of different things)

26.1 Purposes of simile

1. For comparison

Reading a translation is like looking at a tapestry on the wrong side. (Miguel de Cervantes)

The human history is like a long river.

2. For relatedness

In winter, ice crystals decorate the fountains and snow covers Basel like icing sugar. (advertisement for tourism)

3. For emphasis

Carlos Lehder was to cocaine transportation what Henry Ford was to cars.

Note: Carlos Lehder was a Columbia's drug baron; Henry Ford was an automobile businessman.

4. For description

I know it helped put me at ease when I felt like the new kid at school at my first economic summit in Ottawa in 1981.

5. For novelty

Learning is like rowing upstream; not to advance is to drop back.

So as she shows she seems the budding rose,
Yet sweeter far than is earthly flower.

6. For attraction

The clouds float over the mountain and among its peaks and gullies like a sea in which the peaks from time to time appear and disappear, often in the twinkling of a moment, like isolated small islands the cloud sea is even more splendid at sunrise and sunset.

The Red Man has ever fled the approach of the White Man, as the morning mist flees before the morning sun.

7. For vividness

Her constitution was sound as a bell – illness never came near her. (Charlotte Brontë: *Jane Eyre*)

You're like a restless bird in a cage. When you get out of the cage, you'll fly very high. (Charlotte Brontë: *Jane Eyre*)

8. For praise

He is, as it were, a walking dictionary.

If they could not see the Winter Palace with their own eyes, they could dream about it as if in the gloaming they saw a breath-taking masterpiece of art they had never known before – as if above the horizon of European civilization was towering the silhouette of Asian Civilization.

9. For contempt or criticism

The man can't be trusted. He is as slippery as an eel.

She's as dull as a doorknob.

10. For euphemism

He talks like a book all the time.

11. For exaggeration

The criminal drove like a bat out of hell.

You may as well ask for the moon as for a bicycle, because you are not going to get either.

The girl listened as if she had been turned to stone.

12. For humor

He can no more swim than a hammer can.

Previously, if I had been really interested in a book, I would race from page to page, eager to know what came next. Now, I decided, I had to become a miser with words and stretch every sentence like a poor man spending his last dollar.

13. For suggestion

What light is to the eye that knowledge is to the mind.

One might as well throw money into the sea as lend it to William.

26.2 What influences the choice of the target words in different cultures

1. Psychology

When founded in the earth, gemstones are often dull-looking and rough. Cut and polished, they sparkle as with an inner fire.

2. Religious belief

I am as poor as Job, my lord, but not so patient. (William Shakespeare: *Henry IV*)

Note: "Job" is a character in the Bible, who could tolerate poorness.

Those were the words that were to make the world blossom for me, "like

Aaron's rod, with flowers". (Helen Keller: "The Story of My Life")

He looked as if he had just stepped out of my book of fairy tales and had passed me like a spirit.

3. Customs

They will never be able to save money to buy a new house – they both spend money like water.

4. Material culture

He treats his child as the apple in the eye.

He was as drunk as ten bears.

5. Environment

Mary was as merry as a cricket when we saw her at Christmas.

6. Culture

You've been about as cheerful as a cemetery these last few days. (James Baldwin: *This Morning, This Evening, So Soon*)

7. Language

Wit without learning is like a tree without fruit.

26.3 Classification of simile

1. Like

1) like

It has long leaves that sway in the wind like slim fingers reaching to touch something.

For hope grew round me, like the twining vine. (Samuel Taylor Coleridge: "Dejection")

Much of the town was destroyed by bombs in the war but it was rebuilt and in the following decade rose from the ashes like the phoenix.

Using this instrument is like trying to pick up one grain of rice with chopsticks: possible, but difficult for the uninitiated.

2) just like

In the supermarket, the shoppers are just like sharks in search of food.

American dreams come in different sizes just like French fries.

2. As

1) as

He was sorry for MacGownt! There he sat, poor devil – with every one getting up all round him, still; and red as a turkey-cock.

It's as important as a game of cricket.

2) just as

When the propeller turns, it pushes the ship forward just as a woodscrew goes into a piece of wood when it is turned.

3. As ... as

In this structure, people, animal, insect, plant, natural things, religion, class, profession, body, disease, food, clothing, material, metal, mineral, etc. can be used for comparison as follows: as innocent as a baby, as tame as a chicken, as beautiful as a flower, as hard as iron, as cheap as dirt, as deaf as a post, as free as air, as hot as hell, as heavy as lead as silent as grave, as steady as a rock, as weak as water, as cold as death, as sure as Bible, as proud as King, as lean as a skeleton, as brown as a cigar, as white as cotton, as red as coral, as faithful as a dog, as crafty as a fox, as black as a crow, as red as a lobster, as fair as rose, as cold as snow.

The two sisters look very much alike. But in temperament they are as like as chalk and cheese.

He is as cross as a bear.

He runs as fast as lightning.

4. As ... so

As the pot is, so is the cover. (proverb)

As you bake, so shall you eat. (proverb)

5. Might (just) as well ... (as)

He never listens – you might as well talk to a brick (as talk to him).

I might just as well have been in his shoes and he in mine.

6. As if

The boy, who was crying as if his heart would break, said, when I spoke to him, that he was very hungry, because he had had no food for two days.

Why doesn't she buy me a drink? It isn't as if she had no money!

7. As though

He was a beautiful horse that looked as though he had come out of a painting by Velasques. (Ernest Hemingway: *For Whom the Bell Tolls*)

"The church! The church!" she repeated, softly, then darted out of sight, as though the brown wall were but thick brown vapor into which she melted.

8. And (= like)

Truth and rose have thorns about them.

Note: Here "truth and rose" means "truth like rose".

Men and pyramids are not made to stand on their heads.

Note: Here "men and pyramids" means "men like pyramids".

9. What

The pen is to a writer what the gun is to a fighter.

What blood vessels are to a man's body that railways are to the country.

10. More ... than

When in a fury, she is more savage than a tigress.

A home without love is no more than a body without a soul.

11. No less ... than

Our village is no less beautiful than this picture.

12. Be similar to

His strength is similar to a horse.

13. Compare ... to

Shall I compare thee to a summer's day?

Thou art more lovely and more temperate. (William Shakespeare: "Sonnet 18")

Shakespeare compared the world to a stage.

14. Liken

You can liken your eye to a camera.

15. Regard ... as

Samuel Johnson regarded a dictionary as a watch.

16. Remind ... of

His nose was particularly white and his large nostrils, correspondingly dark, reminded me of an oboe when they dilated.

17. Resemble

Her face resembled a silver moon.

18. Seem

So as she shows she seems the budding rose.
Yet sweeter far than is earthly flower ... (R. Greene: "Pandosto")

19. Treat ... as

My employer treated my request as a joke.

20. Plant simile

Colin will come to the party; the chance of a free drink is like a carrot to a donkey to him!

But mature love is like a tree, moving slowly from the seed in the ground to the sheltering splendor of its prime.

The mountain is as green as grass.

21. Animal simile

He walked as slowly as a snail.

Maggie is a very diligent person. She works hard like a beaver.

She can't come to your party this weekend as she is recently as busy as a bee.

I rushed to the dining room like a hungry bear.

In the supermarket, the shoppers are just like sharks in search of food.

26.4 Use of simile

1. In idioms

sleep like a top
drink like a fish
run like a hare
as awful as justice
as far apart as the poles
as barren as winter rain

He's as sly as a fox. You've got to watch him.

All over the country, hands of men had been running like wolves; and today they become more merciless.

2. In proverbs

Wit and humor are to conversation what salt is to food.

Jack is as good as his master. (Jack refers to ordinary people)

Laws are like cobwebs, they catch flies but let hornets / wasps go free.

A man can no more fly than a bird can speak.

3. In novels and short stories

She looked and was – as simple as earth, as good as bread, as transparent as spring water. (Margaret Mitchell: *Gone with the Wind*)

Note: "Bread" is very popular and common in the west.

Mary was driven away and she shivered in the cold. She was pale and trembling with anger. Mary felt dizzy as if the earth shook and the mountain vibrated. (Mary Shelley: *Frankenstein*)

… then, like a volcano bursting forth, his face would suddenly change to an expression of the wildest rage as he shrieked out imprecations on his persecutor. (Mary Shelley: *Frankenstein*)

She looked straight in front of her, and her face was as cold and hard as marble. (Charlotte Brontë: *Jane Eyre*)

4. In poetry

Passions are liken'd best to floods and streams:
The shallow murmur, but the deep are dumb … (Walter Raleigh)

If music and sweet poetry agree
As they must needs (the sister and the brother)
Then must the love be great, 'twist thee and me,
Because thou lov'st the one, and I the other. (Richard Barnfield)

My mother groan'd, my father wept,
Into the dangerous world I leapt:
Helpless, naked, piping loud;
Like a fiend hid in a cloud.

Struggling in my father's hands,
Striving against my swadling bands.
Bound and weary I thought best
To sulk upon my mother's breast. (William Blake: "Infant Sorrow")

I have done it again.
One year in every ten
I manage it –
A sort of walking miracle, my skin
Bright as a Nazi lampshade,
My right foot
A paperweight,
My face a featureless, fine
Jew linen. (Sylvia Plath: "Lady Lazarus")

5. In dramas and movies

No more the thirsty entrance of this soil
Shall daub her lips with her own children's blood;
Nor more shall trenching was channel her fields,
Nor bruise her flowerets with the armed hoofs
Of hostile paces, …
The edge of war, like an ill-sheathed knife,
No more shall cut his master. (William Shakespeare: *Henry IV*)

O, beware, my lord, of jealousy;
It is the green-eyed monster which doth mock
The meat it feeds on;
…
Poor and content is rich and rich enough,
But riches fineless is as poor as winter
To him that ever fears he shall be poor.
Good heaven, the souls of all my tribe defend
From jealousy! (William Shakespeare: *Othello*)

My bounty is as boundless as the sea,
My love as deep; the more I have, the more I give to thee,

The more I have, for both are infinite. (William Shakespeare: *Romeo and Juliet*)

My Mama always said, "Life was like a box of chocolates; you never know what you're gonna get." (*Forrest Gump*)

6. In prose

The professor said that the college grading systems were about as accurate as police estimates of crowds of peace marches.

Today is fair. Tomorrow may be overcast with clouds. My words are like the stars that never change.

But mature love is like a tree, moving slowly from the seed in the ground to the sheltering splendor of its prime.

Three passions, simple but overwhelmingly strong, have governed my life: the longing for love, the search for knowledge, and the unbearable pity for suffering of mankind. These passions, like great winds, have blown me hither and thither, in a wayward course, over a deep ocean of anguish, reaching to the very edge of despair.

7. In speeches

For the people of Scotland to walk away now would be like painstakingly building a home – and then walking out the door and throwing away the keys. (David Cameron: "Address before the Vote for Scotland's Independence")

For blacks and other minorities, it means tying our own struggles for justice to the challenges that a lot of people in this country face – the refugee, the immigrant, the rural poor, the transgender American, and also the middle-aged white man who from the outside may seem like he's got all the advantages, but who's seen his world upended by economic, cultural, and technological change. (Barack Obama: "Farewell Address")

8. In advertisements

Light as a breeze, soft as a cloud. (advertisement for clothes)

Moms depend on Kool-Aid like kids depend on moms. (advertisement for Kool-Aid)

Featherwater: light as a feather. (advertisement for glasses)

Perfect Skin as an Angel. (advertisement for Guerlain)

As soft as mother's hands. (advertisement for shoes)

9. In news headlines

"Pretty as a Picture" (*Time*, June 1996)

"As if by Magic" (*Time*, February 1996)

10. In academic writing

Like a fish in the ocean, man is confined to a very shallow layer of atmosphere.

Time, it is well known, sometimes flies like a bird, sometimes crawls like a worm; but man is wont to be particularly happy when he does not even notice whether it passes quickly or slowly.

Like a solidly hit fall ball, the Big Bang is going-going-going.

The hovercraft is a machine that can rise a short distance above the earth; it is round like a saucer; and it has a short tower in the middle of its upper base.

26.5 Differences between metaphor and simile

Metaphor and simile are two of the best known tropes and are often mentioned together as examples of rhetorical figures. Metaphor and simile are both terms that describe a comparison.

1. Simile uses words such as "like", "as", or "than" to compare, while metaphor does not

The significant difference between a metaphor and a simile is that a simile makes a comparison explicit by using "like", "as", or "than", etc. *The Colombia Encyclopedia* (6th edition) explains the difference as: A simile states that A is like B; a metaphor states that A is B or substitutes B for A. According to this definition, "You are my sunshine" is a metaphor whereas "Your eyes are like the sun" is a simile. Some scholars describe simile as simply a specific type of metaphor.

Usually, similes and metaphors could easily be interchanged as follows:

Death lies on her, like an untimely frost. (William Shakespeare, simile)

Death lies on her, an untimely frost. (metaphor)

The two sentences retain almost exactly the same meaning.

Comparison between simile and metaphor:

Simile	**Metaphor**
He is as cunning as a fox.	He is an old fox.

Happiness is like sunshine; it is made up of very little beams.	The sunshine of life is made up of very little beams.
Habit is like a cable; every day we weave a thread, and soon we cannot break it.	Habit may be a cable; every day we weave a thread, and soon we cannot break it.

2. Using a simile as opposed to a metaphor clarifies the analogy by calling out exactly what is being compared

"He had a posture like a question mark" has one possible interpretation that the shape of the posture is that of a question mark, whereas "His posture was a question mark" has a second interpretation that the reason for the posture is in question.

3. At other times, the use of a simile rather than a metaphor adds meaning by calling to attention the process of comparison

A woman without a man is like a fish without a bicycle. (Irina Dunn)

The point is not to compare a woman to a fish, but to ask the reader to consider how the woman is like the fish.

4. Similes are often more convenient than metaphors when analogizing actions

Wide sleeves fluttering like wings. (Marcel Proust)

It is difficult to change this sentence from simile to metaphor.

Chapter Twenty-seven Metonymy

Metonymy (转喻), from a Greek word, *metonymia*, meaning change of name, is a figure of speech that has to do with the substitution of the name of one thing for that of another. Or it is the use of a word for a concept or object which is associated with the concept / object originally denoted by the word. (Mohanty, 2009) This substituted name may be an attribute of the other or be closely associated with it. In other words, the literal term for one thing is applied to another with which it has become closely associated because of a recurrent relation in common experience. (Abram & Harpham, 2010)

27.1 Purposes of metonymy

1. For comparison

A heavy purse makes a light heart.

The conductor ruled his orchestra with a brilliant ear and an iron fist.

2. For relatedness

She meant to marry money.

Shares rose sharply on Wall Street yesterday.

3. For description

All the wit in the world is not in one hand. (proverb)

A still tongue makes a wise head. (proverb)

4. For vividness

Al spoke with his eyes, "Yes."

The negotiations' eyes and ears are run to everything the counterpart does.

27.2 Classification of metonymy

1. Body part as a name for the sense, behavior or ability

He has a sharp tongue.

A light purse makes a heavy heart.

Brain drain has become the country's number one problem.

Little things amuse little minds.

2. Name of a person as a name for his / her works or style

Bob likes reading Byron.

My students have already read Dickens and Hemingway.

3. Name of a clear sign of an object or a person as a name for the object or the person

Are we boys going to be beaten by a bunch of skirts?

Good clothes open all. (proverb)

Give us our daily bread.

4. Name of a place as a name for something produced or some event that happened there

Would you care for a cup of Longjing?

I like to have a little cayenne for the dish. (Cayenne, a place in French Guiana, is well-known for its chili)

5. Instrument or container as a name for the method, position or substance

Sorry, my pocket cannot afford such a pair of shoes.

Let's have a chat over a bottle.

The kettle is boiling. (water)

Two beers, please. (glass of beer)

6. Trade or brand as a name for the products

When the baby-boomers go on Geritol, where are we going to be?

Note: Geritol is the brandname for an anti-aging drug.

They drove a Volvo around the country.

7. Location of a name for the government, institution or enterprises

The order came directly from the White House.

The Wall Street definitely has more say in their policy making.

8\. Symbol or emblem that substitutes a person or activity

The pen is mightier than the sword.

He has a green thumb.

I have two thousand swords at my disposal. (*The Economist*, 1979)

9\. A type of person for his distinctive quality

One may read husband in his face at this distance.

What kind of sailor are you?

10\. A plant for its distinctive quality to refer to people's characteristics

She is a virgin, a most unspotted lily.

He claimed that his family tree included several noblemen.

11\. An animal for its distinctive quality to refer to people's characteristics

The wolf and the pig mingled together in his face.

An army of lawyers is busy preparing suits against Ashland Oil in the wake of a massive diesel-fuel spill that still is snaking its way down the Ohio River.

12\. A concrete thing for the person related to it in some way

The ham-sandwich at table 11 wants the bill. (The person who has been eating a ham-sandwich)

He has been appointed to the bench.

Note: Here "the bench" refers to the judge.

13\. Color for the thing with the color

He is too yellow to stand up and fight.

The blue eyes walked into the office.

14\. Number for things or people

Most courses have been completely unplayable, except the nineteenth hole.

Note: Here "nineteenth hole" is the nickname for the bar in the golf club as there are eighteen holes in each golf course.

She didn't like working nine to five.

15\. Specialized term for a particular concept

As a defensive-backfield coach for Syracuse University's football team, Randy

Edsall spends hours putting X's and O's on the blackboards and exhorting players in Saturday showdowns. ("X and O" are symbols used by the coach for explaining the positions of football players during the game.)

27.3 Use of metonymy

1. In proverbs

Too much knowledge makes the head bald.

A wise head makes a close mouth.

A faint heart never wins a fair lady.

Absence makes the heart grow fonder.

A belly full of gluttony will never study willingly.

2. In prose

Companies have to do more than just reduce costs, says Thahn. "In a downturn, you need not just cut fat – it's even more important to try to build muscle." (*Asian Business*, Oct. 1997)

Note: Here "fat" and "muscle" refer respectively to "the situation in which there are more handed than needed" and "the ability to resist crises".

The 15 billion USD proposed stock warp with Novell gives Lotus the technical muscle to provide a lot of those connections.

The story about him became smaller and faded from the public eye by and by.

On the road of development, every company has its roses and thorns.

3. In news headlines

"A Royal Pain for the Crown" (*The Times*, 1992)

Note: Crown refers to the queen.

"Uncle Sam's Islands" (*The Economist*, 1989)

Note: Uncle Sam refers to the US.

"Shares Rose Sharply on Wall Street Yesterday.

They bring us to the 64,000-dollar question: By what standards are films selected these days?"

Note: Here "64,000-dollar question" refers to the most difficult one with the highest prize in the American radio prize quiz during the Second World War.

4. In novels and short stories

She had been going up to her room to tidy herself when she had been swallowed in embraces with Luke and Helen and Jane, who had missed her and knew that the crossness and impatience that had ruled the house would now be banished. (Doris Lessing: *The Fifth Child*)

You had a company of the Royal Americans here, in what manner would you set them to work in this business? The bayonet would make a road. Ay, there is white reason in what you say; but a man must ask himself, in this wilderness, how many lives he can spare. No, horse, continued the scout, shaking his head... (James Fenimore Cooper: *The Last of the Mohicans*)

Note: Here "white" refers to the white men.

Joanne burned Player after Player in her nervousness at his father's eccentric and preoccupied driving. (John Updike: *Home*)

Note: Here "Player" is a brand of cigarettes.

5. In poetry

O, for beaker full of the warm south! (John Keats: "Ode to a Nightingale")

Sceptre and crown
Must tumble down,
And in the dust be equal made
With the poor crooked scythe and spade. (James Shirley: "Love's Cruelty")

Note: Here "scepter" and "crown" refer to the king, while "scythe" and "spade" refer to the people, and "dust" refers to death.

6. In dramas

Ye gods, it doth amaze me,
A man of such a feeble temper should
So get the start of the majestic world.
And bear the palm alone. (William Shakespeare: *Julius Caesar*)

Note: Here "palm" is the emblem of victory.

O knight, thou lackest a cup of canary, when did I see you so put down? (William Shakespeare: *The Twelfth Night*)

Note: Here "canary" is a place well-known for its white wine.

For I never knew SO young a body with so old a head.

7. In speeches

I have nothing to offer but blood, toil, tears and sweat. (Winston Churchill)

Note: Blood, tears, sweat are used for sacrifice, sympathy, and hard work.

I have fought against white domination, and I have fought against black domination. I have cherished the ideal of a democratic and free society in which all persons live together in harmony with equal opportunities. It is an ideal which I hope to live for and to see realized. But if needs be, it is an ideal for which I am prepared to die. (John F. Kennedy)

Note: Here "white" and "black" refer respectively to white people and black people.

8. In academic writing

The higher the voltage the more insulation we need, just as we need more copper for more amperes.

Note: The abstract noun "insulation" substitutes the concrete.

A Koepe is used in the main shift?

Note: Koepe refers to a Koepe friction-wheel hoist.

9. In daily conversations

Sorry, my pocket can't afford such a pair of shoes.

The kettle is boiling.

His father is fond of the bottle.

Would you like to have a glass of champagne?

27.4 Differences between metaphor and metonymy

Metaphor stresses two different things that are similar in some abstract respect, while metonymy stresses two things that are closely related in some respect, and the two things are not the same. The following two sentences both have a container, but they belong to different figures of speech.

A little pot is soon hot. (This is a proverb, and the whole sentence is used as metaphor.)

The kettle is boiling over. (Here the kettle is a container, substituting the water in it, and so it is metonymy.)

Chapter Twenty-eight Synecdoche

Synecdoche (提喻), from a Greek word, *syneckdoche*, meaning taking together, is a common figure of speech or trope by which something is referred to indirectly, either by naming only some part or constituent of it or – less often – by naming some more comprehensive entity of which it is a part. (Baldick, 2001) It is often confused with metonymy as both involve substitution. Metonymy involves substitution of the name of one thing for that of another closely associated with it, whereas synecdoche involves the substitution of the part for the whole, or (more rarely) the whole for the part, the specific for the general, the general for the specific, or the material for the thing made from it.

28.1 Purposes of synecdoche

1. For comparison

He is the Newton of this century.

The actress decided to tread to boards once more. (go back to the "stage")

2. For relatedness

They counted fifty sails in the harbor. (ships)

The poor man is now left without a roof. (house)

After suffering two World Wars, the European people and their leaders finally realized the horrors of modern warfare and the absolute necessity to end disputes with the pen and not the sword. (pen = negotiation; sword = war)

3. For description

Did you see that cutthroat? (a kind of killers / assassins)

All the wit and learning of the world were assembled there. (the wise and learned scholars)

4. For vividness

He has many mouths to feed in his family. (people)

Excessive authoritarianism has unhappy consequences, whether it wears skirts or trousers, and the ideal of equal rights and equal responsibilities is pertinent not only to healthy democracy, but also to a healthy family. (women and men)

28.2 Classification of synecdoche

1. The part for the whole

Outside, there is a sea of faces. (people)

The actor looked out from the stage onto a sea of faces. (people)

They were short of hands at harvest time. (workers)

We have a fleet of forty sails over there. (ships)

2. The whole for the part

Canada has beaten Australia at cricket. (Australian team, Canadian team)

He was cut open and his appendix taken out. (his abdomen)

The birds sang to welcome the smiling year. (spring time)

As a Sac and Fox, Jim had the colorful Indian name Wa-Tho-Huck. (an Indian tribe)

3. The abstract for the concrete, or the concrete for the abstract

Life was a wearing to him. (a wearing thing)

He said that it was the most beautiful tongue in the world. (language)

Every time a student sits down to write for us, he has to invent the university or the occasion – invent the university, that is or a branch of it, like history, anthropology or economics or English. He has to learn to speak our language, to speak as we do, to try on the peculiar ways of knowing, selecting, evaluating, reporting, concluding, and arguing that define the discourse of our community. (Batholomae: *Inventing the University*)

Note: "University" here refers to the rote, the rule, the ways a university has to follow.

4. The species for the genus, or the genus for the species / a general class for a specific class, or vise versa

There sits my animal guarding the door to the henhouse. (dog)

They were at tea when I called. (meal with tea in the afternoon)

Mary has just acquired a beautiful Spanish cat. She is very happy with it. As for her husband, he simply cannot bear the animal.

5. A material for an object composed of that material

She was dressed in silk. (silk dress)

Thank God. I still have my plastic. (credit card)

28.3 Use of synecdoche

1. In proverbs

Great minds think alike.

The hand that rocks the cradle rules the world. (women)

Two heads are better than one.

Many hands make light work.

2. In prose

If the term sounds unscientific to 20th century ears, let us remember there is a definite connection between marshy lands and malaria.

Many eyes turned to a tall, 20-year girl on the US team.

They came to live under the same roof.

Scientists now want to build a larger and more modern robot that will be called Jason. The Jason device might some day study the ocean floor, and find submarines and investigate enemy equipment. (a larger and more modern robot = the Jason device)

3. In poetry

They say there's bread and work for all,
　And the sun shines always there;
But I'll not forget old Ireland,
　Were it fifty times as fair. (Helen S. Blackwood)

From fairest creatures we desire increase,
That thereby beauty's rose might never die,
But as the riper should by time decrease,
His tender heir might bear his memory; ... (William Shakespeare: "Sonnet 1")

4. In novels and short stories

On seeing him, the miserable creature fell upon his shoulder, sobbing and crying, and pointing to the fountain, where some women were stooping over the motionless bundle, and moving gently about it. (Charles Dickens: *A Tale of Two Cites*)

Dinner was sent into her. (her = her room) (Jack London: *Anecdotes in the Boat*)

A pale oval face came forward into the light. (James Joyce: *Dubliners*)

Still, if all hands had been got together, they would not have more than half filled the room. (Charles Dickens: *The Uncommercial Traveller*)

We looked up and saw the Union Soldiers ride past the window – the blue coats and the guns. Then we heard the boots and spurs on the porch. (William Faulkner)

Note: All the four nouns, blue coats, guns, boots, and spurs refer to soldiers.

5. In dramas

Lear: Return to her, and fifty men dismiss'd?
No, rather I abjure the enmity o' th' air;
To wage against all roofs, and choose
To be a comrade with the wolf and owl – Necessity's sharp pinch! (William Shakespeare: *King Lear*)

These cease of majesty
Dies not alone, but like a gulf, doth draw what near it with it:
Or it is a messy wheel,
Fix'ed on the summit of the highest mount,
To whose huge spokes ten thousand lesser things
Are mortis' and adjoin'd, which when it falls,
Each small annexment, petty consequence,
Attends the boist'rous ruin. (William Shakespeare: *Hamlet*)

Note: Here "a messy wheel" refers to great cart, with the part for the whole.

Have I in conquest stretch'd my arms so far
To be afraid to tell greybeards the truth? (William Shakespeare)

6. In advertisements

CUTTY SARK SCOTS WHISKY

Some people wear trendy clothes to attract attention. Others drive flashy cars. A glass of Cutty Sark won't turn any heads. But if you insist on creating a stir, you can always ask the bartender for one of them. (advertisement for Scots Whisky)

7. In news headlines

"Cultural Threads" (*Time*, August 2003)

Note: Here "threads" refers to clothes worn by sportspeople.

"Monopolists 'R' Us?" (*Time*, June 1996)

Note: Here "R" refers to the toy retailer "Toys R Us".

8. In daily conversations

What a lovely creature she is.

Have you any coppers?

9. In academic writing

Do not touch the exhibits ... These objects, however, were different. Lined up against the wall, there were long thin wires attached to metal spheres... In the centre of the hall there were a number of tall structures which contained colored lights.

Note: The three underlined words refer to the same thing.

In purely analytical studies, equations are used to calculate unknown variable. However, one cannot always solve a mechanical problem solely by mathematical analysis, sometimes the mathematics becomes too difficult. Often one cannot even mathematically formulate the mechanical phenomenon because the mechanics are too complex for adequate description.

Note: Here "mathematics" refers to "mathematical analysis", and "mechanics" refers to "mechanical phenomenon".

28.4 Differences between metonymy and synecdoche

According to Baldick (2001), synecdoche in which the name of a part is substituted for that of a whole (e.g. hand for worker), or vice versa, is an important kind of metonymy. Mohanty (2009) points out that synecdoche, where a specific part of something is used to refer to the whole, is usually understood as a special kind of metonymy. Both metonymy and synecdoche stress two different things that are closely related in some respect but they are not similar. If the whole is stressed, it is metonymy and if part of it is stressed, it is synecdoche.

You are a noble heart. (Charles Dickens) ("Heart" is used to substitute the person. So it is synecdoche.)

Her heart ruled her head. ("Heart" is used to substitute the function, that is, feelings or emotions, and so they are related but not similar. Thus it is metonymy.)

In the two sentences above, part of the body, that is, heart, is used, but it refers to something different, and thus it belongs to different figures of speech.

The whole class rejoiced at the news. (The whole class is considered as a container which refers to all the students in it. So it is metonymy.)

The world is still ignorant of the fact. (The world is also a place as a whole, but it only refers to part of the people in it. So it is synecdoche.)

The following single sentence can display the use of synecdoche and metonymy.

The hand that rocks the cradle rules the world.

In this simple sentence, "hand" is synecdoche, as it represents the mother of whom is a part; and "the deep" is metonymy, because it represents a child by close association. (Nørgaard et al., 2017)

The following single sentence can display the use of synecdoche, metonymy and metaphor.

Fifty keels ploughed the deep.

In this simple sentence, "keels" is the synecdoche, as it refers to the whole (that is, the ship); "ploughed" is the metaphor, as it substitutes the concept of ploughing a field for moving through the ocean; and "the deep" is the metonymy, because "depth" is an attribute associated with the ocean. (Mohanty, 2009)

Chapter Twenty-nine Antonomasia

Antonomasia (换称), from a Greek word, *antonomazein*, meaning to call by another name, is a figure of speech that replaces a proper name with an epithet, or other indirect description; or one that applies a famous proper name to a person alleged to share some quality associated with it. (Baldick, 2001) Simply put, it is the replacement of a proper name by a common noun, or the replacement of a common noun by a proper noun to refer to a class or type, or one proper noun by another proper noun.

29.1 Purposes of antonomasia

1. For comparison

He was another Cicero of his time.

He is Sherlock Holmes the second.

Note: Sherlock Holmes is a private detective in Conan Doyle's novels.

2. For relatedness

Churchill, a bent Pickwick in blue uniform, looked up at Roosevelt with majestic good humour, much older, more dignified, more assured. (Herman Wouk: *Argentia Bay*)

Note: Pickwick is the main character in the novel *The Pickwick Papers* by Charles Dickens. He is short, stout, good-hearted and benevolent.

3. For vividness

His Waterloo was a woman. ("Waterloo" means "failure".)

With these emblems printed at the top party tickets it was easy for the local politicians to tell the Democrats to vote for the "big chick" or the Republicans to vote for the "bird on the dollar". (Howard L. Hurwitz)

Note: Here "big chick" refers to the US Democratic Party, and "bird on the dollar" refers to the US Republican Party.

29.2 Classification of antonomasia

1. Use of proper names for ordinary people

1) From mythology

It is especially whether of ancient Greek or of Roman mythological origins. For example,

Achilles heel: a person's weak or vulnerable point;

Hercules: a hero of strength and bravery;

Prometheus: a tremendous force;

Trojan horse: a person or thing that enters something secretly in order to attack it.

A misbehaving minister is regarded as a government's Achilles heel.

It was to me the stepping off point of and Odyssey.

2) From religion or the Bible

Daniel: a wise and fair judge;

Eden garden: paradise;

Judas: a traitor;

Mecca: birthplace of Muhammad and chief place of Muslim pilgrimage;

Solomon: a wise man;

Towel of Babel: confusion of languages.

Thailand has become the tourist mecca of Asia.

Note: Here, mecca refers to a place which attracts people of a particular group.

The priests have got a book that says
    But for Adam's sin
Eden's garden would be there
    And I there within. (William Butler Yeats)

3) From history

Gypsy: a member of a nomadic people in Europe, of Hindu origin with dark skin and hair, and speaking a language related to Hindi;

Hitler: tyrant, coming from the leader of Germany, who launched the Second World War;

Julius Caesar: great man, coming from the emperor in ancient Rome;

Napoleon: conqueror, coming from the French emperor.

For nearly six decades, whether the country was at war or at peace, Bob, with a band of Hollywood gypsies, has traveled the globe to entertain our service men and women.

It doesn't take an Einstein to recognize that Albert Einstein's brain was very different from yours and mine.

4) From literature

Frankenstein: a monster to be destroyed by what one creates in Mary Shelley's fiction, *Frankenstein*;

Lilliputian: an island in J. Swift's *Gulliver's Travels* where the inhabitants are six inches tall, that is, extremely small;

Man Friday: faithful servant, a character in Daniel Defoe's novel, *Robinson Crusoe*;

Shylock: a greedy and cruel person in Shakespeare's play, *The Merchant of Venice*.

Lebanon has been led, too long, by a Hamlet. (*The Economist*, 1984)

Everything about the house seemed small, from its front door to its lilliputian furniture.

2. Use of the epithet or title for a proper name

Big chick: for the Democrats in the US;

The Bard: for Shakespeare;

The Big Apple: for the American city New York;

The bird on the dollar: for the Republicans in the US;

The boss: for the employer;

Your Majesty: for the king addressed.

Those ad companies celebrating the Big Apple, those shirts with a heart design proclaiming "I love New York" are signs, pathetic in their desperation, of how the mighty has fallen. (Thomas Griffith: "Loving and Hating New York")

On the fourteenth of March, at a quarter to three in the afternoon, the greatest living thinker ceased to think. (Frederick Engels: "Speech at the Graveside of Karl Marx")

Note: Here, "the greatest living thinker" refers to Carl Marx.

29.3 Use of antonomasia

1. In poetry

Some village Hampden, who, with dauntless breast;
The little tyrant of his fields withstood;
Some mute inglorious Milton here may rest;
Some Cromwell guiltless of his country's blood. (Thomas Gray: "Elegy Written in a Country Churchyard")

Note: the individual one refers to a class.

I am the audience – that witnesses history,
The Napoleons come from me and the Lincolns,
They die,
And then I send forth more Napoleons and Lincolns. (C. Sandburg: "I Am the People, the Mob")

2. In dramas

Shylock: A Daniel come to judgement! Yea, a Daniel!
O wise young judge, how I do honour thee! (William Shakespeare: *The Merchant of Venice*)

Would any of the stock of Barabbas,
Had been her husband rather than a Christian!

Note: "Barabbas" refers to gangsters in the Bible.

3. In novels and short stories

"Listen, young man," he whispered, "I want to ask you something before old pineapple juice comes back."

"Yes, sir," responded Swain attentively. (Rude Goldberg)

Note: Here, a common noun for proper name is also considered as metonymy.

4. In prose

Scientific studies have been made of street-corner society, out of which crime, gangsterdom, and fascism inevitably develop. It is a society with leisure – that is to say, spare time – and without compensatory occupation. It does not need a Satan to find mischief for such idle hands to do. (Herbert Read: "Work & Play")

In "Elegy Written in a Country Churchyard", it read: Some mute inglorious Milton here may rest.

Society lifts its hands in honor, but from age to age the Helens, the Messalinas, the Du Barrys, the Pompadours, the Maintenons and the Nell Gwyns flourish, and point a freer basis of relationship than we have yet been able to square with our lives. (Theodore Dreiser)

5. In news headlines

"Send Uncle Sam a Smaller Slice" (*Time*, December 2001)

Note: "Uncle Sam" refers to the US.

"Has Julia Found a Romeo?" (*Time*, October 1995)

Note: Here Julia refers to the well-known actress Julia Roberts. Her fans are interested in her love affairs. "Romeo" comes from Shakespeare's drama *Romeo and Juliet*, meaning fiance or boyfriend.

6. In daily communication

May I use your Hoover?

He thinks he's a Don Juan, but none of the girls like him.

7. In academic writing

Computer technology may make the car, as we know it, a Simithsonian antique. ("The Age of Miracle Chips")

Note: Simithsonian refers to the Simithsonian Museum of Natural History in Washington, DC, USA.

The efficacy of the vaccines is the Achille's heel of India's anti-polio campaign.

29.4 Differences between metonymy and antonomasia

In metonymy, the proper name is used to substitute a specific person or thing that is unique, while in antonomasia, the proper name is used to refer to a group of people or things, which are great in number.

Whitehall does not seem to care about this problem at all. ("Whitehall" refers to the British government, and so it is metonymy.)

Were it not for your help, I should have met my Waterloo. ("Waterloo" is a place but it refers to a failure. So it is antonomasia.)

"Uncle Sam will not help us," he said in a soft voice. ("Uncle Sam" represents the US only and becomes a proper noun. So it is metonymy.)

Lu Xun is a Gorky of China. ("Gorky" is a kind of writers, but not only he himself. There are many such writers and Lu Xun is one of them. So it is antonomasia.)

Chapter Thirty Personification

Personification (拟人) is a figure of speech by which animals, abstract ideas, or inanimate things are referred to as if they were human. (Baldick, 2001) Simply put, it gives human form, character or feeling to animals, plants or life and personal attributes to inanimate objects, or to ideas and abstractions, by the use of adjectives, verbs, nouns or phrases. In fact, personification is a kind of simile or metaphor. For example,

Walls have ears. (metaphor, and also personification)

An earthquake comes like a thief in the night, without warning. (simile, and also personification)

30.1 Purposes of personification

1. For picturesqueness

The fields breathe sweet, the daisies kiss our feet.

Even my hand balks at the date; I had to push to write it down, just to keep the pen moving on the paper. (Donna Tartt)

2. For vividness

All day long the sea waves sobbed with sorrow.

The car beckoned me from across the showroom.

Three mouthfuls of hot soup convinced him that he could not eat.

3. For humor

His words were bitingly sarcastic.

Mosquitoes were using my ankles for filling stations.

My ears have not yet drunk a hundred words.

4. For conciseness and effectiveness, especially in proverbs

Lies have short legs. (proverb)

Love is blind. (proverb)

5. For wit

Punctuality is the thief of time. (proverb)

The fox knows who flees proves himself guilty. (proverb)

30.2 How to personify

1. By the use of nouns or noun phrases

Poverty or drastically lowered income and old age go hand in hand.

Apple thinks different. (advertisement for Apple)

2. By the use of verbs

My heart aches, and a drowsy numbness pains,
My sense, as though of hemlock I had drunk,
Or emptied some dull opiate to the drains,
One minute past, and Lethe-wards had sunk:
'Tis not through envy of thy happy lot,
But being too happy in thine happiness. (John Keats: "Ode to a Nightingale")

My mind just isn't operating today.

All the machines were coupled to OSCAR, the big computer which did the Professor's translation, handled most of the island's administration and bookkeeping and could play championship chess on demand.

I could already see the shadows of leaves dancing on the ground on a sunny day, a sight that I hadn't seen for a time. (Lin Yutang)

3. By the use of adjectives

Hans shrugged a scornful shoulder.

The run down house appeared depressed.

4. By the use of -ing form or -ed form as adjectives

He crashed down on a protesting chair.

Maycomb was an old town, but it was a tired town when I first knew it.

A royalty is regarded as a wasting asset as copyrights, patents, and mines have limited lives.

I was travelling in China when Samaranch announced in Moscow that the city for hosting the 2008 Olympics was Beijing. All Chinese people were overjoyed; all mountains were overjoyed; all rivers were overjoyed.

5. By the use of personal pronouns

China will always do what she has promised to do.

But nature does not manage it so. She put gold in little fissures in the earth, nobody knows where ... (J. Ruskin)

6. By the use of adverbs

Overhead the stars winked mischievously at us.

The stars danced playfully in the moonlit sky.

7. By the use of prepositional phrases

Prices are low in sympathy with the general depression.

Note: Here "in sympathy with" is usually used for people.

8. Gender and person of personified nouns

Some nouns such as sun, pine, death, time are considered masculine, and other words like ship, car, country, love, nature, earth are usually considered feminine. So different personal pronouns of gender are used for them as follows.

How soon hath Time, the subtle thief of youth, stolen on his wing my three and twentieth year!

Nature's first green is gold,
Her hardest hue to hold
Her early leaf's a flower;
But only so an hour.
Then leaf subsides to leaf.
So Eden sank to grief,
So dawn goes down to day.
Nothing gold can stay. (Robert Frost: "Nothing Gold Can Stay")

30.3 Classification of personification

1. Animals described as people

The crocodile said to the monkey, "I want to eat your heart."

Slowly the lion turned its face and looked at Mrs. Cousins. "Me? A dog?" it seemed to say with its strong body and sharp white teeth.

The wolf knows well what another evil beast thinks.

Dogs don't speak in the future tense. They live in the moment.

2. Plants described as people

The trees are wearing their fall colors.

The next morning when the little tree was awake, it had its needle once more. It was so glad to have them again that it laughed, and all the trees of the forest laughed with it. And always after that the little tree was contented.

3. Inanimate objects or natural things described as people

The flames ate up the house.

The sun kisses the green fields.

The car negotiated around the corner carefully.

Poetry in motion, dancing close to me. (advertisement for Toyota)

There is no month in the whole year, in which nature wears a more beautiful appearance than in the month of August! (Charles Dickens: *The Pickwick Papers*)

4. Abstract ideas or concepts described as people

Fashion wins.

Bitterness fed on the man who had made the world laugh. (Noel Grove: "Mark Twain – Mirror of America")

Truth is the daughter of time.

5. Nouns of time used as subjects

Nouns of time (month, season, spring, summer, year, century, etc.) are used as subjects followed by such verbs as discover, find, notice, see, take, and witness, etc.

Eight springs have flown since last I lay
On seaward Quantock's healthy hills,
Where quiet sounds from hidden rills
Float here and there, likes things astray,

And high o'erhead the skylark shrills. (Samuel Taylor Coleridge: "Recollections of Love")

The first rays of morning tiptoed through the meadow.

The twentieth century saw a population boom never before experienced on our small planet.

Slowly the hours crawled.

6. Nouns of places used as subjects

Nouns of places (countries, cities, mountains, rivers, seas, or lakes, etc.) are used as subjects followed by such verbs as discover, find, notice, see, take, and witness, etc.

A wide range of land and sea recreational facilities awaits you. (advertisement for tourism)

I could hear Hawaii calling my name.

The unplanted fields as yet were only cracked clods of dry earth; the mulberry trees reigned supreme here this time of the year.

France, mother of arts, of warriors, and of law.

The town wears gorgeous clothes for the coming holiday.

30.4 Use of personification

1. In proverbs

Money talks.

Dialogue opens many doors to compromise.

Necessity is the mother of invention.

If a donkey brags at you, don't brag at him.

2. In poetry

Apparently with no surprise
To any happy Flower
The Frost beheads it at its play –
In accidental power –
The blonde Assassin passes on –
The Sun proceeds unmoved
To measure off another Day

For an Approving God (Emily Dickenson)

When love with unconfined wings
Hovers within my gates,
And my divine Althea brings
To whisper at the grates;
When I lie tangled in her hair
And fettered to her eye,
The birds that wonton in the air
Know no such liberty. (Richard Lovelace: "To Althea, From Prison")

He clasps the crag with crooked hands;
Close to the sun in lonely lands,
Ringed with the azure world, he stands.

The wrinkled sea beneath him crawls;
He watches from his mountain walls,
And like a thunderbolt he falls. (Alfred Tennyson: "The Eagle")

Note: "He" refers to the eagle, and is personified, and "the sea" is also personified.

3. In children's stories

The crocodile in the river thought hard and finally he had an idea.

Toto did not like this addition to the party. He smelled around the stuffed man as if he suspected there might be a nest of rats in the straw, and he often growled in an unfriendly way at the Scarecrow. (L. Frank Baum: *The Wizard of Oz*)

Note: Toto is a dog.

"Run downhill!" suggested the cows.
"Run toward me!" yelled the gander.
"Run uphill!" cried the sheep.
"Turn and twist!" honked the goose.
"Jump and dance!" said the rooster.
"Look out for Lurvy!" called the cows.
"Look out for Zuckerman!" yelled the gander.
"Watch out for the dog!" cried the sheep.
"Listen to me, listen to me!" screamed the goose. (E. B. White: *Charlotte's Web*)

"We called him Tortoise because he taught us," said the Mock Turtle angrily. (Lewis Carroll: *Alice in Wonderland*)

4. In prose

The rust is eating up the car.

Knowledge always desires increase: it is like fire which must first be kindled by some external agent, but which will afterwards propagate itself. (Samuel Johnson)

Nature prescribes snow as an occasional antidote to the gasoline habit.

The idea of becoming a writer had come to me off and on since my childhood, but it wasn't until my third year in high school that the possibility took hold.

Inflation is eating up our profits.

But the complexion even of external things seemed to suffer transmutation as her announcement progressed. The fire in the grate looked impish – demoniacally funny, as if it did not care in the least about her strait. The fender grinned idly, as if it too did not care. The light from the water-bottle was merely engaged in a chromatic problem. All material objects around announced their irresponsibility with terrible iteration. And yet nothing had changed since the moments when he had been kissing her; or rather, nothing in the substance of things. But the essence of things had changed.

5. In novels and short stories

Some fishing boats were becalmed just in front of us. Their shadows slept, or almost slept, upon the water, a gentle quivering alone showing that it was not complete sleep, or if sleep, that it was sleep with dreams. (Tao Yuanming: *A Tale of the Fountain of the Peach Blossom Spring*, translated by Mark Rutherford)

"What a delicious shiver is creeping over these times!" said Lancelot, half to himself. (Charles Kingsley: *Yeast: A Problem*)

Sophie felt a knot tighten in her stomach. She was certain of it too. For ten years she had tried to forget the incident that had confirmed that horrifying fact for her. She had witnessed something unthinkable. Unforgivable. (Dan Brown: *The Da Vinci Code*)

A whole village-full of sensuous emotion, scattered abroad all the year long, surged here in a focus for an hour. The forty hearts of those waving couples were beating as they had done since, twelve months before, they had come together in similar jollity. (Thomas Hardy: *The Return of the Native*)

6. In dramas

If music be the food of love, play on;
Give me excess of it, that, surfeiting,
The appetite may sicken, and so die. (William Shakespeare: *The Twelfth Night*)

But though lean hunger and green thirst
Like asp with adder fight. (Wilde)

7. In advertisements

Unlike me, my Rolex never needs a rest. (advertisement for watches)

Last but not least, Beatenberg beckons from high above Lake Thum, a sun terrace par excellence and also the longest village in Europe. (advertisement for tourism)

The world smiles with *Reader's Digest*. (advertisement for the magazine *Reader's Digest*)

With 52 issues, they'll be thinking of you week after week. (advertisement for the magazine *Newsweek*)

8. In news headlines

"The Homework Eat My Family" (*Time*, January 1999)

"Will Walmart Steal Christmas?" (*Time*, December 2003)

9. In daily conversations

Student: Did I get your permission to the conference?
Teacher: Your paper says no.

Student: Could you have a quick look at my exercise?
Teacher: There goes the bell and it hurries me back to the platform.

10. In academic writing

Much of modern technology wouldn't exist if it weren't for the invention of materials nature never thought of.

It is very much like communicating with an accurate robot who has a very small vocabulary and who takes everything literally.

The program ready for computer to read is prepared in a specially designed language.

Chapter Thirty-one Parody

Parody (仿拟) comes from a Greek word, *paroidia*, which means counter-song. It is a mocking imitation of the style of a literary work or works, ridiculing the stylistic habits of an author or school by exaggerated mimicry. In other words, it is a kind of imitation which borrows the style and techniques of a text or writer's idiolect and fits new subject matter to it, and is often used for a humorous or satirical purpose.

According to *Webster's Third New International Dictionary* (2002), parody is a writing in which the language and style of an author of work is closely imitated for comic effect or in ridicule often with certain peculiarities greatly heightened or exaggerated.

According to *Merit Students Encyclopedia*, parody is an imitation of a serious author or literary work designed for comic effect or humorously reveals the peculiarities or excesses of the original work. It may also implicitly criticize the ideas or ideals of a given age or society.

Parodies can be written in verse or prose, and they may take the form of plays. Their humorous effect depends largely on the reader's knowledge of the style or particular work being ridiculed. According to Peters (1995), parody is a humorous or satirical imitation of a literary work (or any work of art). It usually keeps the form and style of the original work, or the genre to which it belongs, and applies them to rather different matter, and is not plagiarism since it makes its debt to its original very clear.

31.1 Purposes of parody

1. For satire

Wall Street owns the country. It is no longer a government of the people, by the people and for the people, but a government of Wall Street, by Wall Street and for Wall Street. (Leo Huberman: *We, the People*)

A: Did you see Hilda at the party last night?

B: Yes, I did. She was really dressed to the teeth!

A: Well, she had on her finest, most elegant clothing because she was out to make a good impression on Bill.

Note: "Dressed to the teeth" comes from "armed to the teeth".

2. For cynical attitude

Don't put off till tomorrow what can be enjoyed today. (Oscar Wilde)

Note: This comes from "Don't put off till tomorrow what can be done today."

The Unbearable Heaviness of Being.

Note: It comes from "The Unbearable Lightness of Being".

3. For fun

"I won't have Ralph upset. After all," she smiled, "a husband in the hand is worth two in the bush."

4. For attraction, especially in advertisements

Two beer or not two beer, that's a question. – Shakesbeer (advertisement for beer)

Note: It comes from "To be, or not to be, that is the question." Even the brand will let people think of Shakespeare.

An apple for everybody keeps worries away. (advertisement for Apple Computer)

Note: It comes from "An apple a day keeps the doctor away."

All roads lead to Holiday Inn. (advertisement for Inn)

Note: It comes from "All roads lead to Rome."

5. To create a new context

Where there is a will, there is a lawsuit.

Note: It comes from "Where there is a will, there is a way."

Art's for heart's sake.

Note: It comes from "Art's for art's sake."

You can fool all of the people all of the time if the advertising is right and the budget is big enough.

Note: It comes from "You can fool one person at one time but you can not fool all of the people all of the time."

6. For contrast

Ugly is only skin-deep. (advertisement for Volkswagen)

Note: It comes from "Beauty is only skin-deep."

Lib and let lib.

Note: It comes from "Live and let live."

7. For brevity

He intended to take an opportunity this afternoon of speaking to Irene. A word in time saves nine. (John Galsworthy)

Note: "A word in time saves nine" comes from a well-known proverb "A stitch in time saves nine." This short sentence is very brief and meaningful.

A Mars a day keeps you work, rest and play. (advertisement for Mars, a chocolate brand)

Note: This advertisement comes from two proverbs – "An apple a day keeps a doctor away" and "All work and no play makes Jack a dull boy". Such a brief advertisement can easily draw the consumers' attention.

31.2 Classification of parody

1. Word parodies

For the first time, Shanghai has officially put forward the concept of "gray-collar workers", which refers to technicians with a high-level of creativity and professional skills, in order to encourage more young people to take up these neglected positions.

Note: Here "gray-collar worker" comes from "white-collar worker".

The rise of the no-collar worker. Did the 90s loom free a legion of white-collar Dilberts, or create a false utopia for a new generation of high-tech drones? ("Unraveling Myth from Reality: The Dream of a Freer, Hipper American Workplace")

Note: "No-collar worker" comes from "white-collar worker".

Farewell to Wall Street

Note: It comes from *Farewell to Arms*, a novel by Hemingway.

He had a clean-cravatish formality of manner and kitchen-porkerness of carriage. (Charles Dickens)

Note: Here "clean-cravatish" comes from "clean-cravat", and "kitchen-porkerness" comes from "kitchen-porker".

2. Phrase parodies

Jane has fallen in love with Jack. It is said that she had hesitated for a long time before she finally walked into love.

Note: Here, "walk into love" comes from "fall in love".

A group of militant ladies are agitating to forbid US newspapers from running separate male and female want ads, and call any ladies who tolerate it "Aunt Tom".

Note: "Aunt Tom" comes from "Uncle Tom" in *Uncle Tom's Cabin* by Harriet Beecher Stowe.

3. Sentence parodies

Smile and the world smiles with you may work in London or Leeds. Smile in Cambridge and see where it gets you. (*The Sunday Times*)

Note: "Smile in Cambridge and see where it gets you" comes from "Smile and the world smile with you."

Money Makes the Mayor Go. (Chandigarh, India, *Tribune News Service Sunday*, 2002-07-22)

Note: "Money Makes the Mayor Go" comes from the proverb "Money Makes the Mare Go".

4. Poem parodies

Bring me your tired,
Worn-out, worthless
Old dollar bills.
I'll trade you for one of
My incredible Wellington
Counterfeit Diamonds

It makes sense in this senseless world. (advertisement for Wellington Counterfeit Diamonds)

Note: This advertisement poem comes from Emma Lazarus's "The New Colossus" as follows:

Give me your tired, your poor,
Your huddled masses yearning to breathe free,
The wretched refuse of your teeming shore,
Send these, the homeless, tempest-tossed to me.
I lift my lamp beside the golden door!

5. Tone parodies

Judge (in the dentist chair): "Do you swear that you will pull the tooth, the whole tooth, and nothing but the tooth?"

The judge says so because he usually uses: Do you swear that you tell the truth, the whole truth, and nothing but the truth?

31.3 How to create parody

1. Change a word or some words to express something new

Better late than the late. (Safety slogan on the US highway)

Note: It comes from "Better late than never."

Clearly, when it comes to marriage, practicing beforehand doesn't make perfect. Give me Green World, or give me yesterday.

Note: It comes from "Give me liberty, or give me death" by P. Henry.

A wolf in Sheik's clothing.

Note: It comes from "a wolf in sheep's clothing".

A Tale of Two Sisters.

Note: It comes from *A Tale of Two Cities* by Dickens.

2. Change the order of the original sentence

He thought of his past, its cold splendour and insouciance. But he knew that for him there was no turning. His boats were burnt.

Note: "His boats were burnt" comes from "burn one's boats", but in passive voice.

3. Add new constituents

Though Henry Adams found Cambridge a "social desert", it flowed with intellectual milk and honey.

Note: "It flowed with intellectual milk and honey" comes from "a land flowing with milk and honey".

4. Change the voice

I came, I saw, I was conquered.

Note: It comes from "I came, I saw, I conquered" by Caesar.

5. Change the words by changing some letters

Government off the people, buy the people, fool the people. (from Abraham Lincoln's speech)

6. From proverbs, or famous sayings by well-known writers

Dollar wise, penny foolish.

Note: It comes from "Penny wise, pound foolish."

Sense and simplicity.

Note: It comes from Jane Austin's *Sense and Sensibility*.

To swim or not to swim, that is the question.

Note: It comes from Shakespeare's "To be, or not to be, that is the question."

7. Use the above means together

Not all cars are created equal. (advertisement for cars made by Toyota)

Note: It comes from "All men are created equal", with one word changed, and another word added.

More examples:

Original sentence	**New one by parody**
One man's meat is another man's poison.	One man's recyclables are another man's masterpiece.
No pains, no gains.	No personalized research, no Noble Prize.
The one who laughs last, laughs best.	He laughs best who runs longest. (advertisement for tires)
Failure is the mother of success.	We need to accumulate experience, for experience is the mother of wisdom.
All roads lead to Rome.	All roads lead to Holiday Inn.
No pains, no gains.	No taxes, no government.
East or west, home is best.	East or west, the Guangzhou cuisine is the best.
Seeing is believing.	Comparing is believing.

All work and no play makes Jack a dull boy.	All work and no play makes a dull stay.
A friend in need is a friend indeed.	A friend in need is a friend to be avoided.

31.4 Use of parody

1. In prose

Mothers know instinctively that for children an ounce of praise is worth a pound of scolding. (*College English*)

Note: It comes from "an ounce of prevention is worth a pound of cure".

It's been cold out. Really cold, not just normal New York, scarf-and-overcoat December cold but Canadian cold, Arctic cold – the kind of cold that insinuates its way through window frames, and whispers under doors, and chills even perpetually overheated New York apartments. The city may have missed the big snows that have been falling elsewhere in America, crushing the roof of the Metrodome and forcing the Giants into a game in Detroit, but with the weather this cold, can the snow be too far off? (Adam Gopnik: "All Alike", in *The New Yorker*, January 3, 2011)

Note: It comes from "If winter comes, can spring be far behind?"

One good launch deserves another. (Blog.msdn.www.sfgate.com)

Note: It comes from "One good turn deserves another".

Reagan's conduct in the Governor's office did at least demonstrate that his conservative bark often carried little bite when he tackled the practical problems governing his state.

Note: "Bark often carried little bite" comes from "His bark is worse than his bite."

To the Mondavi brothers, wine was thicker than blood. They feuded bitterly over control of Charles Krug Winery.

Note: Here "wine was thicker than blood" comes from the proverb "Blood is thicker than water."

2. In novels and short stories

I had no outlook, but an uplook rather. My place in society was at the bottom. (Jack London: *What Life Means to Me*)

No – let me make my last appeal. Listen to this! We've both remarried out of our senses. I was made drunk to it. You were the same. I was gin-drunk; you were creed-drunk. Either form of intoxication takes away the nobler vision ... let us then shake off our mistakes, and run away together! (Thomas Hardy: *Jude the Obscure*)

Note: Hardy created a new word based on gin-drunk.

3. In poetry

"You gallop with a loose rein."
"Pace give life", was the reply.
"I shall write in my diary tonight."
"What!"
"That a burnt child loves the fire."

Note: The last line comes from "A burnt child dreads the fire", and "dread" is changed into "love".

I love a sunburnt country
A land of open drains
Mid-urban sprawl expanded
For cost-accounting gains.
Broad, busy bulldozed acres
Once wastes of ferns and trees
Now rapidly enriching
Investors overseas. (Oscar Krahnvohl)

Note: This poem comes from the following one by Dorothea MacKellar:

I love a sunburnt country
A land of sweeping plains
Of ragged mountain ranges
Of droughts and flooding rains.
I love her far horizons
I love her jewelled sea
Her beauty and her terror
The wide brown land for me.

How doth the little crocodile
  Improve his shining tail
And pour the water of the Nile
  On every golden scale!
How cheerfully he seems to grin

How neatly spreads his claws
And welcomes little fishes in
With gently smiling jaws! (Lewis Carroll: *Alice in Wonderland*)

Note: This poem comes from the following poem by Isaac Watts:

How doth the little busy bee
Improve each shining hour
And gather honey all the day
From every opening flower!
How skillfully she builds her cell!
How neat she spreads the wax
And labors hard to store it well
With the sweet food she makes.

4. In advertisements

My goodness! My Guinness! (advertisement for Ireland's beer: Guinness)

Note: "Goodness" is used in spoken English as an interjection.

Tasting is believing. (advertisement for food, from: Seeing is believing)

Shanghai TV – Watching is believing. (advertisement for TV, from: Seeing is believing)

Just a reminder. This is why you save money. Easy as UCB. (advertisement for United Carolina Bank, from: as easy as ABC)

5. In news headlines

"A Wolf in Shiek's Clothing" (*The Times*, 1981, from: a wolf in sheep's clothing)

"Where There's a Web, There's a Way" (from: where there is a will, there is a way)

"To Lie or Not to Lie – the Doctor's Dilemma" (*College English*)

Note: It comes from "To be, or not to be, that is the question" in *Hamlet* by William Shakespeare.

"Britannia Rues the Waves" (title of an article by Andrew Neil)

Note: It comes from the song of "Rule, Britannia".

6. In academic writing

The ultimate applications of the computer revolution are still around the bend of a silicon circuit.

Note: Here "still around the bend" comes from "still around the corner".

Chapter Thirty-two Synaesthesia

Synaesthesia (通感，移觉), from the Greek prefix "syn-", and the root "aisthesis", means "a union of the senses". As a figure of speech, it is a blending or confusion of different kinds of sense-impression, in which one type of sensation is referred to in terms more appropriate to another. (Baldick, 2001) According to *The Random House College Dictionary*, it refers to the mixing of sensations or the stimulation of one sense that produces a mental impression associated with a different sense.

32.1 Purposes of synaesthesia

1. For vividness

He gave me a sour look.

As round the rose its soft perfume,
Sweet love around her floated;
Admired she grew – while mortal doom
Crept on, unfear'd, unnoted, ... (Hartley Coleridge: "Early Death")

2. For attraction

The same bright face I tasted in my sleep,
Smiling in the clear well ... (John Keats: "Endymion")

Till ev'n his beams sing, and my musick shine. (George Herbert: "Christmas")

3. For beauty

Pretty soon Mat and Beverly burst open the door and came dancing in together, the sweet air of the warm April evening coming in with them, and life grew rose-colored for me in a moment.

These had now ceased from battle for old age, yet were they right good orators, like grasshoppers that in a forest sit upon a tree utter their lily-like voice; even so sat the elders of the Trojans upon the tower. (Homer: *Iliad*)

32.2 Classification of synaesthesia

1. Sense of vision mixed with sense of hearing

The light is braying like an ass.

I heard flowers that sounded. (St. Martin)

2. Sense of vision mixed with sense of touch

In the evening she wears soft rich colours, dark, red, olive green, midnight blue, always of the most supple flowing texture. (V. Sackville-West)

The rooms on the first floor are decorated with cold color.

3. Sense of touch mixed with sense of hearing.

The soft voice was full of menace, the glare of famine and fury was in the burning eyes, and the supple cruelty of the wild beast was in the clenched hands.

Here will we sit and let the sounds of music
Creep in our tears; soft stillness and the night
Become the touches of sweet harmony.
...
With sweetest touches pierce your mistress' ear
And draw her home with music. (William Shakespeare)

4. Sense of taste mixed with sense of hearing

That's a sour joke.

She has a sweet voice.

A loud perfume, which at my entrance cried ... (John Donne: "Elegy")

5. Sense of vision mixed with sense of taste

And between these three and the misty mountain peaks there were a face – not Mat Nivers's, for the first time in all my day-dream – a sweet face with dark eyes looking straight into mine.

All the immediate world was soon swimming in the same liquid green. She was clothed in it. Green shadows almost disguised he face ... (Patrick White: *Voss*)

6. Sense of smelling mixed with sense of taste

… a delicious smell of dew rising from the grass their feet trampled and the bushes they brushed against in passing. The sky was still benign. Were she presently to die, her last thought, would be of watered blue.

Smell how it taste!

7. Sense of smelling mixed with sense of hearing

A loud perfume cried. (John Donne)

Thy voice was a censer that scattered strange perfumes, and when I looked on thee I heard a strange music.

8. Sense of smelling mixed with sense of vision

As the budding grapes' bright perfume, or the sweet grape-flower. (Sitwell)

I can't see what flowers are at my feet,
Nor what soft incense hangs upon the boughs,
But, in embalmed darkness, guess each sweet
Where with the seasonable month endows
The grass, the thicket, and the fruit tree wild. (John Keats)

9. Sense of smelling mixed with sense of touch

Johnson's Baby Power: The Soft Smell. (advertisement for baby powder)

Soft music like a perfume, and sweet light
Golden with audible odours exquisite
Swathe me with cerements for eternity. (Arthur Symons: "The Opium Smoker")

Note: In this poem, actually senses of taste, hearing, smell, vision, and touch are used together in two lines of one poem.

10. Sense of taste mixed with sense of vision

Graig stereo tape deck: Hear the light. (advertisement for stereo tape)

Music, when soft voices die,
Vibrates in the memories
Odors, when sweet violets sicken,
Live within the sense they quicken. (Percy Bysshe Shelley: "When Soft Voice Dies")

11. Different senses are used together

Sweet Thames! Run softly, till I end my song. (Edmund Spenser) (senses of taste, vision, and touch are used together)

When all my five and country senses see,
The fingers will forget green thumbs and mark
How, through the halfmoon's vegetable eye
Husk of young stars and handful zodiac,
Love in the frost is pared and wintered by,
The whispering ears will watch love drummed away
Down breeze and shell to a discordant beach,
And, lashed to syllables, the lynx tongue cry
That her fond wounds are mended bitterly.
My nostrils see her breath burn like a bush.

My one and noble heart has witnesses
In all love's countries, that will grope awake;
And when blind sleep drops on the spying senses,
The heart is sensual, though five eyes break. (Dylan Thomas: "When All My Five and Country Senses See")

Note: The senses of touch, hearing, taste, smelling and vision are used together to show the importance of the noble heart.

32.3 Use of synaesthesia

1. In poetry

O rose, thou art sick:
The invisible worm
That flies in the night,
I the howling storm

Has found out they bed
Of crimson joy;
And his dark secret love
Does they life destroy. (William Blake: "The Sick Rose", from *Song of Experience*)

April, April,
Laugh thy golden laughter,
But, the moment after,
Weep thy golden tear! (William Watson)

The music breathing from her face. (George Gordon Byron)

2. In novels and short stories

"What a delicious shiver is creeping over these times!" said Lancelot, half to himself. (Charles Kingsley: *Yeast: A Problem*)

"I never do those things if I can avoid them," replied the rat sourly. "I prefer to spend my time eating, gnawing, spying and hiding." (E. B. White: *Charlotte's Web*)

3. In prose

Some books are to be tasted, others to be swallowed and some few to be chewed and digested; that is, some books are to be read only in parts, others to be read, but not curiously; and some few to be read wholly, and with diligence and attention. (Francis Bacon: "Of Studies")

Stephen, still trembling at his soul's cry, heard warm running sunlight and in the air behind him friendly words.

4. In dramas

How silver-sweet sound lover's tongues by night, like softest music to attending ears! (William Shakespeare: *Romeo and Juliet*)

That strain again! It had a dying fall;
O, it came o'er my ear like the sweet sound
That breathes upon a bank of violets,
Stealing and giving odour. (William Shakespeare: *The Twelfth Night*)

Freeze, freeze, thou bitter sky,
That dost not bite so nigh
As benefits forgot: ...
Though thou the waters warp,
Thy sting is not so sharp
As friend remembered not. (William Shakespeare: *All's Well That Ends Well*)

5. In advertisements

Posner lipstick music to your lips. (advertisement for lipstick)

Smell how it taste! (advertisement for muffin)

Chapter Thirty-three Transferred Epithet

The word epithet comes from a Greek word, *epitheton*, refers to an adjective or adjectival phrase used to define a characteristic quality or attribute of some person or thing. In the transferred epithet (移就，移位修饰), or called hypallage, an adjective appropriate to one noun is attached to another by association. (Baldick, 2001) Simply put, transferred epithet is a figure of speech in which an adjective properly modifying one noun is shifted to another noun in the same sentence. In choosing epithets, it is important to to consider aptness and brilliant effectiveness. Epithet aims at being fresh, seeking striking images, paying attention to connotative value. Compare the following two pairs of sentences.

1a. She led a solitary life for several years and at that period of time she was in despair.

1b. She spent several years of solitary despair.

2a. They smiled and greeted each other.

2b. They were exchanging smiling words.

Note: The two pairs of sentences mean the same respectively, but the second in each is more vivid and effective, because in 1b, "solitary", an adjective usually used to modify a person, is used to modify an animate noun "despair", and in 2b, "smiling", a word used to refer to people, is used to modify an animate noun "words".

33.1 Purposes of transferred epithet

1. For vividness

He is very tall of his age, with sweet laughing blue eyes, dark eyelashes, and curling hair. (Mary Shelley: *Frankenstein*)

Sometimes they threw (him) bits of food, and got scant thanks; sometimes a mischievous pebble, and a shower of stones and abuses.

2. For emphasis

... and she proceeded to cut slices with a generous hand.

This devotion brought some to an early grave.

3. For attraction

An expensive failure can be made into an asset if you've learnt from it, but Monsanto still has some learning to do.

Rooney, England takes healthy win.

Note: Here "healthy win" means England's soccer team will win.

4. For surprise

His listeners looked at each other with a surprised and perplexed air.

Instantly from the dark holes all round, there was a frenzied rush of Jews.

5. For description

A manned trip to the Mars is not impossible in the future. ("Manned" should be used to describe spaceship, but here is used for trip.)

Darrow walked slowly round the baking court.

33.2 Classification of transferred epithet

1. Parallel relationship

She had a dry humour.

But I saw his face, and I think I can see now the anxiety upon it, the worried impatience.

2. Cause-effect relationship

He saw the look of beneficent happiness on the Old Gentleman's face ... (O. Henry: *Two Thanksgiving Day Gentlemen*)

He behaved with guilty caution and rather enjoyed stealing a march on Doctor Ed.

3. Effect-cause relationship

He wheeled in his pacing, paused and glared at his plate. There was a suspenseful silence.

The warrant officer shook his head in numb astonishment. (Joseph Heller: *Catch-22*)

4. Modifying relationship

1) Adjective as the modifier

I was surprised to find him living in such drab and cheerless surroundings.

I visited Edinburgh with languid eyes and mind.

My heart is a lonely hunter that hunts on a lonely hill.

2) -ing as the modifier

"Don't worry, son, we'll show them a few tricks," Darrow had whispered throwing a reassuring arm around my shoulder as we were waiting for the court to open.

As he extended his hand with a magnificently forgiving air, and as I was broken by illness and unfit to quarrel, I took it. (Charles Dickens: *Great Expectations*)

3) -ed as the modifier

My mind was full of confusing pictures and disturbed emotions.

… this thought pressing on me when I awoke, held other thoughts in a confused concourse at a distance.

4) Adverb as the modifier

I frowningly sat down to my breakfast. (Charles Dickens: *Great Expectations*)

The heat of a July sun beat pitilessly down on the scorching plains. (*Vanguards from the Plain*)

5) "Noun of" as the modifier

He is an oyster of a man.

33.3 How does transferred epithet work

1. Use a modifier for people to describe things

All that sleepless night I replayed the moment those black gloves came up to the car window. (*College English*, Book II, Unit 7)

The old lady lived in a sick room.

The Don railway. A quiet cheerless station, white and solitary in the steppe, with its walls baking in the sun, without a speck of shade, and, it seems, without a human being. The train goes on after leaving one here; the sound of it is scarcely audible and dies away at last. (Anton Pavlovich Chekhov)

2. Use a modifier for one thing to describe another

Whether you are surrounded by the noisy friendliness of a pub or whether you are seated in the peaceful comfort of someone's home, you will be sipping away on a drink. (*New College English*, Unit 4)

But she seemed to sense the cold mockery in their smiles, and the fact that there was no need for her to say any more.

His stories achieved nothing but cheap laughs.

3. Use a modifier for things to describe people

He is not an easy poet. ("Easy" refers to the poet's poems, that is, what the poet writes is not easy to understand.)

All the time the creeping fear that he would never come back to her grew strong within her.

4. Use a modifier for animals to describe things

The American society saw a gnawing poverty during the tears of the Great Depression.

33.4 Use of transferred epithet

1. In prose

One teacher writes that instead of drowning the students' compositions in critical red ink, the teacher will get far more constructive results ... (*College English*, Book II, Unit 10)

... even as I enjoy the clean voluptuousness of the warm breeze on my skin and the cool support of the water. (V. Sackville-West: *No Signposts in the Sea*)

I buried my head under the miserable sheet and rug and cried like a child.

It was the end of my exhausting first day as waitress in a busy New York restaurant.

He passed many anxious hours in the train.

2. In novels and short stories

When I said some reassuring words, she stretched out her tremulous right hands, as though she was going to touch me; ... (Charles Dickens: *Great Expectations*)

It was a thoughtful evening with both of us. (Charles Dickens: *Great Expectations*)

I took John by the hand, bent down on one knee and hugged his sad little face, as his mother (Linda) watched on tearfully. (Budd Hopkins: *Witnessed: Brooklyn UFO Abductions*)

Through sleepless nights and a distraught frame of mind Endicott lost thirty pounds over three of four months in late 1944 and early 1945. (Stephen Endicott: *James G. Endicott: Rebel Out of China*)

3. In poetry

Winter kept us warm, covering
Earth in forgetful snow, feeding
A little life with dried tubers. (T. S. Eliot: *The Waste Land*)

This living hand, now warm and capable
Of earnest grasping, would, if it were cold
And in the icy silence of the tomb,
So haunt thy days and chill thy dreaming nights
That thou would wish thine own heart dry of blood,
So in my veins red life might stream again,
And thou be conscience-calm'd. See, here it is. (John Keats)

In this new place where we may fully
merge we sense often times a loss;
yet to love so will we must give away
treasures of independence, lose that
lonely freedom of my long life road. (Glen Philips: "Face to Face")

4. In dramas

Mama: I was going to tell you. Mathew's on leave and he's in the village, so Papa and I thought it would be a good time to mend our fences. He's coming tonight with Isabel.

Edith: And his fiancée. [gloating]

Mary: What? [with a fairly surprised and heat-broken look]

Mama: Edith…I don't know how helpful you're being. [in a frustrating tone]

Now o'ver the one half-world,
Nature seems dead, and wicked dreams abuse
The curtained sleep, ... (William Shakespeare)

5. In advertisements

The Relentless Pursuit of Perfection. (advertisement for Lexus)

Behind that healthy smile, there's a Crest kid. (advertisement for Crest)

6. In news headlines

"An Old Sweet Song" (*Time*, July 1996)

"The Anxious Skies" (*Time*, October 2001)

Note: This news report appeared after the September 11 tragic to show that many Americans were afraid of travelling by air.

7. In academic writing

One of the painful prices human beings have paid for their predilection for starchy and sugary foods has been the premature decay and loss of teeth.

These twin discoveries were a fitting reward for more than 800 lonely hours of patient patrolling of the skies over six years.

Chapter Thirty-four Analogy

Analogy (类比) comes from a Greek word, *analogia*, meaning proportion. It is illustration of an idea by means of a more familiar idea that is similar or parallel to it in some significant features, and thus said to be analogous to it. (Baldick, 2001) Analogy compares two things, which are alike in various aspects, for the purpose of explaining or clarifying some unfamiliar or complex idea or object by showing how the idea or object is similar to a familiar one. In simile and metaphor, there is usually only one similar point between the target and vehicle. But in analogy, there are usually two or more.

34.1 Purposes of analogy

1. For wit

Only the man who has known fear can be truly brave. (proverb)

Life is compared to a road over the mountains as both have their ups and downs.

War resembles a game of chess in that the whole of society is represented on the playing field.

2. For humor

Money is like muck, not good unless it be spread. (H. W. Fowler: *A Dictionary of Modern English Usage*)

– What did the blind person say when given some matza?

– Who the hell wrote this?

Note: Here "matza" is a kind of thin pancake that has dots on its surface, and is to a page with Braille.

3. For contrast

These coasts remind me of people: either they were forbidding and unapproachable; or else they present no mystery and show all they have to give at a glance. (V. Sackville-West: *No Signposts in the Sea*)

Beauty is as summer fruits, which are easy to corrupt, and cannot last; and, for the most part, it makes a dissolute youth, and an age a little out of countenance; but yet certainly again, if it light well, it maketh virtues shine, and vices blush. (Francis Bacon: "Of Beauty")

4. For emphasis

Beauty without grace is the hook without the bait. (Ralph Waldo Emerson: *The Conduct of Life*)

The more you give, the more you have. (proverb)

34.2 Use of analogy

1. In proverbs

Beauty without grace is the hook without the bait.

Just as the moth is attracted by the light, so he was fascinated by the pretty girl.

2. In prose

As the caterpillar chooses the fairest leaves to lay her eggs on, so the priest lays his curse on the fairest joys. (William Blake: *Aphorism*)

The cultivation of a hobby and new forms of interest is ... not a business that can be undertaken in a day or swiftly improved y a mere command of the will. The growth of alternative mental interests is a long process. The seeds must be carefully chosen; they must fall on good ground; they must be sedulously tended, if the vivifying fruits are to be at hand when needed. (Winston Churchill)

The author compares bluffs along the coast to people, who are forbidding and unapproachable.

3. In poetry

Follow a shadow, it still flies you;
Seem to fly it, it will pursue:
So court a mistress, she denies you;
Let her alone, she will court you. (Ben Jonson)

Roses have thorns, and silver fountains mud;
Clouds and eclipses stain both moon and sun,
And loathsome canker lives in sweetest bud.
All men have faults. (William Shakespeare)

4. In dramas

Shylock: Nay, take my life and all!
Pardon not take the prop
That doth sustain my house. You take my life
When you do take the means whereby I live. (William Shakespeare: *The Merchant of Venice*)

Shylock: To bait fish withal; if it will feed nothing else, it will feed my revenge. He hath disgraced me, and hindered me half a million; laughed at my losses, mocked at my gains, scorned my nation, thwarted my bargains, cooled my friends, heated mine enemies; and what's his reason? I am a Jew. Hath not a Jew eyes? Hath not a Jew hands, organs, dimensions, senses, affections, passions? Fed with the same food, hurt with the same weapons, subject to the same diseases, healed by the same means, warmed and cooled by the same winter and summer, as a Christian is? If you prick us, do we not bleed? If you tickle us, do we not laugh? If you poison us, do we not die? And if you wrong us, shall we not revenge? If we are like you in the rest, we will resemble you in that. If a Jew wrong a Christian, what is his humility? Revenge. If a Christian wrong a Jew, what should his sufferance be by Christian example? Why, revenge. The villainy you teach me, I will execute, and it shall go hard but I will better the instruction. (William Shakespeare: *The Merchant of Venice*)

Good name in man and woman, dear my lord,
Is the immediate jewel of their souls;
Who steals my purse steals trash; ‘tis something, nothing;
’Twas mine, ’tis his, and has been slave to thousands:
But he that filches from me my good name
Robs me of that which not enriches him
And makes me poor indeed.
...
O, beware, my lord, of jealousy;

It is the green-eyed monster which doth mock
The meat it feeds on;
...
Poor and content is rich and rich enough,
But riches fineless is as poor as winter
To him that ever fears he shall be poor.
Good heaven, the souls of all my tribe defend
From jealousy! (William Shakespeare: *Othello*)

5. In well-known quotations

In rivers the water that you touch is the last of that has passed and the first of that which comes; so with time present. (Leonardo da Vinci)

Knowledge always desires increase: it is like fire, which must first be kindled by some external agent, but which will afterwards propagate itself. (Samuel Johnson)

Books are to mankind what memory is to the individual. (John Lubbock)

6. In advertisements

More people choose a dog over any other pet.
More people choose blue over any other color.
More people choose ice cream over any other ice cream.
More people choose cotton over any other fabric.
More people choose football over any other televised sport.
More people choose the Accord over any other car. (advertisement for Accord Coupe)

7. In academic writing

Intellectual assimilation makes time. The mind is not to be enriched as a coal barge is loaded. Whatever is precious in a cargo is carefully on board and carefully placed. Whatever is delicate and fine must be received delicately, and its place in the mind thoroughly assigned. (Arlo Bates)

The human heart is analogous to a pump.

Sound waves are created by the compression of the molecules of air, this compression generated by the origin of the sound. The resulting wave motion is analogous to that created in water when a rock is thrown in a pond. By studying the properties exhibited by water waves, we can become familiar with the properties of all wave motion. First, we note the waves produced on the water by a rock striking it move away at a constant speed. This speed is called the velocity of propagation. Second, we note that the waves have crests and troughs. The distance between successive crests or troughs is called the wavelength. Third, as the waves move past a given point, they cause an up and down motion of the water at this point. This motion is the frequency of the wave.

Part Five

Logical Figures of Speech

Chapter Thirty-five Epigram

The word epigram (警句) derives from Greek. The prefix "epi-" means upon or on, and the root "gram" means something written, or carved. According to Baldick (2001), epigram is a short poem with a witty turn of thought, or a wittily condensed expression in prose. Simply put by *Collins COBUILD English Dictionary* (1998), epigram is a short saying or poem which expresses an idea in a very clever and amusing way. As a kind of rhetorical device, epigram stands for a concise, pointed or sarcastic saying; a terse, sage, witty and often paradoxical insight into certain aspects of human behavior or feelings.

Samuel Taylor Coleridge defines epigram as follows:

What is an epigram? A dwarfish whole;
Its body brevity, and wit its soul.

Martial defines epigram as follows:

Three things must epigrams, like bees, have all –
A sting, and honey, and a body small.

35.1 Purposes of epigram

1. For brevity, especially in proverbs

He laughs best who laughs last.

A little learning is a dangerous thing.

Fair words and foul deeds.

2. For satire

Beauty is but skin-deep.

A blind man will thank you for a looking glass.

Few, save the poor, feel for the poor. (Letitia Elizabeth Landon: "The Poor")

3. For wit

Deeds show what we are; word, what we should be. (proverb)

Well begun is half done. (proverb)

Where there is a will, there is a way. (proverb)

The childhood show the man, as morning shows the day. (John Milton)

4. To indicate paradoxical features

Difficulties are opportunities. (proverb)

A God all mercy is a God unjust. (Edward Young)

35.2 Classification of epigram

1. A short poem as epigram

Lulls swears he is all heart, but you'll suppose
By his proboscis that he is all nose. (Herrick)

Through and through the inspired leaves,
Ye maggots make your windings,
But oh! Respect his lordship's taste,
And spare the golden bindings. (Robert Burns: "The Book Worms")

2. A witty saying or a proverb as epigram

The last suitor wins the maid.

Ill-gotten goods thrive not to the third heir.

Fear has a quick ear.

He that does lend will lose his friend.
After showers Phoebus shines.
Note: Phoebus is the name for Apollo in Greek mythology.

3. A paragraph from an essay as epigram
Hope springs eternal in the human breast:
Man never is, but always to be, blest.
The soul, uneasy and confin'd from home,
Rests and expatiates in a life to come. (Alexander Pope: "On Man")

35.3 Use of epigram

1. In proverbs
Better suffer ill than do ill.

It is easier to buy books than to read them, and easier to read them than to absorb them.

Silence is sometimes more eloquent than words.
He that desires honour is not worthy of honour.
A fault confessed is half redressed.
Books and friends should be few and good.

2. In poetry
If you rattle along like your mistress's tongue,
Your speed will outrival the dart;
But a fly for your load, you'll break down on the road,
If your stuff be as rotten's her heart. (Robert Burns)

You are so witty, profligate, and thin,
At once we think thee Milton, Death, and Sin. (Edward Young)

Here lies a pretty, witty king,
Whose word no man relies on,
Who never said a foolish thing
Nor ever did a wise one. (Earl of Rochester)

3. In dramas
The only way to get rid of a temptation is to yield to it. (Oscar Wilde: *The*

Picture of Dorian Gray)

It is silly of you, for there is only one thing in the world worse than being talked about, and that is not being talked about. (Oscar Wilde: *The Picture of Dorian Gray*)

4. In prose

All men think all men mortal, but themselves. (Edward Young)

Language is the art of concealing thought. (La Rochefoucauld)

They who drink beer will think beer. (Washington Irving)

Knowledge is power. (Francis Bacon)

5. In news headlines

Some journalists like to use proverbs or part of proverbs in news headlines to attract readers as follows.

"A Friend in Need" (*Time*, February 1996)

Note: This comes from the proverb "A friend in need is a friend indeed."

"Where Money Talks" (*Time*, June 1996)

Note: This comes from the proverb "Money talks."

Chapter Thirty-six Hyperbole

Hyperbole (夸张) comes from a Greek word, *hyperbole*, which means a throwing beyond, or excess, or overshooting. As a figure of speech, it is bold overstatement, or the extravagant exaggeration of fact or of possibility. (Abrams & Harpham, 2010) Hyperbole aims to describe something and make it more than it really is to achieve emphasis, to intensify emotion, to sharpen the image and impression, or to achieve humorous effect, etc.

36.1 Purposes of hyperbole

1. To exaggerate

You are sitting on a volcano, which might erupt any moment.

We are dying to know what has happened to him.

"At'em, all hands, all hands!" He roared, in a voice of thunder.

Nay, he said-yes you did-deny it if you can, that you would not have confessed the truth, though the master had cut you to pieces.

2. To praise

Two months later, I got a postcard with a picture of the Yangtze River, postmarked Chungking, China. "Are you still making me proud of you, my little brave one?" it asked. If anyone had given me a million dollars, it couldn't have made me more proud. (*College English*, Book III, Unit 5)

Antony: His legs bestrid the ocean: his reared arm

Crested the world. (William Shakespeare: *Antony and Cleopatra*)

Yes, young men. Italy owes to you an undertaking which has merited the applause of the universe.

3. To satirize or criticize

Her voice was horribly sweet and false.

We must work to live, and they give us such mean wage that we die.

She was clever, of course – wickedly clever.

4. To indicate surprise

It took a mere twenty-year flick of time to double the limit again.

They murdered us at the negotiating session.

5. To indicate humor

John: Did Lucy eat so little?

Tom: No, she can eat an elephant of meal.

He ran down the avenue, making a noise like ten horses at a gallop.

6. To sharpen the image and impression

Seventy times has the lady been divorced.

My ears are bleeding!

One day apart seems three autumns.

7. To contrast

The one-eyed man mocks the man who squints. (proverb)

What makes the finest tasting coffee in the world? The roaster's art. (advertisement for coffee)

You know it's easier to get killed by a terrorist than get married over the age of 40. (*Sleepless in Seattle*)

Comparison:

Ordinary way	**Exaggerated way**
She cried terribly.	She cried her eyes out.
He laughed heartily.	He split his sides.
I am awfully thirsty.	I am dying of thirst.
She felt extremely anxious.	She had her heart in her mouth.
I was shocked at the terrible accident.	I was frozen with horror at the terrible accident.
His eloquence was excellent.	His eloquence would split rocks.
The cheers became louder and louder.	The cheers reached the stars.

He has come to the truth.	He could not have come nearer to the truth.
He has a great many sorrows.	He has an ocean of sorrows.
She is a pretty girl.	She is the prettiest girl in the world.
I'm quite contented.	I couldn't be more contented.
I have many many things to do.	I have a thousand and one things to do.
Alice likes the new dress very much.	Alice is hysterical over the new dress.
Mary cried bitterly at the loss of the watch.	Mary cried her eyes out at the loss of the watch.

36.2 Classification of hyperbole

1. By the use of numerals

She is a girl in a million.

Mary and her sister are different in a thousand and one ways.

You are right a hundred times.

On Sunday I have a thousand and one things to do.

Cheese, the oil, makes too much of itself. It wants the whole boat to itself ... and with a two hundred horsepower scent about them that might have been warranted to carry three miles, and knock a man over at two hundred yard. (K. Jerome: *Three Men in a Boat*)

2. By the use of nouns

Usually extreme words such as acre, ages, amount, cloud, flood, heap, mass, miles, multitude, myriad, ocean, pile, pole, sea, stack, storm, world, etc. are used to denote a very high degree.

The two views are miles / poles / worlds apart.

We had a whale of good time in the countryside.

I have worlds to say about what is happening there.

Heaven on Earth (advertisement for BMW)

She wept oceans of tears.

3. By the use of adjectives

Most Americans remember Mark Twain as the father of Huck Finn's idyllic cruise through external boyhood and Tom Sawyer's endless summer of freedom and adventure. (*Advanced English*)

The wind was dead against us.

The cost amounted to astronomical figures.

4. By the use of adverbs

Adverbs such as ape, awfully, dreadfully, fearfully, frightfully, ghostly, horribly, savagely, terribly, etc. can be used to indicate exaggeration.

"Do you like your house?"

"Oh, fearfully. Won't you come and see it?"

He was ghostly obvious about most things.

The nation watched agape Friday as the stock market suffered a history making collapse that shook professional and armchair investors alike.

I must watch this ghastly countenance – these blue, still lips forbidden to unclose – these eyes now shutting now opening. (Charlotte Brontë: *Jane Eyre*)

5. By the use of superlative degree

The most effective water power in the world – women's tears.

His character was decided. He was the proudest, most disagreeable man in the world, and everybody hoped that he would never come there again. (Jane Austin: *Pride and Prejudice*)

The Orangemostest Drink in the world. (advertisement for orange juice)

Jesse went out. The whole world seemed to have turned golden. He limped slowly, with the blood pounding his temples, and a wild incommunicable joy in his heart. "I'm the happiest man in the world," he whispered to himself, "I'm the happiest man in the world." (Albert Maltz)

6. By the use of comparative degree

Two fiery dragons could not have been more furious than they were.

The party couldn't have been more successful.

No criticism could be more to the point.

7. By the use of prepositions such as beyond, past, to, without, etc.

I'm full to the throat.

They lauded him to the skies.

Hangzhou's beauty is beyond imagination.

I will follow you to the last gasp with truth and loyalty. (William Shakespeare)

It's beyond my wildest dream.

8. By the use of verbs which exaggerate

He nearly exploded with indignation.

They bombarded me with a number of questions.

They murdered us at the negotiating session.

She was blinded with rage.

What he said made my blood freeze.

9. By the use of words of the "dead" group

I'm sick to death of your endless criticism.

Mary felt dead on her feet and didn't have the energy to question them further.

The students sat there in deadly silence.

I'm dying to know what happened to them.

We were tired to death on reaching the peak.

10. By the use of words of the "terror / horror" group

The service in the restaurant is terrible.

It is terribly kind of you to do so.

The experiment went horribly wrong.

I stood up to speak and – horror of horrors – realized I had left my notes behind.

11. By the use of real or unreal conditionals

Here was wealth beyond computation, almost beyond imagination – and here were human habitations so abominable that they could have disgraced a race of alley rats. (H. L. Mencken)

I could have cried to see how thin and pale and old she looked.

"... if none of the rest of you dare," she said, "Jim and I dare. Back we will go, the way we came, and small thanks to you big, hulking, chicken hearted men. We'll have that chest open, if we die for it. And I'll thank you for that bag, Mrs. Crossley, to bring back our lawful money in ..." (Robert Louis Stevenson: *Treasure Island*)

12. By the use of exaggerated simile

The old man smoked like a chimney.

The news came like a bolt from the blue.

The criminal drove like a bat out of hell.

Perfect Skin as an Angel. (advertisement for Guerlain)

13. By the use of exaggerated metaphor

Bob was in that part of South America before the revolution began. He knew he was sitting on a volcano.

Sometimes a person who presents himself as kind and gentle can in private turn out to be a dragon, who breathes fire.

14. By the use of idiomatic expressions

The sound of drums and gongs reached the stars.

Once in a blue moon, you will find a valuable book in the secondhand book stores.

The young girl brought the house down with a ballet dance.

The speaker gave the audience plenty of time to rave itself out. (Thomas Mann)

When the reporter telephoned in his message, the editor said, "That's hot stuff."

I was no end pleased with her response to my question.

15. By the use of repeating the same word

Down dropt the breeze, the sails dropt down
'T was sad as sad could be;
And we did speak only to break
The silence of the sea! (Samuel Taylor Coleridge)

She is poor as poor can be. (William Makepeace Thackeray)

This slander is indeed the wickedest of the wicked.

Grain is the treasure of treasures.

He seemed so beautiful with his eyes gone dark, and looking as if they were deep as the deepest well.

16. Increased hyperbole

Daisy is clever beyond comparison.

In the dock, she found scores of arrows piercing her chest.

17. Decreased hyperbole

Words of small quantity or little degree such as atom, flicker, fraction, glimmer, grain, hint, inch, jot, minute, morsel, muscle, ounce, particle, rag, scrap, shadow, shred, spark, speck, trace, etc. can be used to indicate exaggeration, usually used with negative words such as hardly, scarcely, never, no, not, without, etc.

She was not really afraid of the wild beast, but she did not wish to perform an atom more service than she had been paid for. (Saki: *Mr. Packletide's Tiger*)

For want of a nail the kingdom was lost. (proverb)

Mother had no ghost of an idea of what happened to her daughter.

Oh, Tom, don't lie … it only makes things a hundred time worse. (Mark Twain: *The Adventures of Tom Sawyer*)

I wouldn't give him one red cent for that car.

36.3 Use of hyperbole

1. In proverbs

Every lover sees a thousand graces in the beloved object.

A dozen horses can't overtake the tongue.

One would not be alone even in Paradise.

Laziness travels so slowly that poverty overtakes him.

2. In novels and short stories

When our visitors would say, "Well, upon my word, Mrs. Primrose, you have the finest children in the whole country."

"Ah, neighbour," she would answer, "they are as heaven made them, handsome enough, if they be good enough; for handsome is that handsome does." (Oliver Goldsmith: *The Reverend Wakefield*)

Oliva, now about eighteen, had that luxuriancy of beauty with which painters generally draw Hebe; open, sprightly, and commanding. (Oliver Goldsmith: *The Reverend Wakefield*)

The satellite was directed into an area known as Manhattan (named after the great Venusian astronomer Prof. Manhattan, who first discovered it with his telescope 20,000 light years ago). (*College English*, Book II)

So we dug and dug with the case-knives till most midnight; and then we was dog-tired, and our hands was blistered, and yet you couldn't see we'd done anything hardly. At last I says: "This ain't no thirty-seven year job; …" (Mark Twain: *The*

Adventures of Huckleberry Finn)

She's better than ninety-nine folk out of a hundred, I tell you! She's BETTER, she is! She's fair, she's honest, she's straight! There isn't anything underhand or superior about her. Don't be mean about her! (D. H. Lawrence: *Sons and Lovers*)

3. In dramas

Neptune's ocean wash this blood
Clean from my hand? No. This my hand will rather
The multitudinous seas incarnadine,
Making the green one red. (William Shakespeare: *Macbeth*)

Hamlet: I loved Ophelia, forty thousand brothers could not, with all their quantity of love, make up my sum. (William Shakespeare: *Hamlet*)

To be, or not to be, that is the question;
Whether 'tis nobler in the mind to suffer
The slings and arrows of outrageous fortune
Or to take arms against a sea of troubles,
And by opposing end them? (William Shakespeare: *Hamlet*)

4. In poetry

Sound, sound the clarion, fill the fife!
To all the sensual world proclaim,
One crowded hour of glorious life
Is worth an age without a name. (Walter Scott: "Clarion")

Was this the face that launched a thousand ships,
And burnt the topless towers of Ilium?
Sweet Helen, make me immortal with a kiss!
…
O, thou art fairer than the evening star,
Clad in the beauty of a thousand star. (Christopher Marlowe)

5. In prose

There is no paradise on earth equal to the union of love and innocence. (Rousseau)

There were thousands and thousands of elephants, all running toward us. (J. B. Heaton & J. P. Stocks)

Most Americans remember Mark Twain as the father of Huck Finn's idyllic cruise through eternal boyhood and Tom Sawyer's endless summer of freedom and adventure. (Noel Grove: "Mark Twain – Mirror of America")

Splendid cheeses they were, ripe and mellow, and with a two hundred house-power scent about them that might have been warranted to carry three miles, and knock a man over at two hundred yards. (J. K. Jerome: "The Odour of Cheese")

We are resolved to destroy Hitler and every vestige of the Nazi regime. (Winston Churchill: "Speech on Hitler's Invasion of the U.S.S.R.")

6. In advertisements

We have hidden a garden of vegetables where you'd never expect. In a pie. (advertisement for vegetable pies)

Give us 20 minutes, we give you the whole world. (advertisement for WINS Broadcasting)

Her smile could heat up a nation. Her fragrance captured a country. (advertisement for perfume)

We take the world's greatest pictures. (advertisement for Nikon camera)

You name it, we've got it. (advertisement for a supermarket)

At 60 miles per hour, the loudest noise in the new Rolls-Royce comes from the electric clock. (advertisement for Roll-Royce)

Winning the hearts of the world. (advertisement for Air France)

Challenge the Limits. (advertisement for Samsung)

Everything you've heard is true. (advertisement for automobiles)

They face Everest without oxygen. But not without Rolex. (advertisement for Rolex)

7. In news headlines

"Dell Wants Your Home" (*Time*, March 2003)

"Atomic Guitar" (*Time*, August 1997)

8. In daily communication

We have a hundred things to do.

Seventy times has the woman been abroad.

She has twenty things to tell her father about her new school.

My passion for you is beyond any words.

I only have eyes for you.

You swept me off my feet.

I'm about to explode.

That's the stupidest thing I've ever heard!

9. In academic writing

If there really were millions of times more comet strikes than we believe, the moon's surface would be much more heavily crater, and Earth's stratosphere would be saturated with water. It's quite dry.

The strongest spring leads to fatigue caused by excessive high stress.

Illness brought her a strange restlessness and made her all the more eager to cling to life and squeeze from it the last drop of happiness. It made her envy health, but it also made her sentimental over a leaf that the wind had blown into her room.

Anyone who has ever ridden on a railroad knows how rapidly another train flashes by when it is traveling in the opposite direction and conversely how it may look almost motionless when it is moving in the same direction.

Chapter Thirty-seven Understatement

Understatement (低调陈述), the opposite of hyperbole or overstatement, deliberately represents something as very much less in magnitude or importance than it really is (Abram & Harpham, 2010), or it is the presentation of something as being smaller or less good or important than it really is (Pearsall, 2001). According to *Collins CIBUILD English Dictionary* (Sinclair, 1998), it is the practice of suggesting that things have much less of a particular quality than they really have.

Understatement includes litotes, and meiosis. Actually, modern scholars tend to treat the three terms as synonymous, for example, *The New Oxford Dictionary of English* (2001) says, meiosis is another term for litotes, Lanham (1968) points out that meiosis is sometimes the same as litotes. Nicholas (2016) points out that understatement is a figure of speech sometimes known as meiosis, in which a speaker expresses a stronger meaning than his words carry in themselves. According to Baldick (2001), meiosis is the Greek term for understatement or "belittling": a rhetorical figure by which something is referred to in terms less important than it really deserves, and the favored form of meiosis is litotes, in which an affirmation is made indirectly by denying its opposite. Thus we can use understatement as the name of this figure of speech for all the three, and it can be said that litotes is understatement by the use of negatives while meiosis is understatement without the use of negatives.

37.1 Purposes of understatement

1. To be polite

Please refrain from smoking in this room.

You must excuse my saying anything more on the subject. (= Forgive me for not saying anything more on the subject.)

I don't think this guy is quite dishonest.

2. To exaggerate

There isn't a weapon he doesn't know the use of.

The face wasn't a bad face; it had what they called charm. (John Galsworthy)

I wasn't overimpressed by her speech.

3. For euphemism

He didn't try it in vain.

Jack is not quite a gentleman.

4. To praise

Mr. Smith is no bad musician. (=He is a very good musician)

They are no ordinary people. (=They are important people.)

In fact she was everything you have never read about her.

5. To criticize or satirize

He pointed out, "The United Nations Organization has not so far justified the hopes which the people of the world set on it."

Why should you be so late today?

I wish you could write better next time.

He is nothing if not polite.

6. To complain

If only you could help us.

The old lady is just a bit inquisitive.

7. For emphasis

The man is no fool.

I wasn't born yesterday.

8. To indicate suspension

The apartment and furniture would have been nothing extraordinary as belonging to a homely, northern farmer, with a stubborn countenance, and stalwart limbs set out to advantage in knee-breeches and gaiters. (Emily Brontë: *Wuthering Heights*)

Belinda won a little bit of money at the Blackjack tables.

37.2 Litotes

Litotes (反叙) is a figure of speech by which an affirmation is made indirectly by denying its opposite, usually with an effect of understatement. (Baldick, 2001) Or it is ironical understatement in which an affirmative is expressed by of the negative of its contrary. (Pearsall, 2001)

Litotes can be classified as follows.

1. Two negations = affirmative

He didn't study English for nothing.

One has no right to speak without investigation.

It is impossible for an Englishman to open his mouth without making some other Englishmen despise him. (George Bernard Shaw)

Vigorous writing is concise. A sentence should contain no unnecessary words, a paragraph no unnecessary sentences. (William Strunk Jr.: *The Elements of Style*)

2. Use of not / no / never / none + negative word / phrase / adjective or adverb of comparative degree

He has no small chance of success.

He never spared himself and so he made me work hard.

He is not too thin.

3. Use of a bit, almost, a little, etc., to say something less important

By this time they were a little anxious.

My shoe has been pressing against my foot, so it hurts a bit.

It rained a bit more than usual.

My friend was a bit upset.

4. Use of can't but, can't help, can't ... too / enough / sufficiently / sufficient, can't ... more, no sooner ... than

I can't but admire your courage.

You can never be too careful.

5. Use of not ... until

It was not until the 18th century that man realized that the whole of the brain was involved in the workings of the mind. (*College English*, Book I)

I hadn't realized she wasn't English until she spoke.

6. Use of in no time (at all), none other than (no one else but), nothing / nobody but, as often as not, more often than not (frequently), as soon as not

I would as soon stay here as not.

It was none other than the king.

7. Use of rhetorical questions

Who can not rely on such an honest man? (= Everyone can rely on him.)

Isn't it a marvelous book?

37.3 Meiosis

By meiosis (弱叙), is a word from Greek, meaning lessening, by which a degrading epithet is used to belittle (Lanham, 1968), that is, the impression is intentionally conveyed that a thing is less in size, importance, etc. than it really is.

Meiosis can be classified as follows.

1. Use of hardly, rarely, scarcely

There was hardly any bread at home.

John could hardly sit up straight after the accident.

2. Use of almost, quite, pretty, rather

She is rather good-looking.

The explanation is pretty thin.

3. Use of a bit, a few, a little, kinda, kind of, some, something of, sort of

He is something of a philosopher.

I'm kind of disappointed at your failure.

37.4 Use of understatement

1. In poetry

As lean was his horse as is a rake,
And he was not right fat,
I undertake. (Geoffrey Chaucer)

I've studied human nature, and

I know a thing or two;
Though a girl may fondly love
a living gent, as many do,
A feeling of disgust upon her
senses there will fall
When she looks upon his body
Chopped particularly small. (William Schwenck Gilbert)

2. In novels and short stories

Let it deceive them then, a little longer, it can not deceive them too much. (Charles Dickens: *A Tale of Two Cities*)

"You would not bring me a bad telegram," she said. "You are a good boy – like my little Juanito when he was a little boy. Eat another piece. (William Saroyan: *The Human Comedy*)

I've let the cat out of the bag already, Mr. Corthell, and I might as well tell the whole thing now. (F. Norris: *The Pit*)

3. In dramas and movies

Lady Macbeth: Thou wouldst be great
Art not without ambition but without
The illness should attend it. (William Shakespeare: *Macbeth*)

It is impossible for an Englishman to open his mouth without making some other Englishmen despise him. (George Bernard Shaw)

She smiled at him weakly as he came over and stared at the shrieking Neely.

"This is Neely. She's a little upset."

"I'd say that was a classic understatement." (Jacqueline Susann: *Valley of the Dolls*)

But at fourscore it is too late a week. (William Shakespeare)

It is no mean happiness, therefore, to be seated in the mean. (William Shakespeare)

4. In prose

It has not escaped our notice that the specific pairing we have postulated immediately suggests a possible copying mechanism for genetic material.

He conducted the experiment with no little enthusiasm.

His recent book is no small accomplishment.

Margo didn't sleep a wink before her big test.

5. In advertisements

We are having problems with Guests who won't leave. (advertisement for a hotel)

6. In daily communication

Sorry, this is more than I can promise.

TV reporter: Do you think all the programs are good?

One of the audience: Well, some are interesting, some could be better, and some are almost sort of rubbish.

Chapter Thirty-eight Irony

Irony (反讽), from a Greek word, *eironeia*, means dissembler in speech, or dissimulation. As a figure of speech, it is a subtly humorous perception of inconsistency, in which an apparently straightforward statement or event is undermined by its context so as to give it a very different significance. According to *The New Oxford Dictionary of English* (2001), irony is the expression of one's meaning by using language that normally signifies the opposite, typically for humorous or emphatic effect. Simply put, according to *Oxford Concise Dictionary of Linguistics* (1997), it is a figure of speech in which one thing is said but the opposite is meant. It is an effective literary device because it gives the impression of great restraint. Irony intends to criticize or condemn.

The context is important to decide whether it is irony or not. For example,

a. I love people who signal.

Note: Usually it is not irony. But if you are the driver, and someone on the backseat tells you to do this and that, and you say so, then it is irony.

b. I've had a great morning!

Note: If the person says so after he has worked so hard a whole morning, it is irony.

c. Peter: I was told Bill has great learning. He has read quite a lot of books.

Mary: Well, Bill is a well-read man indeed. He has even heard of Shakespeare.

Note: If this is said between two English people, it is irony.

d. Liu Lin: Li Feng is a well-read and learned man.

Mei Xin: He is erudite indeed. He has learned of Shakespeare.

Note: When this is said between two Chinese people, usually it is not irony; but if Li Feng is a student majoring in English, it can be considered as irony.

38.1 Purposes of irony

1. For depreciation

This morning, I was late for work; at noon, I had my bike stolen; on the way home this afternoon, I slipped down in the street. So today, I am certainly enjoying myself.

The colonel was gorgeous. He had a cavernous mouth, cavernous cheeks, cavernous, sad, mildewed eyes. His face was the color of clouded silver. (Joseph Heller: *Catch-22*)

2. For emphasis

She is not the ugliest around.

3. For criticism

You are capable indeed. You even made profit out of your father's pocket.

4. For appreciation

It would be a fine thing indeed not knowing that what time it was in the morning.

5. For humor

The last writing teacher I had was generous in helping me fossilize poor writing habits.

You've got us into a nice mess.

What a glorious mess!

6. For praise

She was clever, of course – wickedly clever.

7. For contempt

It is impossible for an Englishman to open his mouth without making some other Englishmen despise him. (George Bernard Shaw)

38.2 How to use irony

1. Say other than what one means

If I were as pretty as you are!

There is no easy job in language learning.

2. Mean the opposite of what is said

How clean you are! (spoken by a mother to her dirty child)

This diligent student seldom reads more than an hour per month.

– I'm sorry I've spoiled your computer, but there has been something wrong with it before I operated it.

– Then, I should express my gratitude for you!

38.3 Classification of irony

1. Verbal irony

Verbal irony involves a discrepancy between what is said and what is really meant, as in its crude form, sarcasm. (Baldick, 2001) It is a statement of the opposite of what one means. Verbal irony is used to veil feelings in a subtle way, using words of praise to condemn. In verbal irony, people say the opposite of what they mean. Most people use or hear verbal irony daily. For example,

If the day has been terrible, you may say, "Boy, this has been a great day!" The hearer knows that it is ironic because of your tone of voice or bodily expressions or because of this discrepancy between statement and actuality.

1) Light irony

Light irony is used to achieve humor.

It must be delightful to find oneself in a foreign country without a penny in one's pocket.

How unselfish you are!

He is as welcome as a storm.

There is no easy job in language learning.

I left my bag in the restaurant, and someone kindly walked off with it. (The implied meaning: Someone unkindly stole my bag.)

2) Heavy irony

Heavy irony is used for satire, denunciation or criticism.

Blessed are the young, for they shall inherit the national debt.

She was not so young as I expected and in appearance imposing rather than attractive.

She is as slender in the middle as a cow in the waist.

He seldom failed to order a bleeding.

We send missionaries to China so the Chinese can get to heaven, but we don't let them into our country. (Pearl S. Buck)

The Chinese should thank Acheson also because he has fabricated wild tales about modern Chinese history.

2. Situational irony

Situational irony occurs when there is a discrepancy between what appears, or is believed, to be the case and the real state of affair. Situational irony is usually used in literature.

Slowly the old lady stooped to pick the cheque up. Her present, her lovely present, with trembling fingers she tore it into little bits. (*College English*)

Mrs. Zhang: How about our daughter in the school lately?

Mrs. Li: Don't mention it, her score is so good that her teacher wants to talk with me about her three times.

When the doctors came, they said she had died of heart disease – of joy that kills.

Well, of course, I knew that gentlemen like you carry only large notes. (Mark Twain)

"We are a nation that must beg to stay alive," said a foreign economist.

Womba mocks the way Normans impose their language on the Anglo-Saxons, and the way the English nobility absorb the language of their conquerors.

3. Dramatic irony

Dramatic irony refers to the fact that the audience knows more about a character's situation than the character does, foreseeing an outcome contrary to the character's expectations, and thus ascribing a sharply different sense to some of the character's own statements; in tragedies, this is called tragic irony. The term cosmic irony is sometimes used to denote a view of people as the dupes of a cruelly mocking Fate, as in the novels of Thomas Hardy. (Baldick, 2001) This is concerned with contrast between the audience and the actors. The actor who speaks in the play believes what he says is true, and the actor who listens in the play also believes that it is true, but the audience who knows the cause and effect knows that is not true, thus leading to irony.

A: I've been trying to figure out how to work the machine for 8 hours. But just look at this instruction sheet.

B: What a useful piece of paper! (= useless)

4. Attitudinal irony

Situational irony results from what most people expect, whereas attitudinal irony results from what one person expects. In attitudinal irony, an individual thinks that reality is one way when, in fact, it is very different. A frequent example in literature is naive characters such as Cervantes's Don Quijote, or Dickens's Mr. Micawber, who think that everyone is upright and that everything will turn out for the best, when in fact people they encounter treat them unfairly and events are hurtful.

38.4 Figures of speech and other ways used in irony

Any grammatical form can indicate irony in an appropriate linguistic situation. Hyperbole, understatement, interjection, citation, etc. can also indicate irony.

1. Interjection is used to indicate irony

Ah, Tuesday in May!

2. Citation is used to indicate irony

Oh to be in England
Now that April's there. (Robert Browning: "Home Thoughts from Abroad")
Note: Actually, spring is not a good time for living in England.

3. Understatement is used to indicate irony

He is something of an economist.
They did not study history for nothing.
Two people are caught in a downpour … "It seems to be raining."

4. Hyperbole is used to indicate irony

Her voice was horribly sweet and false.

5. Parody is used to indicate irony

America's allies – always there when they need you.

Note: This comes from "always there when they need them", a slogan by British police, and is used to criticize that the allies depend too much on the US but the US gives much less help.

6. Exclamatory sentences

What a clever idea! (actually it is not)

7. Grammatical structures

A precious lot you care about my wallflowers.

8. Stylistic way

Could you do me the favor of shutting up? (too polite and so it sounds irony)

Mother said to her son: Would you mind if I asked you to please consider cleaning up your room this month? (too polite and so it is irony)

9. Phonetic way

Peter: John has lost your pen.

Jack: Well, I like THAT ! (As Jack stresses "that", he indicates irony / anger.)

38.5 Use of irony

1. In proverbs

Your friends in need come to you when they need you.

The man who curses prays to the devil.

A man of wealth is a slave to his possessions.

2. In novels and short stories

What a noble illustration of the tender laws of this favorable country! – They let the paupers go to sleep. (Charles Dickens)

She ransacking the stores for Jim's present. (O. Henry: *The Gift of Magi*)

Sir Pitt Crawley was a philosopher with taste for what is called low life. His first marriage with the daughter of the noble Binkie had been made under the auspices of his parents; and as he often told Lady Crawley in her lifetime she was such a confounded quarrel – some high-bred jade that when she died he was hanged if he would ever take another of her sort, and at the ladyship's demise he kept his promise, and selected for a second wife Miss Rose Dawson, daughter of Mr. John Thomas Dawson, iron monger, of Mudbury. What a happy woman was Rose to be my Lady Crawley. (William Makepeace Thackeray: *Vanity Fair*)

You and the girls may go, or you may send them by themselves, which perhaps will be still better, as you are as handsome as any of them, Mr. Bingley might like you the best of the party. (Jane Austin: *Pride and Prejudice*)

3. In prose

When a man is tired of London, he is tired of life. (James Boswell: *Life of Johnson*)

I realize now that as a child I sat by, through the years, and literally watched my father kill himself; surely one such victory in my family, for the prosperous leaders who own the tobacco companies, is enough. (*New Horizon English*, Book II)

Laws are like cobwebs, which catch small flies, but let wasps and hornets break through. (Jonathan Swift)

4. In poetry

Water, water, everywhere,
And all the boards did shrink;
Water, water, everywhere,
Not any drop to drink. (Samuel Taylor Coleridge)

The decent docent doesn't doze;
He teaches standing on his toes,
His student doesn't doze – and does,
And that's what teaching is and was. (David McCord: "History of Education")

So let me have the rouge again,
And comb my hair the curly way.
The poor young men, the dear young men
They'll all be here by noon today.

So bring my scarlet slippers, then,
And fetch the powder puff to me.
The dear young men, the poor young men –
They think I'm only seventy. (Dorothy Parker: "Ninon de Lenclos, on Her Last Birthday")

Note: The poet criticizes an old lady's way as a young girl. The last two lines are the key to understand this as irony.

5. In dramas

As flies to wanton boys are we to the gods;
They kill us for their sport. (William Shakespeare)

Go ask his name: if he be married.

My grave is like to be my wedding bed. (William Shakespeare: *Romeo and Juliet*)

Note: Juliet commands her nurse to find out who Romeo was and says so. The audience know that she is going to die on her wedding bed.

6. In advertisements

Nobody is perfect. (advertisement for Fitness equipment)

If people keep telling you to quit smoking cigarettes, do not listen … They are probably trying to trick you into living. (public anti-cancer advertisement)

7. In news headlines

"America's Bomb Culture" (*Time*, May 1995)

Note: "Bomb culture" is used to show the fact that the US has dropped so many bombs in different wars, and the fact that terrorists use and even produce bombs, and so everybody can get access to news and information about bombs.

"Here's My Marijuana Card" (*Time*, May 1999)

Note: In 1996, California passed the Compassionate Act on using drugs in medical care, but without a detailed explanation about how to apply it, thus leading to troubles. The news report under this title criticized it.

8. In daily communication

We are lucky. It's the other side on the thirteenth of December. That makes us feel real good.

Teacher: Your brain is perfectly OK.

Student: How come?

Teacher: Everybody's brain is not separated so perfect, but yours is an exception.

Student: Why?

Teacher: There is nothing right in your left brain, and there is nothing left in your right brain.

Teacher: When do you intend to turn in your paper today?

Student: I have a terrible headache.

Teacher: Your headache is in time.

A: The boy has broken another glass.

B: A fine thing.

Chapter Thirty-nine Euphemism

Euphemism (委婉), from a Greek word, *euphēmismos* ("eu-" means good, and "phēmē" means voice or speak), refers to an inoffensive expression used in place of a blunt one that is felt to be disagreeable or embarrassing, and euphemisms occur frequently with reference to such subjects as religion, death, bodily functions and sex. (Abrams & Harpham, 2010) According to *The New Oxford Dictionary of English* (2001), euphemism is a mild or indirect word or expression substituted for one considered to be too harsh or blunt when referring to something unpleasant or embarrassing.

39.1 Purposes of euphemism

1. For covering cruel or unacceptable facts

The company had to deal the industrial action. (=strike)

She had a series of affairs before marriage.

His old friend is sleeping here – but forever.

He has been job waiting (between jobs / waiting for a better job) for several months.

His family is less well off / less than better off.

His mother passed away last night.

Millions of heroes have laid down their lives for the liberation of mankind.

McCartney, 59, lost his first wife Linda to breast cancer in 1998.

2. For avoidance of hurting other's feelings

I feel very sorry for the loss of your husband.

He is advanced in age. (old)

He is a big slow for his age. (It means he is foolish.)

He is hard of hearing. (It means he is deaf.)

He depends on others to do his work.

3. For avoidance of bad association

They are planning to see their grandfather in the memory garden. (who is lying in peace among trees)

He was in the restroom.

He has opened his eyes with the sun at dawn, scratched, done his business like a dog at the roadside, washed at the public fountain?

Beniamin, are you having an affair with someone?

Jack was boarded at the expense of the state.

Peter is in embarrassing obligation to my brother.

Mary is in strained circumstances.

4. For politeness

As an office administrator, her duties are sending sales invoices, paying purchase invoices and processing staff expenses. (Actually, she is a secretary.)

He can do better work with help. (Actually, he is stupid.)

Henry used an Anglo-Saxon word.

– How do you like my painting.

– I don't have an eye for beauty, I'm afraid.

Peter: How do you like my new sweater?

Mary: [a second silence] I love it!

Peter: Oh, you don't like it.

Note: Here, silence indicates dislike but for politeness.

Would you mind answering the phone?

5. For suggestion

A: Let's get the kids something.

B: OK, but I'm against I-C-E-C-R-E-A-M.

A: Lily, could you help me with the cooking?

B: Alice can do it better, I think.

6. For humor

She fought the battle of the bulge. (weight)

He has been self-employed for a few months.

Tom's father is a butcher. Whenever somebody asks him what his father is, Tom answers with a great confidence. "He works on dissection on animals."

That hooligan liked ripping off when he could.

He is always misinformed.

7. For satire

"I used to think I was poor," she wrote. "Then they told me I was not poor; I was needy. Then they said it was self-defeating to think of myself as needy, that I was culturally deprived. Then they told me deprived was a bad image, that I was underprivileged. Then they told me that underprivileged was overused, that I was disadvantaged. I still do not have a dime – but I have a great vocabulary!"

Speaking at the last night's Mansion House banquet in London, Owen said no one should be in any doubt about the true nature of the Soviet and Cuba intervention in the Horn of Africa and why it placed such a large question mark over the future of detente.

He lived upon nothing for a year. (William Makepeace Thackeray: *Vanity Fair*)

All music is alike to him.

8. For criticism

You should know better.

You should have been here earlier.

Your article is full in content, but it would be better if it were a little more original.

Your report is OK, but wouldn't it better that you pay more attention to details?

His manners are still to be polished.

– The weatherman said it would be warm.

– He must take his readings in a bathroom.

39.2 Classification of euphemism

1. About jobs and professions of low social standing

secretary – administrative assistant

hairdresser – beautician

cook – chef

housewife – domestic engineer

dustman – sanitation engineer

plumber – pipe engineer

auto mechanic – auto engineer

secretary – administrative assistant

waitress – hostess

foreman – supervisor

salesman – sales representative

prison guard – correctional officer

2. About social identity

bastard – love child

old age – advanced in age; get on in years; golden ager / years; senior citizen; seasoned man; second childhood; sunset years; third age; well-preserved person

home for old people – home for adults; nursing home; private hospital; rest home

stupid student – slow learner; under-achiever

disabled student – special student

3. About poverty and unemployment

unemployed worker; person out of work – forgotten man; welfare worker

poor – modest

the poor – the disadvantaged

penniless – in difficulties

strike – industrial action

out of work – at liberty

dismiss – give sb. the walking ticket; give sb. the sack; give sb. the mitten

4. About death

die / dead – be called to God; be at rest; be promoted to glory; be taken to paradise; cross over the great Divide; feel one's age; go to one's grass; join one's ancestors; leave this world; play one's harp; pass away; return to dust; take one's departure; yield up the ghost / breath

death notice – prepared biography

dead house – mortuary; funeral parlor

graveyard – cemetery

suicide – brief illness

5. About illness

crippled – afflicted

cancer – big C; long illness; malignancy; prolonged illness

fall ill – be in a bad way; be out of order; be taken bad; be unwell; feel off color; under the weather

illness – complaint; conditions; disorder; infirmity; problem; trouble

6. About insanity

mad / not good in mind – be a little confused; be a little eccentric; feeble-minded; go bananas; mentally handicapped/ ill; nervous breakdown; off the track; off one's nut / base / head; simple-minded; soft in the head; unbalanced; unhinged

lunatic asylum – mental hospital; rehabilitation centre; rest house; sanatorium

7. About drunkenness

drunk – fuddled; merry; in his cups; top-heavy; reeling; tanked up; soaked; lubricated

8. About sexuality

love – business; action; love-making; practice; connection; conversation; occupy; congress; copulate; make love; sleep together; go to bed with; slip a length; hide the egg roll; be intimate with, dip the wick

whore / prostitute – street girl; call-girl; business girl; street walker; trading girl

naked – buff

rape – assault

9. About urination and defecation / indelicate things

urinate – make water; number one

defecate – move the bowels; number two

Also not so direct as follows:

answer / pay a call of nature; go to the bathroom / restroom; do one's business / needs; visit the necessary; cash a clerk, spend penny, relieve oneself; wash one's hands; because nature calls; get some fresh air; answer nature's calls

10. About pregnancy

She is in an interesting condition.

She is in a delicate condition.

She is in a family way.

She is expecting.

11. About the body

belly – abdomen

breast – bosom; bust; chest

false teeth – artificial dentures

copse / body – remains

butt – seat

fat person – weight watcher; calorie counter

thin woman – willowy woman

fat – stout; ample

overweight – plump

obesity – classic proportion

12. About crimes

prisoner – detainee; intern

death penalty – capital punishment

murder / kill – take care of; dispose of; rub out; put out; put away; waste; remove; put away; do away with; bump off

commit suicide – make away with oneself; take one's own life

thieves – finger man; fork; gentleman of the road; lifter; night man; tea leaf

bribery – grease one's palm; jobbery; kickback; meat eater; questionable payment

sex offence – abuse; assault; attack; defile; ill-treat; ill-use; maltreat; personal violence; statutory offense

gambling – commission agent; controller; speculator

narcotics – a-bomb; angel dust; antifreeze; bog bloke; big C; black stuff; blue sage; cold and hot; cookie; dope; dreamgum; dynamite; giggle smoke; hemp; joy stick; love weed; midnight oil; ope; pep pill; snort dust; STP; white nurse; witchhazel

drug-taking – bang in the arm; blow a stick; lie down; pop it; shoot up; sniff;

snort

drug user – a-head; campfire boy; gongbeater; grasshopper; hippy; smoker; sniffer; tripper; viper

13. About cursing with religious expressions

God – golly / gosh

Jesus – gee

goddam – doggone

good god – good grief

14. About cursing with devils

damn – dang; darm; dam it

hell – heck; jesse

devil / stan – deuce; god of this world; His Sable Majesty; old gentleman in black

15. About business

pawn shop – loan office

secondhand store – resale store; super; giant; special

cheap – economical; budget; low-cost

expensive – premium-priced

used car – pre-owned car

commercial – message

16. About war and military action

defeat / lose – break off contact with the enemy

war – conflict; pacification

invasion – rescue mission

air raid – surgical strikes

retreat – adjust the front

17. About politics and diplomacy

backward country – underdeveloped country; developing country; emerging country

economic crisis – recession; depression

slum – substandard housing

nuclear arms race – strategic competition
racial extinction– final solution
policeman – peace officer
failure – incomplete success

39.3 Ways of creating euphemism

1. Lexical ways

1) blending: goes under – gezudna
2) acronym: bowel movement – BM; cancer – the Big C
3) clipping: lavatory – lav
4) synonym: skinny – slim; stingy – tight
5) borrowing: underwear – chemise / lingerie (French words)
6) negation: stupid – unwise
7) words with bigger idea for ones with smaller idea
belly – Abdomen; leg – limb
8) use of abbreviation
venereal disease – VD; body odor – BO; shit of luck – SOL; garbage man – G-man
9) suffixes for jobs of lower level
Suffixes such as -ician, -ologlist, -ist, -ian are used for euphemism.
cobbler – shoetrician
butcher – meat technologist
garbage collector – garbologist
barber – beautician
10) Latin suffix -or is for some jobs of higher/ better level
adviser – advisor
wild animal trainer – wild animal trainor
furnitor – furniture dealer
teacher – educator

2. Metaphorical ways

1) metaphorical transfer: die – go to sleep forever
2) metonymical transfer: breast – chest
3) understatement: stinking – smelly

4) periphrasis: drop – adjustment downward

5) phonetic distortion: god – gosh

6) punctuation: son of a bitch – son of a

7) use of idioms and allusion: for death: go west, go to heaven, go to one's Maker, be with God, go to the way of all flesh, return to dust, cross the Jordan

3. Grammatical ways

1) by the use of "if" clause

I'll open the window if you don't mind.

2) by the use of subjunctive mood

It is time we got up.

3) by the use of "would like"

Would you like to close the window?

4) by the use of negative clause

Won't it be better for us to start off a little earlier?

5) by the use of "mind"

Would you mind my opening the window?

6) by the use of model verbs

It might be a good idea for us to hold two separate meetings for the two problems.

7) by the use of "please"

Could you please pass me that pen?

8) by the use of questions

Could you please open the door?

9) by the use of comparative or superlative degree

She has seen happier times.

Some of the items are good, but others might be better.

10) by the use of superlative degree

It is the idea farthest from my thoughts.

39.4 Use of euphemism

1. In business

Unfortunately, we <u>could not accept</u> your offer. Your prices are prohibitive.

<u>Would you please</u> inform us by return of the price, discounts, terms of payment

and the time when you can deliver?

We were discussing the terms of payment and the shipment.

May we suggest that you make some allowance on your quoted prices so as to enable us to introduce your goods to our customers?

I hope our verbal offer, if accepted by you, cold be confirmed by sales confirmation or contract within three days.

We presume that there must be some reason for your having trouble with this article.

Your compliance with our request will be highly appreciated.

2. In public notice

Commit No Nuisance!

Actually, don't litter here or piss here, which is better than No dumping or No pissing.

We don't swim in your toilet – please don't pee in our pool. (a notice at a swimming pool)

3. In dramas

She shall not be a maid unless things be cut shorter. (William Shakespeare: *King Lear*)

But that the dread of something after death –
The undiscover'd country, from whose bourn
No traveler returns – puzzles the will (William Shakespeare: *Hamlet*)
Note: The underlined part refers to death.

Portia: If I live to be as old as Sibylla, I will die as chaste as Diana, unless I be obtained by the manner of my father's will. I am glad this parcel of wooers are so reasonable, for there is not one among them but I dote on his very absence, and I pray God grant them a fair departure. (William Shakespeare: *The Merchant of Venice*)

Note: Portia uses the underlined part to show that she doesn't like to have the suitors.

Hamlet: ... to die – to sleep –
To sleep! Perchance to dream: – ay, there is the rub;
For in that sleep of death what dream may come;

When we have shuffled off this mortal coil
Must give us pause. (William Shakespeare: *Hamlet*)

4. In prose

Thousands of people flocked to the hospital to pay their respect to the remains of the great film star.

When boys and girls are old enough, their parents will tell them the birds and the bees and where babies come from.

A congressman or senator may give a loyal aide or campaigner a plum.

This is a new appointment with a compact company. (*Daily Telegraph*, 1976) (small)

We have been building a compact team of young engineers. (*The Times*, 1976) (small)

5. In speeches

We have come to dedicate a portion of that field as a final resting place for those who here gave their lives that nation might live. (Abraham Lincoln)

On the fourteenth of March, at a quarter to three in the afternoon, the greatest living thinker (Carl Marx) ceased to think. He had been left alone for scarcely two minutes, and when we came back we found him in his armchair, peacefully gone to sleep – but forever. (Frederick Engels: "Speech at the Graveside of Karl Marx")

Note: Here, "the greatest living thinker" refers to Carl Marx.

6. In novels and short stories

Mrs. Thompson flares up easily at that time of month.

"… Is it not sufficient for your infernal selfishness, that while you are at peace I shall writhe in the torments of hell?"

"I shall not be at peace," moaned Catherine … (Emily Brontë: *Wuthering Heights*)

Note: It is also pun. The first "at peace" means death, while the second "at peace" means peace in mind.

"Now I'll tell you, young Copperfield," said he, "the wine shall be kept to wet your whistle when you are storytelling." (Charles Dickens: *David Copperfield*)

Note: Here "wet your whistle" means "drink wine".

Dictating his autobiography late in life, he commented with a crushing sense of despair on men's final release from earthly struggles: "... they vanish from a world where they were of no consequence; where they achieved nothing; where they were a mistake and a failure and a foolishness, ..." (Noel Grove: "Mark Twain: Mirror of America")

I was prepared for my life to be taken from me. Instead the birds accepted to eat out of my hands. There was no sign of hatred or fear while we were encircled. (Patrick White: *The Eye of Storm*)

There was jewelry of stars such as Ellen Roxburgh believed she might be seeing for the last time before a lid was closed, and persistent, if in no way malicious, breezes for an instant halted her in the steps of memory. (Patrick White: *A Fringe of Leaves*)

7. In poetry

Then a soldier
Full of strange oaths, and bearded like the pard,
Jealous in honour, sudden and quick in quarrel,
Seeking the bubble reputation,
Even in the cannon's mouth. (William Shakespeare)

Not the least or the worst of his equipment
Was the sword the herald of Hrothgar loaned in his hour of need. (Beowulf)

8. In daily conversations

A: Accident happened to Mary, they say.
B: I saw she was big, but I didn't know she was that way.
Note: Both "accident" and "that way" refer to pregnancy.

A: I bought a new black skirt.
B: It looks nice. You would look better if it is red, I suppose.

A: How about my shoes?
B: I don't have an eye for beauty, I'm afraid.

You must not fancy I am sick, only overdriven and under weather.

9. In advertisements

Continued driving with a failed bearing could result in disengagement of the axle shaft & adversely affect vehicle control. (advertisement for Ford)

10. In news headlines

"Lost at Sea" (*Time*, July 1999)

Note: "Lost" is a euphemism, which refers to the death of John Kennedy Jr.

"A Bit of a Fit over Pitt Split" (*Time*, June 1997)

Note: Here "split" is a euphemism, which refers to Actor Brad Pitt's separation with his fiancee Gwyneth Paltrow.

11. In academic writing

We're all of the opinion that the quality of your equipment is competitive.

Well, according to our experience, the optimizing control project nowadays can usually be started some years after the start-up of the basic and stabilizing controls.

Chapter Forty　Paradox

Paradox (悖论) comes from a Greek word, *paradoxon*, meaning against opinion. A paradox is a statement or expression so surprisingly self-contradictory as to provoke us into seeking another sense or context in which it would be true (although some paradoxes cannot be resolved into truths, remaining flatly self-contradictory. (Baldick, 2001) Simply put, it is a statement, which is apparently self-contradictory statement, the underlying meaning of which is revealed only by careful scrutiny.

40.1　Purposes of paradox

1. To reveal value and truth

More haste, less speed. (proverb)

He who praises everybody praises nobody. (proverb)

2. To blame

Man is born free and everywhere is in chains.

Advice after mischief is like medicine after death. (proverb)

3. To make comment on political matters

A lover of peace emerged as a magnificent leader of war.

Let him who desires peace, prepare for war.

4. To reveal life experience

Too much experience is a dangerous thing. (Oscar Wilde)

The child is father of the man. – William Wordsworth

I'm nobody.

You can save money by spending it. (proverb)

5. For satire

He who is full of himself is very empty. (Donne)

War is peace. Freedom is slavery. Ignorance is strength. (George Orwell, *Nineteen Eighty-Four*)

6. For contrast

Adversity makes man, prosperity monsters. (proverb)

The afflicted person was once thought sacred but now he's considered a fool. (proverb)

40.2 Use of paradox

1. In proverbs

The more you learn, the less you know.

One man's meat is another man's poison.

He who makes no mistakes makes nothing.

The falling out of loves is the renewing of love.

Cheapest is the dearest.

A hedge between keeps friendship green.

A little leak will sink a great ship.

No news is good news.

2. In news headline

"John McEnroe: The Champ You Love to Hate" (*Newsweek*, September 7, 1981)

Note: It implies that the fans like his tennis skills but dislike his temper during the game.

3. In advertisements

One of the First Things about Owning It Is Selling It. (advertisement for Volkswagen)

Can The Socks Go from Golf Course to Cocktail Party without Changing People? (advertisement for socks)

4. In prose

The suspense is terrible. I hope it will last. (Oscar Wilde)

Humans, having conquered nature, will remain enslaved to nature.

Translations are like women – when they are faithful they are not beautiful, when they are beautiful they are not faithful.

5. In poetry

Caesar: Cowards die many times before their deaths;
The valiant never tastes death but once. (William Shakespeare: *Julius Caesar*)

One short sleep past, we wake eternally
And death shall be no more;
Death, thou shall die. (John Donne: "Death, Be Not Proud")

The child is father of the man. (William Wordsworth)

NO lover saith, I love, nor any other
  Can judge a perfect lover;
He thinks that else none can or will agree,
  That any loves but he;
I cannot say I loved, for who can say
  He was kill'd yesterday.
Love with excess of heat, more young than old,
  Death kills with too much cold;
We die but once, and who loved last did die,
  He that saith, twice, doth lie;
For though he seem to move, and stir a while,
  It doth the sense beguile.
Such life is like the light which bideth yet
  When the life's light is set,
Or like the heat which fire in solid matter
  Leaves behind, two hours after.
Once I loved and died; and am now become
  Mine epitaph and tomb;
Here dead men speak their last, and so do I;
  Love-slain, lo! Here I die. (John Donne: "The Paradox")

6. In novels and short stories

All animals are equal, but some animals are more equal than others. (George Orwell: *Animal Farm*)

Homeless, they have a hundred homes. (O. Henry: *The Furnished Room*)

Even Kohler, whom they said knew everything at CERN, clearly had no idea about the project. (Dan Brown: *Angels and Demons*)

7. In dramas

Mrs. Cheveley: Oh, no! I can't stand your English house parties. In England people actually try to be brilliant at breakfast. That is so dreadful of them! Only dull people are brilliant at breakfast. (George Bernard Shaw: *Ideal Husband*)

What a pity that youth must be wasted on the young. (George Bernard Shaw)

Chapter Forty-one Oxymoron

Oxymoron (矛盾修辞) comes from a Greek word, *oxymoron* ("oxy" means sharp, acute, pointed; and "moron" means foolish, silly, dull), meaning acutely silly, or pointedly foolish. So the word *oxymoron* itself is an oxymoron. Oxymoron is a combination of contradictory or incongruous words. (Mohanty, 2009) It usually produces an ironic contrast when things have gone contrary to expectation, belief, desire or assertion, or when your position is opposite to another's which you are discussing, and it can also achieve the rhetorical effect of a sense of irony, humor and a sense of absurdness as well as fun.

41.1 Purposes of oxymoron

1. For fun

There was an elegant plainness in this small house.

The dear woman, she knew he had talent; and if affection made her overestimate the size of it a little, surely it was a sweet and gentle crime ... (Mark Twain)

2. For emphasis

Parting is such sweet sorrow. (William Shakespeare)

There is a deafening silence in the room.

3. For wit

Faith unfaithful kept him falsely true.

Every advantage has its disadvantage.

4. For irony

Senator Rosebud calls this a useless plan; if so, it is the most helpful useless plan we have ever enacted.

Mary's husband now seems to be an intimate stranger to her.

5. For contrast

For years, they are of a love-hate relationship.

In fact, it appears that the teachers of English teach English so poorly largely because they teach grammar so well.

The whole night she felt so restless and worried that she couldn't go to sleep when her husband returned, all wet through, giving her a delightful surprise.

6. For implicit feeling

I think the host was behaving in a cold pleasant manner toward us today.

7. For attraction

Bad Good News (*Time*, May 1981)

The World Cup is a peaceful war.

41.2 Formation of oxymoron

1. Adjective-noun

Old news; just war; abundant poverty; adult child; baby giant; bankrupt millionaire; cold fever; cruel kindness; friendly enemy; girly man; icy hot; liquid gas; light-heavy weight; little giant; open secret; orderly chaos; priceless junk; restless sleep; silent scream; wise fool.

I like a smuggler. He is the only honest thief. (Charles Lamb)

Modern dancing is so old-fashioned. (Samuel Goldwyn)

During his useful life he often felt he was useless.

The cost-saving program became an expensive economy.

In recent years yet another breed of financial entrepreneur has emerged. Enemies of the industrial status quo, they are takeover artists and spinoff specialists who have forced nothing less than the restructuring of corporate America. They are bringing about the "creative destruction" by which capitalism regenerates itself.

2. Adverbial-adjective

Almost candid; awfully good; bitterly happy; cheerfully mournful; dead right; equally diverse; falsely true; half true; increasingly little; nearly complete; pretty ugly; upside down; unbelievably real; wickedly good.

His honor rooted in dishonor stood,
And faith unfaithful kept him falsely true. (Alfred Tennyson)
His new novel is terribly good.

3. Verb-adverbial

Act naturally; burn cold; climb down; diet ice cream; fail safe; fight for peace; go nowhere; grow small; hasten slowly; progress backward; sit up.

Some radical environmentalists are trying save trees with sabotage. "Tree spiking – driving spikes into trees to ruin sawmill equipment – is reported rising. Other tactics; stringing tripwires across trails used by oil explorers and cutting brake lines in trucks. But so far, there have been only a handful of arrests.

4. -ing + noun

Doubting believer; chilling fever; living dead; loving hate; shouting whisper; talking mime; working vacation.

O dark, dark, dark amid the blaze of noon,
Irrecoverably dark …
As in the land of darkness, yet in light,
To live a life half dead, a living death,
And buried … (John Milton: *Samson Agonistes*)

5. -ed + noun

Crowded solitude; expected surprise; forgotten memories; fried roast; grounded airplane; stunted growth; united nations; unknown knowledge; unsolved mystery; unspoken suggestion.

They were still overjoyed at the expected surprise.

The United Nations could do nothing about the matter.

6. Noun + noun

Anti-missile missile; budget deficit; fish farm; freezer burn; speed limit; standard deviation; suicide victim; union worker; veiled accusation; wilderness management; work party; zero deficit.

They had a love-hate relationship.

That is a life-and-death struggle.

7. Adjective-adjective

Bitter sweet memories; historical current event; little big man; short tall tale.

The poor boy spent a miserable merry holiday.

8. Noun + prep. + noun

The sound of silence.

I could not help feeling the despair of hope itself.

9. -ed + adverbial

Born dead; buried alive; found missing.

The little boy was found missing.

They found the dog was buried alive.

10. Verb + object complement

The power of money to make the stupid wise, the ugly beautiful, and in general, black white had been a satirical commonplace since antiquity.

8. Words of the same root

Changeless change, deathless death; helpless help; expressionless expression.

Enoch had a pleasant day with his ten-year-old son. But, anxiously, he found him a changeless change. (D. H. Lawrence: *The Rainbow*)

9. Verb + object

I can resist anything, except temptation. (Oscar Wilde)

I have made mistakes, but have never made the mistake of claiming I never made one. (James G. Bennett)

Hegel was right when he said that we learn from history that man never learns anything from history. (George Bernard Shaw)

10. Oxymoron with three or more words

Better than new; group of individuals; quickly slowing down; sweet and sour; history of the future; one hundred percent plus; shout in a whisper; the sweet and the bitter of life; the sweets and bitters of life.

How can that be? It is one hundred percent plus.

The old man has experienced all the sweet and the bitter of life.

41.3 Use of oxymoron

1. In compounding words

Bittersweet

Butthead

Childproof

Homework

Recreate

Spendthrift

Superette

Weekday

Wholesome

He doesn't like his father's spendthrift ways of living.

The food is filling and wholesome.

2. In proverbs

Dying is a part of life.

Misfortune tells us what fortune is.

Love is a sweet torment.

3. In titles of books and articles

"A Miserable, Merry Christmas"(*College English*, Book I, Unit 5)(also alliteration)

"My Wonderful, Lousy Poem" (*College English*)

4. In news headlines

"Lethal Lovers?" (*Time*, December 1997)

Note: "Lethal Lovers" refers to Aurore Martin and Peter Uwe Schimitt, who tricked single women into marrying them, and then they killed these women for huge insurance premiums.

"Little Big Man" (*Time*, September 1997)

Note: "Little Big Man" refers to Allen Iverson, a well-known basketball player.

5. In speeches

The second office of the government is honorable and easy, the first is but a splendid misery. (Thomas Jefferson: "Comparing the Vice-presidency with the Presidency")

Nothing in all the world is more dangerous than sincere ignorance and conscientious stupidity. (Martin Luther King, Jr.: "Strength to Love")

6. In prose

Often it is fatal to live too long. (Racine)

It usually takes more than three weeks to prepare a good impromptu speech. (Mark Twain)

I do here make humbly bold to present them with a short account of themselves and their art ... (Jonathan Swift)

7. In poetry

His honor rooted in dishonor stood,
And faith unfaithful kept him falsely true. (Alfred Tennyson)

Speaking silence, dumb confusion,
Passion's birth, and infant's play. (Burns: "To a Kiss")

Oh dark, dark, amid the blaze of noon,
Irrecoverably dark ...
As in the land of darkness, yet in light
To live a life half dead, a living death,
And buried; but, O yet more miserable. (John Milton: *Samson Agonistes*)

8. In novels and short stories

I despise its very vastness and power. It (New York) has the poorest millionaires, the littlest great man, the haughtiest beggars, the plainest beauties, the lowest skyscrapers, the dolefulest pleasures of any town I ever saw. (O Henry: *The Duel*)

He went out of the doorless door. (James Davell: *King Rat*)

They have been indorsed and reinforced by his own eloquent silence. (Mark Twain: *Running for Governor*)

9. In dramas

Here is much to do with hate, but more with love:
Why then, O brawling love, O loving hate,
O anything of nothing first create;
O heavy lightness, serious vanity,

Misshapen chaos of well-seeming forms
Feather of lead, bright smoke, cold fire, sick health,
Still-waking sleep, that is not what it is! (William Shakespeare: *Romeo and Juliet*)

A tedious brief scene of young Pyramus
And his love Thisbe; very tragical mirth.
Merry and tragical! Tedious and brief!
That is, hot ice and wondrous strange snow.
How shall we find the concord of this discord? (William Shakespeare: *A Midsummer Night's Dream*)

Othello: Why, anything!
An honorable murder, if you will,
For nought I did in hate, but all in honor. (William Shakespeare: *Othello*)

41.4 Differences between oxymoron and paradox

According to Baldick (2001), oxymoron is a figure of speech that combines two usually contradictory terms in a compressed paradox, that is, oxymoron is a paradox reduced to usually two words, often in an adjective-noun or adverb-adjective relationship. According to Corbett & Coonors (1999), paradox is like oxymoron in that both are built on contradictories, but paradox may not be a trope at all, because it involves not so much a "turn" of meaning in juxtaposed words as a "turn" of meaning in the whole statement.

In oxymoron, usually only two words that are opposite are put together to be a unity of contradiction. For example,

Can enemies become mortal friends?

Dudley Fields Malone called my conviction a "victorious defeat". (John Scopes: *The Trial That Rocked the World*)

However, paradox consists of a whole sentence or a paragraph, in which two opposite ideas are put together to be self-contradictory. For example,

He who praises everybody praises nobody.

My only love sprung from my only hate. (William Shakespeare)

Art is a form of lying in order to tell the truth. (Pablo Picasso)

Chapter Forty-two Allusion

Allusion (典故), from a Latin word, *allusio*, meaning playing with, is an indirect or passing reference to some event, person, place, or artistic work, the nature and relevance of which is not explained by the writer but relies on the reader's familiarity with what is thus mentioned. (Baldick, 2001) Or simply put, it is usually a casual, brief and implicit reference to a famous historical or literary figure or a well-known historical event, which the writer assumes to be familiar to his readers.

42.1 Purposes of allusion

1. For attraction

He chose a mournful <u>Muse</u>
Soft pity to infuse. (John Dryden: "Alexander's Feast")

What an <u>Arcadia</u> you live in!

Note: Arcadia is a mountainous area in Ancient Greece, where people had a simple and pastoral life.

2. For brevity

He is a frugal man, the furnishings of his home are truly <u>Spartan</u>.

His Achilles heel was his pride – he would get angry if anyone criticized his work.

3. For fun

Poor Charlie! Of all the girls in the world, he should have fallen in love with the daughter of a <u>Judas</u>!

There are some officials who are only dogs in the manger.

Note: Here "a dog in the manger" comes from *Aesop's Fables*, meaning a person who prevents others from enjoying something that is useless to himself.

4. For praise

Nature and Nature's Laws lay hid in Night,

GOD said, Let Newton be! and all was Light. (Alexander Pope: "Epitaph Intended for Sir Isaac Newton")

These Odysseys were not purely escapism. They were also callisthenics for the future, ... (*The Rockefellers – An American Dynasty*)

Note: Odysseus is a Greek hero, who Homer wrote an epic *Odysseys* to praise his deed.

5. For vividness

Being a teacher is being present at the creation, when the clay begins to breathe. (Peter G. Beidler: *Why I Teach*) ("The clay begins to breathe" comes from the Bible.)

Either complete frankness; or complete ignoring – and that meant living with the sword of Damocles above his head! (John Galsworthy: *The White Monkey*)

6. For association with the readers or listeners

Their boss pays the highest wages, but he wants his pound of flesh in return and makes them work hard.

Note: English people are quite familiar with Shakespeare's play *The Merchant of Venice*, in which "pound of flesh" is used.

They gave us a number of very large pictures as a wedding present, but as we live in a very small flat the present was a white elephant.

Note: English people are quite familiar with the story of white elephant, which means something very expensive but worthless to its owner.

42.2 Origins of allusion

1. From myths and legends, especially Greek & Roman mythology, and biblical stories

Last week President Bush tried to reclaim his long-established reputation as a free trader. "I would avoid the Siren's call of protection that suggests the way for us to get strong is to put on quotes and start managing trade." (*Time*, January 27, 1992) (*Siren* comes from Greek legends.)

The hopeful young person soared into so pleasing a Cupid as to constitute the chief delight of the maternal part of the spectators.

Upon my word, Basil, I didn't know you were so vain; and I really can't see any resemblance between you, with your rugged strong face and your coal-black hair, and this young Adonis, who looks as if he was made out of ivory and rose-leaves.

Note: Adonis is a handsome young child in Greek legends.

If we try to implement these harebrained ideas (that English should be replaced by Hindi and the 15 recognized state languages), India will become a Tower of Babel.

Note: It is from the Tower of Babel, where people are arranged by God to speak different languages and could not understand each other.

The boy's laziness all summer got his father's goat.

Note: In the Bible, God forces Satan to burn Job's herd of sheep so as to get Satan angry to see whether he is loyal to God, and now "get one's goat" means "get one angry".

2. From fairy tales and fables

But because we cannot satisfy the desires of our hearts – why should we try "sour grapes" at them? (Herbert George Wells)

Note: Here "sour grapes" comes from Aesop's Fable, meaning one cannot get what he / she wants.

Lou, you can't bury your head in the sand about your health – please, make an appointment with your doctor and get that rash checked out!

Note: Here "bury one's head in the sand" alludes to an ostrich, which is believed incorrectly to hide its head in a hole in the ground when it sees danger.

3. From literary works, especially English and American literary works

He is another Shylock. (William Shakespeare: *The Merchant of Venice*)

You want your pound of flesh, don't you? (William Shakespeare: *The Merchant of Venice*)

The movement is getting infiltrated by youngish Toms. Militancy is a joke and protest an afterthought. (Harriet Beecher Stowe: *Uncle Tom's Cabin*)

People who came into my club don't worry about somebody telling Big Brother. (George Orwell: *Nineteen Eighty-Four*)

Note: "Big Brother" in the novel listens to everything and nothing can escape his ears.

4. From modern and contemporary sources

His army pulled a Pearl Harbor on the enemy. (Pearl Harbor is a place where the Japanese navy attacked the US navy.)

Prime Minister Indira Gandhi decided to go heavy-handed from the outset ... This crisis would never grow into an Indian Watergate. (from the political scandal of the US president Nixon)

5. From historical figures or places

McArthur was American Caesar.

The government has found it easy to persuade the employer to accept its place, but it is expected that during discussions with the trade unions the government may meet its Waterloo. (Waterloo is the place where Napoleon was defeated, thus meaning defeat.)

42.3 Forms of allusion

1. In the form of words

Getting small appliance fixed is *Catch-22*.

Note: "Catch-22" is the title of a novel, written by Joseph Heller:, which means self-contradictory rules or regulations, any situation which puts one in a dilemma.

2. In the form of phrases

All your piteous words for the tenants are no more than crocodile tears.

Note: Here "crocodile tears" is an idiom. If someone sheds (cries) crocodile tears, they pretend to be sad about something, but they are not really sad at all.

3. In the form of sentences

Now that he felt the die really cast, and Megan gave up, hated himself, and almost hated the Holidays and their atmosphere of healthy, happy English homes. (John Galsworthy: *The Apple Tree*)

Note: Here "the die really cast" comes from "the die is cast", used by Caesar when he decided to fight, and now it is used to say that an event has happened or a decision has been made that cannot be changed.

42.4 Use of allusion

1. In prose

The result of a <u>*Catch-22*</u> dilemma: health care costs must be contained in order to encourage corporations to take on full-time workers, but the process could curtail growth in the one job sector that has been robust. (*Time*, Feb. 1, 1993)

It (world frog) spends its winters interned in subzero sleep, its tissues steel-rigid, and revives in the spring raring to go. It's the <u>Rip van Winkle</u> of the animal world. (*Discover*, Feb. 2005)

Note: "Rip van Winkle" is the hero of the short story *The Legend of Sleeping Hollow* written by Washington Irving. He slept for 20 years because of drunkenness and when he woke up he became old and found that the world has change a lot.

She sat there all night as silent as the <u>sphinx</u>.

2. In poetry

A little mouth, or ere those shoes were old
With which she followed my poor father's body,
Like <u>Niobe</u>, all tears. (William Shakespeare)
Note: Niobe is a Greek god.

When Pearse summoned Cuchulain to his side
What stalked through the Post Office? (William Butler Yeats: "The Statues")

Note: William Butler Yeats alludes both to the hero of Celtic legend (Cuchulain) and to the new historical hero (Patrick Pearse) of the 1916 Easter Rising, in which the revolutionaries captured the Dublin Post Office. In addition to such topical allusions to recent events, Yeats often uses personal allusions to aspects of his own life and circle of friends.

3. In novels and short stories

... for want might be a temptation to them to disagree, or not to think themselves delivered, otherwise than out of one difficulty into another. "You know," says he, "<u>the children of Israel, though they rejoiced at first for being delivered out of Egypt, yet rebelled even against God Himself that delivered them, when they</u>

came to want bread in the wilderness. (Daniel Defoe: *Robinson Crusoe*)

Note: The underlined part comes from the Bible, telling the story of Moses leading the Israelis out of Egypt.

"It is true that the enemy won the battle, but theirs is a Pyrrhic victory," said the general.

4. In dramas

Would any of the stock of Barabbas,

Had been her husband rather than a Christian! (William Shakespeare: *The Merchant of Venice*)

Note: Barabbas is a bandit in the Bible.

So excellent a king; that was, to this,
Hyperion to a satyr; so loving to my mother
That he might not beteem the winds of heaven
Visit her face too roughly. Heaven and earth! (William Shakespeare: *Hamlet*)

Note: "Hyperion" comes from Greek methodology.

5. In news headlines

"A Law by Any Other Name"

Note: This comes from 'A law is a law by any other name', meaning a law is a law no matter what name it is given, an allusion to Juliet's words in Shakespeare's play *Romeo and Juliet*.

"The Electric Car's Achilles's Axle" (*The Economist*, 1992) (from Greek mythology)

6. In daily conversations

Is she really sick or is she just crying wolf? ("To cry wolf" comes from *Aesop's Fable*.)

A: How has Peter been handling the break-up?

B: Oh, just burying his head in the sand and ignoring his feelings.

7. In academic writing

The computer is the Proteus of machines, as it takes on a thousand forms and serves a thousand functions.

Note: "Proteus" is the sea god in Greek mythology, who would change constantly.

"Anyone who needs the literature in this field with an open mind soon discovers that the emperor has no clothes," Ravnskov writes. (*Discover*, Feb. 2004)

Note: The writer uses Anderson's story "The Emperor's New Clothes" to show that one can find the truth without prejudice.

Part Six

Application of Figures of Speech

Chapter Forty-three Single Application and Comprehensive Application of Figures of Speech

43.1 Single application of figures of speech

The single application of figures of speech (修辞格的单用) refers to the use of only one figure of speech in one word, phrase, or sentence, which is the basic form of the use of figures of speech. (Chen Rudong, 2000) Single application of figures of speech can be found in different language levels, styles and genres of writing.

1. In compounding words

ram-jam (assonance)
dumdum (assonance)
ding-dong (alliteration)

2. In idioms

through thick and thin (alliteration)

3. In phrases

make a mistake (alliteration)

take place (assonance)

4. In proverbs

Practice what you preach. (alliteration)

Laughter is the best medicine. (metaphor)

5. In news headlines

"Smoke Signals" (*Time*, June 1998, alliteration)

"Sex, Lies and Free Speech" (*Time*, March 1996, parallelism)

6. In titles of books and movies / plays

Pride and Prejudice (a novel by Jane Austin; alliteration)

All Roads Lead to Socialism (a play by George Bernard Shaw; parody)

7. In well-known quotations

The biggest human temptation is to settle for too little. (Thomas Merton; assonance)

Life is not a spectacle or a feast; it is a predicament. (George Santayana; metaphor)

8. In prose

There is no greater nor keener pleasure than that of body love – and none which is more irrational. (Plato; homeoteleuton)

The teacher cracked him on the hand with a ruler. (onomatopoeia)

9. In poetry

"Yo ho, yo ho, the pirate life,
The flag o'skull and bones,
A merry hour, a hempen rope,
And hey for Davy Jones. (James Matthew Barrie: "Peter Pan in Kensington Gardens"; onomatopoeia)

This is the forest primeval. (Henry Wadsworth Longfellow: "Evangeline"; anastrophe)

10. In novels and short stories

O charity, O philanthropy, descend to the Spike and take a lesson from Ginger!

(Jack London; apostrophe)

I'm a pris'ner, gen'l'm'n. Confined, as the lady said. (Charles Dickens: *The Pickwick Papers*)

Note: Here "confined" has two meanings: pregnant, and enclosed. It is pun.

11. In dramas

Will all great Neptune's ocean wash this blood
Clean from my hand? No. This my hand will rather
The multitudinous seas incarnadine,
Making the green one red. (William Shakespeare: *Macbeth*; rhetorical question)

Lord Goring. Afraid I can't, thanks. I have promised to look in at the Hartlocks. I believe they have got a mauve Hungarian band that plays mauve Hungarian music. (Oscar Wilde: *An Ideal Husband*; synaesthesia)

12. In speeches

I'm not going to stick to my laurels. (Kate Winslet: "Speech at the Academy Awards in 2002"; metaphor)

We remain a young nation, but in the words of Scripture, the time has come to set aside childish things. (Barack Obama; allusion)

Note: "Scripture" refers to the Bible.

13. In advertisements

It's more than just new. It's smaller. It's lighter. (advertisement for Sharp xerox; homeoteleuton)

That Baume & Mercier is thinner than ever, isn't it? (advertisement for a Swiss watch; rhetorical question)

14. In academic writing

All grammars leak. (metaphor)

There are many factors which contribute to the problem of road safety. Although cars legally must be fitted with seat belts, it is not compulsory to wear them. In spite of a great deal of publicity people still drive after drinking alcohol and the legislation on this is not sufficiently strong. A major factor in accidents is speed and there are obvious ways of limiting that. Lastly, one of the most serious problems is that the police and the courts are unable to enforce adequately current legislation. (parallelism)

43.2 Definition of comprehensive application of figures of speech

The effectiveness of the use of only one figure of speech is limited, and only one figure used by itself could not express the complexity and diversity of people's feelings and the complicated nature and society, and we can find that more than one figure of speech can be found in many of the examples used in this book, or we can even say that there are more examples of comprehensive application of figures of speech than those of single application.

The combination of two or more figures of speech in a sentence or a segment of language is called the comprehensive application of figures of speech (修辞格的综合运用) for the purpose of expression. (Luo Xiaosuo, 2010)

As stated by Chen Congyun (2014), in specific speech activities, some of the figures of speech are used alone, and some of the figures of speech are used more than once or more than one kind of figures of speech in a sentence or a language fragment. When these figures of speech are used in combination, it is called the comprehensive application of figures of speech.

According to Wang Yang (2013), in actual language use, due to a certain need of expression, several figures of speech are often combined and used together. In other words, in a paragraph or even a sentence, several figures of speech are often used at the same time.

The comprehensive application of figures of speech is aimed to describe people or objective things in a more vivid, expressive, and effective way in order to draw attention of readers or listeners for a more metaphorical effect.

43.3 Purposes of comprehensive application of figures of speech

1. For vividness

In the garden the sparrow chants – a desultory second courtship, a subdued passion, in keeping with the great heat, love in summertime, relaxed and languorous.

Note: Two figures of speech are used in this sentence. "chant" is onomatopoeia; and "desultory second courtship" is metaphor.

2. For attraction

Homeless, they have a hundred homes. (O. Henry: *The Furnished Room*)

Note: The sentence as a whole is paradox. Besides, "a hundred homes" is hyperbole; and "homeless, have, hundred, and homes" is alliteration.

3. For emphasis

There is a deafening silence in the room.

Note: Here "deafening silence" can be considered as oxymoron and hyperbole.

4. For brevity

He who makes no mistakes makes nothing. (proverb)

Note: In this short proverb, there is paradox (the whole sentence); alliteration (makes, mistakes); repetition (makes); and alliteration (no, nothing). The whole sentence as a proverb can also be considered as epigram.

5. For description of more complicated feelings

The poor boy spent a miserable merry holiday.

Note: Here "miserable merry" can be considered as alliteration and oxymoron.

6. For description of more complicated matter

The sunlight pushing its way through the window splattered against a barricade of boxes. Like a fluorescent river, it streamed down the sides and flooded the cracks of the cold, cement floor. I stood in the doorway between the house and garage and wondered if the sunlight would ever again penetrate the memories packed inside those boxes. For an instant, the cardboard boxes appeared as tombstones, monuments to those memories.

Note: "The sunlight pushing its way through the window, streamed down the side and flooded ..." and "the sunlight would ... penetrate ..." are personification and also parallelism; "splattered" and "cracks" are onomatopoeia; "barricade of boxes" is metaphor; "like a fluorescent river" is simile; "stood ... wondered" is parallelism; and "as tombstones, monuments" is simile.

43.4 Classification of comprehensive application of figures of speech

1. Continuous use of figures of speech

The continuous use of figures of speech (修辞格的连用) generally refers to the continuous use of similar figures of speech or heterogeneous figures of speech in a paragraph; or it refers to the continuous use of several figures of speech in a paragraph or a longer sentence, and there is no inclusive relationship or integration between them, and they are only used one by one. (Wang Yang, 2013) Each figure of speech has its own form, and the relationship between each rhetorical means is parallel and parallel. (Luo Xiaosuo, 2010) The relationship between the figures of speech used looks like the following figure.

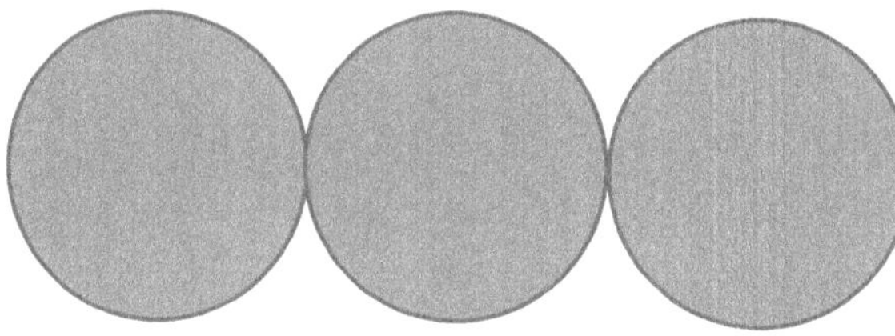

Slowly, patiently, skillfully, James Van Metre's wife fanned the spark of life that flickered in Henry Bedell. ("The Woman Who Would Not Tell", in *College English*, Book III)

Note: Three figures of speech are used in this sentence. "Slowly, patiently, skillfully" is parallelism, "fanned the spark of life" is metaphor, and "flicker" is onomatopoeia.

Who can say of a particular sea that it is old? Distilled by the sun, kneaded by the moon, it is renewed in a year, in a day, or in an hour. The sea changed, the fields changed, the rivers, the villages, and the people changed, yet Egden remained. (Thomas Hardy: *The Return of the Native*)

Note: "Who can say of a particular sea that it is old?" is rhetorical question; "Distilled by the sun, kneaded by the moon" is parallelism; "in a year, in a day, or in an hour" is climax; "The sea changed, the fields changed, the rivers, the villages, and the people changed" is parallelism; and "The sea changed, the fields changed, the rivers, the villages, and the people changed, yet Egden remained" is anticlimax.

2. Dual use of a figure of speech

The dual use of a figure of speech (修辞格的兼用) refers to one word, phrase, or sentence, which can be considered as two or more figures of speech. The characteristic of such use is that the one word, phrase, or sentence is considered as this kind of figure of speech from a certain angle, but another figure of speech from another angle. Several figures of speech are interdependent and harmonious in the same one word, phrase, or sentence, and thus the rhetoric effect is more prominent than that of a single figure of speech. (Chen Congyun, 2014) The relationship between the figures of speech used looks like the following figure.

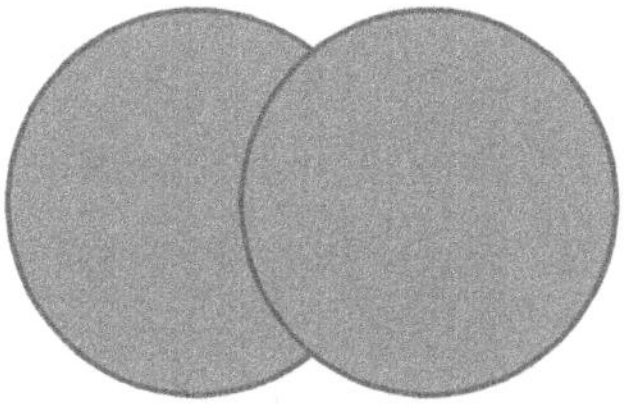

What a life? Today, tomorrow, the week, next week, this month, next month, next year … forever! ("Life Is Boring", in *College English* – Listening, Book II, Lesson 15)

Note: As a whole, "Today, tomorrow, the week, next week, this month, next month, next year … forever!" can be considered as parallelism, repetition (repetition of "week", of "month", and of "next"), and climax. Besides, "What a life?" is rhetorical question. "Today and tomorrow" and "can and considered" can be considered as alliteration.

For glances beget ogles, ogles sighs,
Sighs wishes, wishes words, and words a letter. (George Gordon Byron: "Beppo")

Note: As a whole, the two lines can be considered as climax and also anadiplosis. Besides, "wishes and words" is alliteration, and the repeated pairs of words are repetition.

Am I a free man in England and do I become a slave in six hours by crossing the Channels? (Jonathan Swift)

Note: As a whole, this sentence is rhetorical question, antithesis, and irony. Besides, "crossing the Channels" is alliteration.

3. Inclusive application of figures of speech

The inclusive application of figures of speech (修辞格的套用) generally means that one or more figures of speech are included within another figure of speech so that the layers are intertwined; or it refers to a paragraph or a sentence that uses one figure of speech as a whole, and each part of them uses another. (Wang Liyan, 1998) The relationship between the figures of speech used looks like the following figure.

Faith is a good guide, reason is a better guide, truth is the best guide.

Note: The whole proverb is climax, in which there is repetition (of guide) and alliteration (good and guide; better and best).

Scientists have learned a great deal about the kinds of food people need. They say that there are several kinds of food that people should eat every day. What are these classes of food? They are (1) green vegetables of all kinds, such as string beans, peas, lettuces and cabbages; (2) fruits such as apples, peaches and bananas; (3) other vegetables, examples of these are beets, onions, carrots, tomatoes and so on; (4) meat of all kinds, fish and eggs; (5) milk and food made from milk, such as butter, cheese and ice-cream; (6) bread or cereal. Rice is also in this class of food. (*Focus Listening*, Book IV, Lesson 16)

Note: Here "They are (1) ... (6) bread or cereal" is parallelism, which includes five smaller groups of parallelism in (1) to (5). Besides, "What are these classes of food?" is rhetorical question.

4. Contiguous application of figures of speech

The contiguous application of figures of speech (修辞格的承接) refers to the use of figures of speech, in which the former is the basis of the latter, and the latter is based on the former and depends on the former. The relationship between the figures of speech used looks like the following figure.

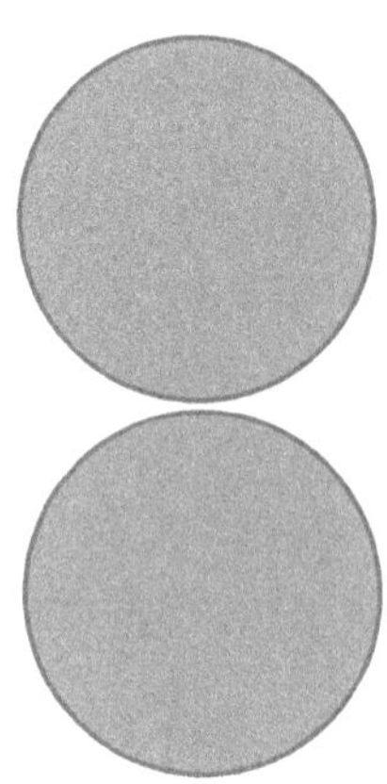

All animals are equal, but some animals are more equal than others. (George Orwell: *Animal Farm*)

Note: The first part "All animals are equal" is parody from "All men are created equal", and there is paradox, which is based on the parody.

… and the sun was a huge flashlight of a billion batteries with a tube so long it never ended … The Flashlight, by Eldridge Cleaver

Note: Here "the sun was a huge flashlight of a billion batteries with a tube" is metaphor, which is the basis of hyperbole (a tube so long it never ended).

If practice makes perfect, and no one's perfect, then why practice? (Billy Corgan)

Note: First "practice makes perfect" is parody, then there rhetorical question, which is based on the parody. Besides, there is also alliteration (practice and perfect).

5. Combined use of the above ways

We can also use two or more of the above ways together to achieve more emphatic and striking effects. The relationship between the figures of speech used looks like one of the following figures.

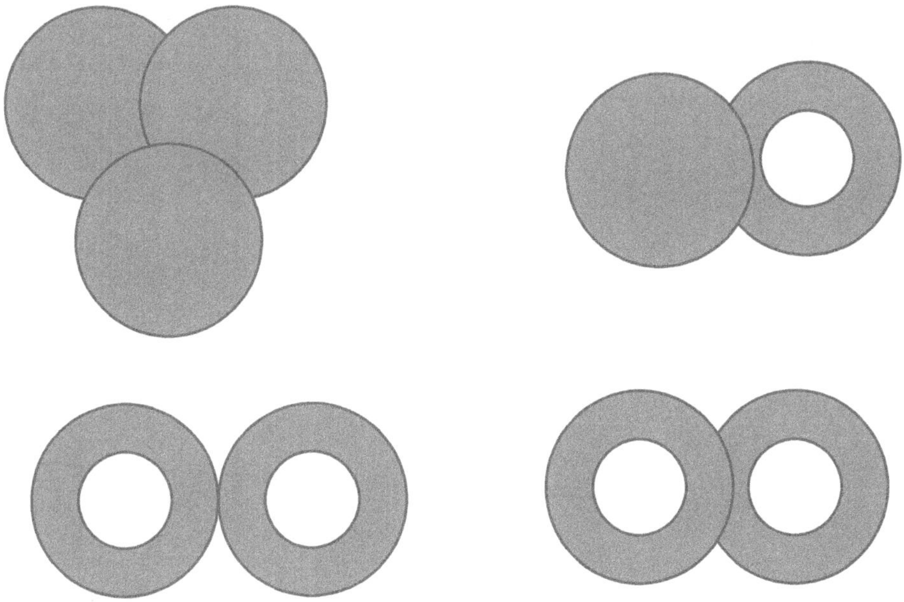

Good, better, best, never get rest.

Note: In this very short slogan, we can find five figures: climax (as a whole), parallelism (as a whole), alliteration (good and get), assonance (better, best, never, get, and rest), and consonance (best, get, and rest).

Love in her sunny eyes does basking play;

Love walks the pleasant mazes of her hair;
Love does on both her lips for ever stray;
And sows and reaps a thousand kisses there. (Cowley)

Note: In this poem, we can find repetition, and also assonance, metaphor, personification, and hyperbole.

The blue heaven, holding its one golden orb, pouring down crystal wash of warm light. (Theodore Dreiser: *Sister Carrie*)

Note: Here "golden orb" is metonymy (referring to the sun), which is the doer of "pouring … light (it is metaphor)". Without the doer, the metaphor could not be created. Besides, "wash and warm" is alliteration; and "warm light" is synaesthesia.

Did I strap red nude, red rump, also slap murdered underparts? I did!

Note: As a whole, this sentence is palindrome, in which "Did I ... underparts?" is rhetorical question; "red" and "did" are repeated twice respectively; "strap" and "slap" are assonance and also consonance; "red nude, red rump" is parallelism; "strap red nude, red rump, ... slap murdered underparts" is parallelism; "strap red nude, red rump" and "also slap murdered underparts" connected with a comma not "and" is asyndeton.

参考文献
References

Abrams, M. H. & Harpham, G. G. *A Glossary of Literary Terms* [M]. 北京：外语教学与研究出版社，2010.

Baldick, C. *The Concise Oxford Dictionary of Literary Terms* [M]. Oxford: Oxford University Press, 2001.

Childs, P. & Fowler, R. *The Routledge Dictionary of Literary Terms* [M]. Rev. ed. Abingdon, Oxon: Routledge & Kegan Paul Ltd., 2006.

Corbett, R. P. J. & Coonors, R. J. *Classical Rhetoric for the Modern Student* [M]. Oxford: Oxford University Press, 1999.

Deignan, A. *Metaphor* [M]. 北京：外文出版社 / 香港：商务印书馆，2001.

Lakoff, G. & Johnson, M. *Metaphors We Live By* [M]. Chicago: University of Chicago Press, 1980.

Lanham, R. A. *A Handlist of Rhetorical Terms* [M]. Berkeley & Los Angeles: University of California Press, 1968.

Minsky, M. *Society of Mind* [M]. New York: Simon & Schuster, 1986.

Mohanty, U. *Literal and Figurative English* [M]. Delhi, India: Pacific Books International, 2009.

Nicholas, A. *Key Terms in Pragmatics* (语用学核心术语)[M]. 北京：外语教学与研究出版社，2016.

Nørgaard, N., Montoro, R. & Busse, B. *Key Terms in Stylistics* (文体学核心术语)[M]. 北京：外语教学与研究出版社，2017.

Pearsall, J. *The New Oxford Dictionary of English* [M]. Oxford: Oxford University Press / 上海：上海外语教育出版社, 2001.

Peters, P. *The Cambridge Australian English Style Guide* [M]. Melbourne: Cambridge University Press, 1995.

Quirk, R. *Longman Dictionary of Contemporary English* [M]. London: Longman Group UK Limited, 1997.

Richards, I. A. *The Philosophy of Rhetoric* [M]. Oxford: Oxford University Press, 1936.

Sinclair, J. *Collins COBUILD English Dictionary* [M]. London: HarperCollins Publishers, 1998.

Theodore, S. *The Art of Translation* [M]. London: Jonathan Cape, 1975.

Webster's Third New International Dictionary [M]. Springfield: G.&C. Merriam Company, 2002.

Wehmeier, S. *Oxford Advanced Learner's English-Chinese Dictionary* [M]. 8th ed. Oxford: Oxford University Press / Beijing: The Commercial Press, 2014.

陈丛耘. 现代汉语修辞学[M]. 武汉：华中科技大学出版社，2014.

陈科芳. 英汉修辞格比较与翻译[M]. 北京：中国社会科学出版社，2017.

陈汝东. 对外汉语修辞学[M]. 南宁：广西教育出版社，2000.

陈淑华. 英语修辞与翻译[M]. 北京：北京邮电学院出版社，1990.

陈望道. 修辞学发凡[M]. 上海：上海教育出版社，1976.

冯翠华. 英语修辞大全[M]. 北京：外语教学与研究出版社，2005.

韩仲谦. 英语倒转、音韵和置换辞格探究[M]. 北京：中国书籍出版社，2017.

黄衡田. 英语辞格辨析[M]. 武汉：华中科技大学出版社，2016.

李明. 美国《时代周刊》标题修辞研究[M]. 昆明：云南大学出版社，2009.

李阳，覃先美. 英语修辞学概论[M]. 长沙：湖南师范大学出版社，2006.

李银芳，刘启成. 英语修辞格浅论[M]. 长春：吉林大学出版社，2009.

林承璋，刘世平. 英语词汇学引论[M]. 3 版. 武汉：武汉大学出版社，2005.

刘焕辉. 修辞学纲要[M]. 南昌：百花洲文艺出版社，1990.

刘亚猛. 语用学研究：语用与修辞[J]. 浙江外国语学院学报，2015(3): 1.

骆小所. 现代修辞学[M]. 昆明：云南人民出版社，1994.

吕煦. 实用英语修辞[M]. 北京：清华大学出版社，2004.

钱冠连. 汉语文化语用学[M]. 北京：清华大学出版社，1997.

覃海洋. 英语修辞学教程[M]. 杭州：浙江大学出版社，1998.

束定芳. 隐喻学研究[M]. 上海：上海外语教育出版社，2000.

汪丽炎. 汉语修辞[M]. 上海：上海大学出版社，1998.

汪洋. 语文修辞[M]. 上海：上海交通大学出版社，2013.

王广荪. 简明英语修辞词典[M]. 北京：北京语言学院出版社，1992.
王希杰. 汉语修辞学[M]. 3 版. 北京：商务印书馆，2014.
王晓军，孟凡艳，孟庆梅，等. 英语修辞学[M]. 济南：山东人民出版社，2014.
文军. 英语修辞格词典[M]. 重庆：重庆大学出版社，1992.
吴平. 英汉修辞手段比较[M]. 合肥：安徽教育出版社，2001.
徐鹏. 英语辞格[M]. 北京：商务印书馆，1996.
喻翔生. 英语汉语修辞格式举要[M]. 昆明：云南民族出版社，2006.
张金泉. 英语辞格导论[M]. 武汉：华中科技大学出版社，2013.
张文庭. 英语修辞及惯用法[M]. 长沙：湖南师范大学出版社，1996.
张秀国. 英语修辞学[M]. 北京：清华大学出版社/北京交通大学出版社，2019.
周瑞英. 高级英语常用修辞格赏析[M]. 北京：中国农业科学技术出版社，2012.